7/2/30

1939

1939

1940

'41

'42

EZRA MEEKER RETRACING THE OREGON TRAIL IN 1910, AND
CHIMNEY ROCK, THE FAMOUS LANDMARK OF THE PIONEERS

The
OVERLAND TRAIL

THE EPIC PATH OF THE PIONEERS TO OREGON

By AGNES C. LAUT

Author of "Conquest of the Great Northwest,"
"Pathfinders," "Vikings," etc.

WITH FORTY-NINE ILLUSTRATIONS FROM PHOTOGRAPHS,
TWO MAPS AND TWO DIAGRAMS

FREDERICK A. STOKES COMPANY
NEW YORK   MCMXXIX

Second Printing, January 31, 1930

Printed in the United States of America

HUMANIZED HISTORY

The story of America's greatest trail moves vibrantly through the pages of this worthy book. It depicts with fidelity one of the most important phases of the master epic of the making of America.

HOWARD R. DRIGGS, *President*

OREGON TRAIL MEMORIAL ASSOCIATION, INC.
95 Madison Avenue, New York City

CONTENTS

PART I

FROM THE MISSOURI TO THE ROCKIES UP THE PLATTE

I—KANSAS CITY

II—OLD FORT LEAVENWORTH

III—OMAHA—"ABOVE THE WATERS"

PART III

DOWN THE COLUMBIA RIVER TO THE PACIFIC

XVII—ON TO THE ENDS OF THE EARTH

LIST OF ILLUSTRATIONS

FOREWORD TO THE SECOND EDITION

It would perhaps clarify the aim of this volume for the purely historical student to emphasize the fact—the title is Overland Trail, not exclusively Oregon Trail.

The Overland Trail is a broad highway with many branches. The Oregon Trail is also a broad highway, both past and present, but it follows in the main one path, except where two cut-offs or diagonal short-cuts come in. All that is attempted, or could be attempted in a volume for the general reader, is a faint reflex from the most brilliant spot-lights coming down from the past on that Trail. More detailed accounts must be looked for in more specialized histories, for obvious reasons that will be given presently.

How many movements in all went over that trail? If you want to be meticulously accurate, you will have to begin with an aged Gulf of Mexico Indian of whom Du Pratz tells. He ascended the Mississippi and Missouri and some river resembling the Platte, crossed the Rockies and so came to the great Salt Sea of the Setting Sun. His dates you cannot follow, but the tribes described you can easily recognize. Or you may care to begin with Coronado's famous search for the seven mythical cities; but of latter day movements you have first, of course, Lewis and Clark. They did not come into the Trail till they had crossed the main ridge of the Rockies and then traversed a strip of what is modern Western Montana, North Idaho and so came into Oregon, or what is now Washington. Then came the fur traders, the Astorians first, the St. Louis merchants, the Missionaries, the Pioneers, the Mormons, the Santa Fé caravans, the Californians, the rail builders.

These movements did not go in distinct groups. They paralleled. They intermingled. They broke off here and there, to turn back, or diverge from their first aim to another lure of fortune. The best example of these I know is brought out in a book by Mr. F. N. Fletcher of Nevada. It explains how in a year when Laramie and Kearney counted passing caravans in many thousands, the North-West population showed accessions of only a little over a thousand. Was it a case of the small boy's "a thousand cats in the back yard" when there were only his own cat and another? It was not. The traders of Kansas City and Omaha and Kearney and Laramie were not growing rich on that kind of imaginary population. They were growing rich on real buyers. Mr. Fletcher points out that in the rush to California, many Overlanders instead of going by Bridger's Cut Off from South Pass across the broad belt of the

Desert—Utah and Nevada—went right on North-West to Fort Hall, then across the narrow belt of the desert to the Sierras. At Fort Hall, they met our Hudson's Bay friend, Grant of Pioneer Days, and received advice from him as to water holes, good springs and safe camps. This explains the amazing differences given as to people passing Laramie and those reaching Nez Percé or Walla Walla.

I am somewhat explicit on this because I read claims of one Western State as the exclusive out-fitting point for all Mormons, and the same claim for another State. Yet there lies beneath my hand a letter from an aged Mormon, who made the trip, describing the first camping place as Council Bluffs, then the next outfitting post as Florence, and the main water front of Omaha "as dead" be-cause the outfitters had jumped West to Florence. This old gentleman with two comrades made the trip at the rate of thirteen miles a day, using oxen on a wagon, with two cows to the rear.

It is equally impossible, in a general book, to take up in detail the shifting in the sites of the various old forts. There were three Laramies, at least four Kearneys, four Boisés, four Vancouvers, four Walla Wallas or Nez Percés. The wise course would seem to be for the modern traveler to go to the modern town and from that point go to the ancient site noted for its heroism. In no case but one, will that run-out require longer than from New York or Chicago to a suburban home. That one exception is the Fort Phil Kearny from which the jumping off place was Laramie. It was built to protect the miners going into Idaho and Montana and should be as sacred in history as the Dollard Site of the Long Sault, Ottawa, or the Alamo in Texas, or Walla Walla of the Whitman Shrine. I have stated as explicitly as I could that it was *not* on the Overland Trail but ought to be included in any itinerary of that highway.

There were peculiar reasons why the authorities of the Army at Washington could not permit the full blaze of the heroism in the Fetterman Massacre to come out, nor the fuller blaze of the victory in the Waggon Box Fight. The public was rabid at the time. A correspondent for *Leslie's* had been murdered and scalped by the Sioux, so wild exaggeration ran into flame. What would the public say about a little fort set down in the most dangerous section of the West, with the rawest of raw recruits, only forty rounds of shells per man, very skittish horses, and deplorably old type rifles? An Army inspector had come up from Laramie in the fall and promised reinforcements as to equipment and men. Not a pound of equipment had come, nor a horse, though men and horses were being sniped off by the Sioux every day from the first, and Red Cloud boasted that "in two moons" he would "leave neither man nor beast on the hoof." What the Army could do with proper equipment was proved in the Waggon Box Fight the next summer. Another point the Army had to consider. To advertise the weakness of many frontier posts would have invited attack by the Indians.

A grandson of Philip Kearny, nephew of Stephen Kearney, writes me that no authentic lives of either famous officers exist, though two statues stand in honor of the younger Kearny. He explains that Phil never used the *e* in his name, though the uncle did and after him the other Kearneys were named. Stephen died in 1848, Phil was killed in 1862. With the exceedingly sad controversy between Kearny and Fremont, which finally flared up over California matters in Leavenworth, this volume has nothing to do.

The four Boisés which might be confused are the modern, to which the traveler should go, and the Pioneer Boisé right on the Snake. The other two hardly need mention. One preceded the modern and was shifted, the other was far up Little Wood River. Only its foundations existed in Professor Coues' day and to this day I do not know a soul who can explain who built it, why or when. The different Walla Wallas and Vancouvers are plainly given in this volume. Pocatello's name is ascribed to an old Indian chief. The Hancock in this volume, it need hardly be told, was not General Hancock.

Mr. Ayres of Boisé gives the most logical explanation of the Snake River Indian name. The prairie tribes used a sign language almost akin to our deaf and dumb language, except that the Indian sign was a full word or an idea. The Inland Empire or Intermountain tribes used a sign language more descriptive of things than ideas. When asked about the river, they made "wiggly" motions with their fingers to show its tortuous course, and so the river and the Indians were called the Snakes in the vernacular. I have talked with the Hopis and Acomas of the South-West in that gesture language, and we understood one another perfectly in a half day visit; but I could no more talk the finger and thumb language of the prairie people than I could the deaf and dumb signs.

Most of us know that two states are at friendly enmity for the honor of little Sacajawea's narrow burial plot. Now it seems two other states are at holy war over the last peaceful resting place of little Holy Rainbow, the wife of Dorion. The last Dorion died only a few years ago near Pierre, South Dakota. A letter lies beside me from Miss Leila McKay of Portland, granddaughter of the splendid Tom McKay of Oregon fame and great-granddaughter of the martyred McKay of the Astorians.

It is not from lack of romance and adventure the great Overland Trail suffers. On the contrary, it abounds in such a wealth of material that it is difficult to know what to select and what to omit, and yet not confuse the general reader.

A. C. L.

January, 1930.

INTRODUCTION

One cannot better describe that great racial Highway of Humanity, that conquest of civilization over savagery, beginning its movement ever westward in the days of Abraham, going up the Euphrates from Ur on the Persian Gulf 2,000 B.C., and ending in our own days on the shores of the Pacific over the Pioneer Oregon Trail, than in the Memorial address given by Dr. Howard R. Driggs on the death of Ezra Meeker, one of the last of the Overlanders:

"It touches closely every part of our country, North, South, East and West. Every state in the Union has some heroic son or daughter who has played a valiant part in the trail-blazing, home-building story of the Far West.

"What is the West? It is merely the transplanted East. It is the blended North and South. We sometimes hear the song, 'Out Where the West Begins.' Frankly, I do not know where the West begins, but I do know where it began. It began along the shores of the stormy Atlantic. Our American pioneers were descendants of those who planted our thirteen American colonies and who afterward fought to establish this nation dedicated to freedom. It was the descendants of these stalwart defenders of liberty who carried America Westward. They followed the Indian trails through the passes of the Alleghenies along the national highways to the Mississippi; thence they wended their way over prairies and plains and mountains and deserts to the shores of the Pacific, there to plant our great Empire States beyond the Rockies. It is not commonly known how great this migration was. We get a mere suggestion of it when we learn from conservative estimates that fully three hundred and fifty thousand Americans took these trails during the days of the covered wagon—from 1836, when Marcus Whitman and his wife first made their way to Oregon, to 1869, when the Golden Spike linking the Union Pacific and the Central Pacific was driven at Promontory Point, at the north end of the great Salt Lake in Utah.

"We are brought a little closer to the tragic cost of it all when we realize that fully twenty thousand lost their lives in the effort to reach the Golden West. You can appreciate that I have a tender interest in the story when I tell you that somewhere among the velvety hills of old Iowa four of my great-grandparents lie in unmarked graves. They had no means of marking the graves of the dead in those prairie stretches. They might have put at the mound of the loved one laid away the skull of a buffalo, the end gate of a wagon or some other temporary marker, but mainly what they did was to scatter the ashes of their camp-fires over these resting places to keep the bodies of their dear ones from being dug up by the wolves.

"Very few graves out of all the twenty thousand, so far as we know, are surely marked. One of these is the grave of the pioneer mother near Scott's Bluffs, Nebraska. When Rebecca Winters passed away, one of the company had the happy forethought to pick up an old wagon tire that lay along the trail. Bending it into an oval he set the tire within the grave. On the top of the tire was chiseled the mother's name and age. For more than three-score years it stood over the mound. Finally a party of surveyors laying out a railroad along the old North Platte, by mere chance happened to run their line right over the mother's grave. As they read the inscription on the old wagon tire, they were touched by the love of a mother's heart. They telegraphed into Salt Lake City, because it was on the old Salt Lake branch of the Oregon Trail, and relatives of the pioneer mother wired back who she was. Then the railroad builders protected the grave, erecting a neat, substantial fence about it. A monument, inscribed briefly with the story, was sent from Utah and set beside the old wagon tire, which still arches above the mound.

"Some years ago, I was in the Museum in Portland, Oregon, listening to George Himes, Secretary of the Oregon Historical Association, tell the story of the coming of the pioneres into the then

Territory of Washington. I shall never forget
the vivid recital of an experience he had as a boy
of ten with the trail-blazers into the far Northwest
when they had to kill three of their oxen to use
their hides to splice two ropes to let their twenty-
nine wagons down a cliff that barred their way.
Mr. Himes showed me during this visit one of the
corners of the Museum in which he had relics that
had come from every state east of the Mississippi
River. 'Here,' said he, 'is a clock that used to
tick time in Vermont; here is a Franklin stove
with which they used to warm themselves in Pennsylvania; here is a cradle in which they rocked
the baby across the plains from Indiana and here
is a scythe with which they mowed blue grass in
Kentucky.' 'Yes, Mr. Himes,' said I, 'these people
came bearing not only their scythes, and their stoves,
their clocks and their cradles; they came carrying
America across our continent; they came sprin-
kling the names of American towns and cities dear
to their hearts upon the map of every state that
they crossed; they came planting their school
houses and churches; they came telling their children of the making of America; they came with
American ideals throbbing in their hearts. They
came, if you please, stretching the warp of our
national life from one end of our country to the
other. They stretched it stout and taut and true.

"The vital question with you and me and with
every American now is, 'Will the warp hold?' It

will, provided we can keep alive the sacred stories of the pioneer builders of this nation in the hearts of American boys and girls. If we would save our country we must see to it that we save this invaluable heritage. An incident comes to my mind which would serve to make concrete the thought I would impress. It chances that recently I was giving an address in a high school in the Bronx, New York City, on America's Greatest Trail. At the close of this address there came to me a young man, whose name was so foreign that I could not pronounce it, and he said with tears in his voice, 'Mr. Driggs, if we could have our history taught to us like that, we would feel like saluting the flag. They tell us to salute the flag. We don't know what they are talking about.' "

Could Americans grasp what an enormous achievement that was—accomplishing in a hundred years what neither Europe nor Asia had achieved in four thousand years—the Oregon Trail would be marked as one of the most famous in history. It would be regarded from end to end as the fulfilment of that Divine Prophecy "when His Dominions shall extend from the rivers to the ends of the earth." It would be beautified, revered, consecrated as a Great National Highway. It would be visited and traversed by every traveler in the land. And it was not built by slave labor as were older highways in ancient lands. It was cut across the sand-blown desert, hewn through the solid rocks of the mountain passes, sculptured against the walls of river canyons by wagon rims of the penniless pioneer going West, ever West; of his Divine urge following the fantom hopes of his own heart to a Newer, Better, Promised Land.

Great epochs in history like mountain peaks in the receding sun lengthen their shadows as they recede. Tardily, very tardily, the Overland Trail is coming into its own. Its full history will never be told; it is lost in the dumb, inarticulate heroism of the dead; for pioneers did not ride "cock-horse on parade" like ancient conquerors. They marched on and died in silence as they marched, and the next band of marchers passed on; but enough of its heroism can be told to stir every heart. Enough of its dauntless adventuring can be recorded to keep its epic achievement fragrant and marvelous in memory. That is all attempted here—just enough to recall the shadowy figures of a Past that created the Present—ghost figures they may be but ghost figures that can never be degraded by cynic sneer; for these ghosts claimed no heroism. They just did their stint of work in life's span and laid them down to sleep with good work well done.

A. C. L.

THE DEVELOPMENT OF THE OVER-LAND TRAIL

PART I

FROM THE MISSOURI TO THE ROCKIES UP THE PLATTE

OLD SPANISH EXPLORERS (1510-1542)
Crossed the country toward the mouth of the Missouri before the voyages of Henry Hudson or Drake, or the Settlement on the James River were made. A Spanish stirrup of Coronado's time was dug up in the streets of Omaha.

LEWIS AND CLARK (1804-1806)
Made a scientific exploration commissioned by Jefferson; its results became important in the long quarrel between Great Britain and the United States over the latter's claims to the Oregon country.

ASTORIANS ON THE WAY TO OR FROM THE PACIFIC (1811-1813)
These were fur traders sent by John Jacob Astor to establish a post on the Pacific Coast.

MISSOURI FUR TRADERS (1816-1840)
Adventurers from St. Louis who came up by the Platte and Three Forks after the Astorians surrendered, to fight the Hudson's Bay men for the rich furs.

LATER EXPLORING PARTIES (1842-1848)

The most noted were those of Frémont "the Pathfinder" in 1842 and 1843. Frémont camped at Independence Rock, and from there went on to the ascent of Frémont Peak in August, 1842.

PIONEER MOVEMENTS WEST (1835-1856)

Missionary, led by Dr. Whitman (1835-1843) ; Mormon, led by Joseph Smith (1846 on) ; Santa Fé caravans, a trade movement at its height in the late forties and early fifties; the California Gold Stampede which in one year (1849) raised the population of California from six thousand to hundreds of thousands; the Oregon fever (1847 to 1856) caused by hard times.

MILITARY OCCUPATION (1823 to present)

From Col. Leavenworth's expedition against the Aricara Indians in 1823 through the eras of migration overland and railway building down to that of Howard against the Nez Percés in 1877, the army was called on to guard the trail. The Fetterman and Wagon-Box fights took place near Fort Kearney in 1866 and 1867.

RAIL PIONEERS (1856-1893)

Long and hazardous surveying preceded the era of actual roadbuilding in the sixties. The Union Pacific advertised in 1868: "track laid and trains running within ten miles of the Rockies."

CHAPTER I

KANSAS CITY

THERE stand in America three great obelisks.

One is in Washington, the Federal Capital. It is the Washington Monument. It marks the beginning of a great nation in its expansion from the Atlantic to the Pacific. It commemorates also one of the noblest leaders, who ever guided that nation in its Destiny.

The second is in Kansas City. It commemorates the soldiers, who perished in the World War; but it also marks the beginning of a great racial path in that expansion from the Atlantic to the Pacific. That racial path is the Overland Trail. Here set out in the last trek of humanity westward, not an army of soldiers in rank formation, but an army of Pioneers, who conquered a wilderness and transformed a desert into a garden; and they accomplished in a little more than half a century, what the Old World did not achieve in sixty centuries. They conquered by sheer dogged dauntless courage an empire half the area of Europe. Five thousand people—men, women, children—perished from hunger, from hardship, from Indian raids, in a single year on the Oregon Trail. If you want

to realize the epic heroism of such pioneer heroism, compare that mortality loss to the army death
list of a single little war in Europe over some
principality not the size of a single county in the
states bordering the Overland Trail! Then you
grasp what the great racial highway means in
American history. You realize why to the West,
it is sacred as the very altar stairs of a saint's monument in Asia or Europe. It, too, is dyed in sacrificial martyr blood. It, too, is worn by the pilgrims' feet in traces which time can never efface.

The third obelisk stands at the final outlet of
Columbia River to the Pacific. It is known as
the Astor Monolith. It marks the end of the
Oregon Pioneer Trail. It commemorates far
more. It symbolizes the final destination of man's
trek round the world from East to West for six
thousand years.

One may grasp the significance of these things
best, perhaps, by telescoping back from the present
to the past and seeing how all evolved from simple
beginnings.

Whether you travel by rail or by motor, pause
midway above the long viaduct across the yeasty
muddy floods of the river flats at Kansas City.
Here shunt in a never-stop shuttle the trains of a
dozen big rail systems. Ask yourself some questions.

Did the three Kansas Cities and their one suburb
jump from a center of a few hundred thousands

to a population of seven hundred thousand through man's dauntless spirit or their own geographic position as the center of a Western Empire much vaster than all Central Europe or for that matter than all New England with New York and Pennsylvania included?

It is a mighty interesting question and its answer is an epic of human progress in a century unparalleled in the records of the race.

When I was there but a few years before the World War, and again just after the War, Kansas City was elated by a population of less than three hundred thousand. Here today are almost three-quarters of a million; and here tomorrow may be —what? I hesitate to answer—a Berlin, a Paris, a Chicago.

Less than seventy-five years ago, a man and his family with prophetic fore-vision might have sat down on a village lot sold at twenty-five dollars or given to anyone who would build and improve the property, and by sheer persistence in sitting on a little nest-egg without letting it go addled before it hatched, waken up to a fortune that would have left Rip Van Winkle rubbing his sleepy eyes, or King Midas feeling cheap. There are lots in Kansas City today as valuable as the best in New York, or richer far than any principality of the Old World. But the man would have needed more than prophetic fore-vision. He must needs have faith in his vision, faith based on facts.

Don't regard Kansas City, Missouri, as the one Kansas City. Kansas City includes also Kansas City, Kansas, and Westport and suburbs beyond each, and Independence farther out, where many workers live and motor to and from home each day.

If you have eyes that see and comprehend what they see, the architecture tells the whole story of the city as it always does.

There are the most recent bank and public buildings and schools of the Grecian column and Chaldean lions with the wings of the spirit from the shoulders of power, with the acanthus leaves above the columns and not a line on the façade more or less than adds to beauty. Then there are the Gothic types, twenty stories with the towers and minarets cutting the clouds, resembling the highest structures of New York and Chicago. Older still are the good substantial red brick defying time in their squatty stolid ugliness—holding their own like good old burghers resisting change as a device of the devil and mighty useful in the wholesale and warehouse sections, where train smoke and the fogs of the rivers would blacken up my lady's fine attire of frills now sported in the beautiful structures of the higher levels.

Take a look down from the causeway bridge, itself no mean viaduct of one and a quarter miles, where but a few years ago a bridge of one or two thousand feet was a marvel. Below the causeway, besides the ordinary freight car for general merchandise, lumber, coal, you see again the whole story of Kansas City's growth. Oil from Oklahoma and Kansas. Cattle, sheep, hogs from the packing plants. Wheat from the great wheat plains north, south, west. Though oil will be piped for a century yet to the great oil distributing point of Kansas City which is the hub of a vast wheel, oil is a will o' the wisp, which no science can foretell or forecast. It is a gusher today and an exhausted pool tomorrow. But the farm—the general farm of dairy, wheat, potato, fruit—there is the hub of Kansas City prosperity; and by the same token, that was what created Kansas as a rich state.

Apart from political plans to mend the farmers' plight—and it is very real—put in a few lines the real farm problem of the fourteen states encircling Kansas City. Say the farmers—Give us a home market for all we sell and all we buy so we won't be eaten alive by middlemen profits, and we'll undertake to make ourselves prosperous. Say the manufacturers implored to come in and create such a home market—Give us a larger farming population to buy all we manufacture and to supply us with raw material, and we'll come in. There is the eternal see-saw and Kansas City plans to meet both demands. Can she do it? She has in the past.

When the founder of the Santa Fé railroad—

Halliday—came west and jumped off the back of nowhere, he found a place called Topeka—Indian word for "where potatoes will grow." Where potatoes will grow, almost any staple farm product will grow; so he planted his meager fortune in the future capital of the State and incidentally, let it be added, quadrupled it and got him busy interesting friends in a rail line to center traffic in Kansas. The Civil War ditched his plans but did not stop them. When the first spadeful of earth was turned for the railroad and a little later a poor lame duck of a train came wabbling over twelve miles of rattling track bed and Halliday spread his arms and predicted his line would yet reach Chicago to the northeast and the Gulf of Mexico to the south and San Francisco to the west, a cowboy who had imbibed too freely of "tangle-foot" threw himself on the ground, kicked up his heels in the air and yelled "the blank old fool." The old-in-head but young-in-years fool lived to see that cowboy become the mayor of Topeka.

Kansas City's name tells its history much as its public buildings do. Before the squat brick structures were the warehouses of the fur traders on the flats and the French-Canadian little dormer-window cottages on the upper levels, of which only three remain today. The Indians who used to come padding in their moccasins up from the river flats where canoes lay beached called themselves

Kon-zas. The French-Canadian voyageur had a trick of slurring his *ins* and *awns* and *ons* and called these Indians *Kahns*. Then when the Americans came, the Indians were known as the Kansas, and the Kaw River as the Kansas.

Or better still than the causeway as a look-out on the Kansas world, motor over to the Soldiers' Memorial Column above the bluffs. You can ascend inside by an elevator. From its dome where flashes the most beautiful dark rose-red light each night, you see an empire fading on the horizon in the distance on all sides—literally an ocean of what was but yesterday sage brush and buffalo grass; but what is even more interesting than the marvelous growth of the city in its brief past is what may be its future.

Look down to the river flats. The Kansas River comes in here like a baby snake following its mother, the great looped python of the Missouri. From what looks like an island of sand in the broad mid-current but isn't an island at all—rather an isthmus of sand accumulated in centuries by the two rivers, rise birds—the most beautiful birds in the world—sky-blue, blue wings of immense expanse, with the beautiful streamer lines of a gigantic aerial fish cleaving the air in whirls and spins, or poise like great hawks, with a roar of propellers that sets the atmosphere vibrating.

This is one of the great half-way stations across the continent for air flight. Will the air trans-

portation do for Kansas City in the future what
the steel rail has done in half a century? Quien
sabe: as the Mexicans say. Remembering that
"tangle-foot" cowboy's derision and the crowd's
"boos" at the founder of the Santa Fé railroad,
who can play prophet? Later, motor down to the
Aviation Field. Now I know a little—very little
—about aviation. I visited every great aeroplane
factory during the War and once took a flight
across one of the most dangerous sections of the
Rockies. The improvements in aviation have left
me gasping. War aeroplanes were built to kill or
be killed—light of wing, too light for safety, light
of cockpit, much too light for anything but war,
but powerful of engine for speed. Now, the aeroplanes are built more powerful of engine, stronger
in cockpit and body, with the wings of enormous
spread in which may be carried extra gasoline to
be tapped as needed. The take-offs are not the
impossible bumpy-humpy land spots, which jarred
going up and jolted the car to bits coming down,
but long runways of concrete, smooth-surfaced as
a billiard table; and experiments are in process
whether these cannot be made softer to avoid jars
in quick landing by the use of tars and asphalts
and heavy fabrics as a binder. It is very much
like the improvement of the railroad bed in a
century, when granite ties and road beds jolted
rail cars to wrecks and the nerves of passengers
so that Boston papers pronounced all rails a posi-

From "The Life of Frémont." From collection Dr. G. C. Hebard, Wyoming Univ.

FRÉMONT ADDRESSING THE INDIANS AT FORT LARAMIE

From Dr. G. C. Hebard's Collection

FORT LARAMIE

FIRST STONE ERECTED IN NEBRASKA TO MARK THE OVERLAND
TRAIL AND FAMOUS U. S. ARMY HEROES

Courtesy Union Pacific Historical Museum

UNION PACIFIC EXCURSION TRAIN, 1866, AT 100TH MERIDIAN.
LOCATED AT POINT 14.7 FEET EAST OF EAST FACE OF PRESENT
DEPOT AT COZAD, NEBR.

tive menace to sanity. There are fourteen air lines now centering in Kansas City.

Then coming up from the flats, pause midway on another viaduct and look down. Here are not switching yards but the dwellings of Mexican laborers—houses in adobé bricks with little yards and the usual assortment of children and puppy dogs and chickens. If you have ever visited a truly Mexican suburb for day labor of the unskilled sort, you know the smells are almost as variegated as the mosaic of colors but by no means so lovely. They assail you in a hot blast of anything but perfume. Look down on these Mexican workers' dwellings—yards clean as a good kitchen floor, children in clean bright multicolored calicoes; no pulque drunks; no poverty. Kansas City does not entrust the Americanizing of her foreign unskilled labor to study-chair theory. She sends down either as public school teacher, or social settlement worker, or deaconess, or nun—according to the dwellers' religion—someone to train these foreigners into American citizens; and of foreigners as foreigners, Kansas City today numbers less than eight per cent. The rest of her population has in a generation been so completely absorbed in American types, it cannot be distinguished from the home born and home bred type.

That is great work and it is more than talk.

Coming back one evening past a playground for children, I saw sitting banked against the green slope several thousand youngsters below a public school that looked like a university. It was as composite a group of what has made America as I have ever seen. The lank lean-horse type predominated; but what impressed most was that there was not a pasty faced weakling among them. These were fine little citizens and their children and their children's children augur well for future Americans.

I wish I had space to tell of other things Kansas City is doing and what they mean in future growth.

Is it possible that only one city in what was called Indian Territory at the time of the Louisiana Purchase at fifteen million dollars has now an assessed property valuation of almost seven hundred millions? Was it gained by man's dauntless spirit or was it the geographic position? People talk as though these two factors in human progress were distinct. The more you contemplate the opening and development of the West, the more you will be forced to the conclusion that with all our wild jumps hither and thither from the prods of necessity, with all our blind fumbling blunders following perhaps an illusion through fog and sunshine, with all our selfish brute instincts and all our fealty to an ideal that may resemble a rainbow and shifts from the glorious tints of heavenly light to the darkest shades of hopeless storm, something higher than self is shaping our zigzag course to a Divine Purpose. Shakespeare

said this long ago. So has every prophet from
Moses to John.

But keep on circling the city with both eyes open
and your memory alert.

Where you come up from the viaduct across the
river flats on a rocky ledge above the road stands
a sentinel of the century—one of the finest bronze
monuments in America of an Indian on horseback.
It used to stand where now points the Soldiers'
Monument to the sky, but was appropriately
moved here, above the very road where padded
the fur traders in moccasins, the first Oregon Pioneers—missionaries and settlers—the gold-crazed
hosts stampeding to California, later the Santa Fé
traders in mule and horse-drawn covered wagon,
and still later, after the Civil War, settlers of
every nationality in swarms like locusts to take
up homesteads preceding or following the lines
of the transcontinental rails beginning to belt the
land in loops of steel. Perhaps I should say in
hoops of steel, for it was the rail bound East and
West in unity.

What is the Indian, sitting so intent, thinking
about? Fur traders—yes—he understood them.
He had known fur traders from the time Lewis
and Clark passed west early in the century. They
wanted his peltries. He wanted their firearms.
With these firearms, he could hold his own against
Indian raiders from the south. He could raid
the south tribes, himself, for more Spanish horses.

He could defy the Crows and the Sioux and the Blackfeet on the north. He could pen the Snake Indians in the mountains and compel them to buy supplies from him as middleman between East and West. Who was this Indian? He might have been any one of a dozen tribes gradually moved by white man pressure from the East to the plains —a Shawnee, a Kaw, a Delaware, a Pawnee, an Osage, a Cherokee, a Sac, a Fox. A pathetic figure, too, he is. He knew what the coming of the white man meant. Kill or be killed, hold your ground or lose it—his code from times unrecorded —was to be applied to himself. Live by the sword and you die by the sword—an inexorable law. Should he resist these new comers? He could see where the traders left their canoes beached, or their flatboats moored to trees, or the puff puff "mill that walked on water," the first steamboat snubbed up as close ashore as the sand flats would permit. In the billowing grass of the flats, horses pastured in thousands near water and carried up the fur traders' packets for the traverse across the plains. No, he would not resist these traders, though he scalped and robbed them as he could. These fur traders had already gone west far as the Rockies. They had crossed the Rockies—they had a post just west of the Rockies, known as Henry's Fort, on an upper branch of Snake River. To be sure, it was only a collection of tumble-down log huts; but it marked the fur traders' advance across the Rockies.

But these missionaries and settlers. He could recall, perhaps, those Flatheads from the Far North going down to General Clark in St. Louis and asking for white men to teach them the Trail to Heaven from the Sacred Book. But these settlers on horseback, in covered wagons, on foot, with mountain men as guides, and women and children, with rifles on shoulders, rifles in cases and bullets in belt or pouch, who encamped in circles surrounded by their wagons, with cows for milk and oxen of broad spreading hoofs to ford the quicksand beds and not so likely to mix up in a buffalo stampede as horses—what did they mean? He knew only too well what they meant. To the rear of the Soldiers' Monument, you will see another statue, finer than the Indian on horseback. It is the settler's young wife on horseback with her husband on one side trudging doggedly, blindly into the unknown, the mountain man guide on the other side, alert for foe as a coyote for rabbit. Well, the Indian could rob and raid them, too. Their oxen and cows would give him winter beef. Sometimes they came in bands of a hundred, sometimes in bands of thousands, with cattle in thousands; but why did these mountain men out for furs guide these settlers, who would destroy hunting grounds? The mountain men wore red shirts or red handkerchiefs around their long hair. He

knew why.   Many had married Indian wives,
partly to assure them of protection from the tribe,
partly to have women to make and mend buckskin
suits, tents, moccasins, to cure buffalo into pemmican, to gather berries and fruits to be dried and
pounded to flour.   While the red shirt or head
gear was a good target for enemies, it was equally
good protection for friendly raiders from mistaking a man for game on the dusky plains.   Curious
these mountain men befriended settlers.   There
was Boone, whose grandson lived out at Westport
on the ridge above the river.   There was a Joe
Meek, who learned the white man's letters by
chalking them on a paddle and then learned to
read from the Sacred Book and later—though the
Indian didn't know anything about that—from
Shakespeare and Scott.   Then there was Jim
Bridger whose family lived at Westport.   These
men were all hunters and had married Indian
wives.   Why did they guide the settlers?   The
Indian was no fool.   He knew what it meant.   It
meant the end of the hunting era.   Particularly,
he knew when the Civil War came on and these
white men began fighting among themselves.
That was the Indian's last chance.   From that time
on, every plains tribe pot-shotted, raided, massacred where and what he could.   He didn't do
it en masse.   Indeed, their wise older chiefs op-
posed the younger rash warriors; but the chiefs
could not control young bucks out on the war path;

and the very contest they provoked hastened the end inevitable. But keep clear in your mind, the fault was not all with the Indian. White-man rum lashed up the worst in the Indian. No one compelled him to drink it; but tribes highly stimulated by an ozone atmosphere and diet too purely of concentrated meats had a passion for liquor from the first taste. White-men thugs pot-shotted Indians for the fun of seeing them spin. To them the only good Indian was a dead Indian. Of this you will get some terrible examples presently when you reach Omaha—and of the terrible nemesis that punished such acts. From Lewis and Clark's day, the Washington Government had frowned on the use of liquor in Indian trade; but who was to enforce law in a no-man's land? The profits were too great for the individual consciences of independent traders. Only four dollars value of liquor could be diluted with water, then "doped" with drugs of a maddening sort to sell for sixteen dollars; and the keg traded at five dollars a pelt worth twenty.

And right here from the look-out of the lone Indian, you get the very birth and growth of Kansas City. The river flats of the fur traders. Independence, where presently clustered and grew the blacksmith shops to shoe horses and oxen and repair wagons. Then the traders' shops to supply goers and comers. Then some enterprising citizens took another jump to Westport to get the trade away from Independence. Thence, the city grew and spread from buckskin tents a century ago on river flats to seven hundred thousand people today.

Why did not the Oregon Trail jump into the unknown from St. Louis, from which Lewis and Clark had set out? Because Kansas City by the river's windings was five hundred miles from the outlet of the Missouri. By cutting off the loops of the river, the Overlanders from the East could save some two to three hundred miles in their traverse across the plains. One was the circumference of the half circle. The other was the diameter.

Here in a steady stream every spring—usually in the months of April and May—from 1843 to 1853, converged lines of emigrant wagons in thousands. They came in neighborhood groups from various states and territories. One group might be from Missouri—one hundred, two hundred, to the group. Another band might be Illinois or Iowa families; yet another old South and Middle South frontiersmen; and in the Whitman Missionary era, from 1839 to 1849, families from as far east as New York State and New England. Motives were as various as the groups; but the lure was the same as from the beginning—the lure of the Western Sea. Missionary zeal, hard times back East, youth's love of adventure, the chance of fortune in gold mine or land might be the bayonet prod of necessity; but the Oregon stampede had become what the New York *Tribune* called "an insanity." *

* To acknowledge all the authorities from whom data for the story of the Overland Trail have been drawn would be to cumber pages with a modern and ancient bibliography. Mrs. Paine, Stella Drumm, Doane Robinson, Grace Hebard, T. C. Elliot, Judge Carey, Mr. Himes, Professor Meaney, Ezra Meeker, Dr. Driggs, Alter,—the names of moderns are almost countless. I give these because they lived on the spot and knew descendants of the old heroes and the few of the old heroes who today survive, though nearing the century mark. I remember among my own personal friends two or three of these dear old people. One passed away, while I was writing this book. I spent the first twenty-five years of my life in the West, where many of the old fur traders had retired, and passed my school days with their children and grandchildren. The traditions of their descendants were already fading and it was comical to hear how many of the old generation differed as violently as to dates and spelling and this and that as modern study-chair critics. I have seen old fellows almost coming to blows over whom and what to blame; and I have tried in this narrative to take no sides but to set down as far as possible facts. On certain types of facts, the definite can never be set down and for obvious reasons, to anyone who has gone on long camping trips, whether by horseback or canoe. Down to at least the 1860's, the daily brigades of fur traders, colonists, surveyors, dotted their notes on anything from dry parchment to tissue paper criss-crossed with a goose quill pen or carpenter pencil. Their notes could not be made daily as any traveler knows, and I myself, have found. They got in at night always dog tired, often drenched to the skin, frequently in haste to get up camps against an impending storm. Often notes had to be made a week after the places named were passed, or the day of the event happening to stamp their memory. This accounts for many of the differences as to places and dates. Take a man away from calendars for six months— yes, a month—and if absorbed by adventures of a life and death struggle, he will lose track of dates, even days of the week. If he didn't you would have good ground for regarding his entire record as "doctored" afterward. Also what one man along the trail saw, another man in the same group missed. One man might be on the south shore of a river, the other on the north. Both were struggling through sage brush, over fallen trees,—perhaps running for dear life from a charging buffalo bull, or cocking a rifle at an ugly bear contesting the path. Would these two men remember the same episode? They would not. I say no more of that type of difference.

More puzzling and confusing are the almost countless different names and sites given to the same forts. The reason is apparent, almost transparent on the spot. Sometimes, the first fort was so close to flood waters it had to be shifted back up the hill. Again, on the crest of the bank it was too easy and exposed a target for Indian raiders, or too vulnerable to violent storms; and the next fort would take the name of the army commander supervising the new structure, only to be razed for another later. In the majority of the cases, but not all, the name that emerged has been the old one, though the modern city may be from five to twenty miles from the first site. Laramie, Fort Hall, Boisé, Walla Walla are all examples of this; but monuments now mark most of the old sites but not all. That has been impossible. Farmhouses, barns, dam sites, water backed up by dam sites covered the old sites. I think of one great modern city, which in its history has had five different fort names. Again, I shall say no more of these differences. They are all along the Trail and do not detract in the least from the tremendous significance of this epic highway. Where I do not give the differences, it is only because they confuse the mind and needlessly cumber the memory, when what really matters is the intensely interesting document of heroism on the Trail.

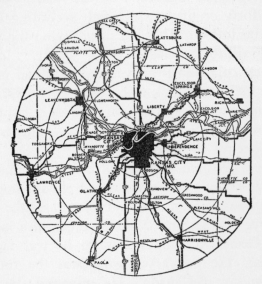

METROPOLITAN KANSAS CITY

CHAPTER II

Old Fort Leavenworth

IS it worth while to run out and see Fort Leavenworth?

That depends on what you want to see.

If you want to see things as they are, the answer is that of the canny Scot—"mebee yes—mebee no."

If you want to see the shell of the acorn from which the mighty oak grew—decidedly yes.

Leavenworth is directly on the road to Omaha about forty or fifty miles north according to the road you follow. It is not properly on the Overland Trail, for here again the snaky rivers loop in countless coils and the Overlanders bound for the Platte ultimately took a short cut northwest from the Kansas to the Platte. On the way out you will see how Uncle Sam's Treasury—the Army branch of it—spends tax money.

When I visited Leavenworth I was amused at my taxi driver's insistence that I should stop and see the Penitentiary. I didn't want to see the Penitentiary. This reminded me too much of a joke on King George of England when he was visiting Canada. He was asked what was the funniest thing he saw in Canada. He answered, the word "Welcome" in gorgeous coloring across the gate to a penitentiary. But the Soldiers' Home and Hospital are certainly worth seeing. The Home did not know I was taking a look at it; so I was not displayed the bright spots, while the dark spots were hidden behind an official screen of discretion.

What I first saw was the men—few faces from the old Civil War era if any; some—fewer and fewer each year—of the Indian War era down to the 1880's; a greater number from the Cuban and Philippine War; and still more from the last War —an invalid class. The faces were happy and contented. The clothing was neat, spick and span, as if in army service. Where not crippled by war, the figures were agile. The grounds—trees, lawns, flowers—in one of the most backward seasons the West has ever known, were a glory of beauty, peace, restfulness, repose. I do not believe any man could live in those surroundings and retain a permanent grouch—the inferiority complex. Nearly all the men have pocket money from pensions or savings for the little comforts of tobacco, knick-knacks and what not. The spotless hospital beds, the recreation halls, the reading rooms, the bed and board are better than many a hotel for which I have paid five dollars a day. They are far and away better than the majority of the men ever knew in their own private homes. I hate to call those soldiers "inmates." They are not. They are retired veterans from service for the public good. Some sat on the benches spinning yarns of the old

days. I wish I could have sat down with them for
a week without their knowing I was a writer so
they would cut loose. When you hear two old fellows scrapping over a point, you may not take sides
but you get a mighty human slant on exactly what
did happen and how at that point. Others wandering among the flower borders pointed out with
their jaunty canes especially fine pansies or pinks
or spiræa. Others I saw pointing crutches at various trees—imported trees like purple beeches, or
California pines, or silver maples. They were interested in life and that is the main thing to keep
going and well.

The highway out from Kansas City is as good as
Riverside Drive, New York, or Chicago's Boulevard. In the rush hours from 7 A.M. to 5 P.M., it
is pretty heavily traveled—tourists, workmen
building bungalows reaching out from the city,
army trucks en route to and from the fort; but toward the west is the same ocean of green prairies
as from the beginning, now in fields of alfalfa and
clover scenting the air as did the old prairie roses.

We had just had such a plunging rain as used to
leave this road, then of log corduroy and mud
holes, a horror; and where the sticky adobé mud
had splashed across the pavement, the swerve of
our car to the grease of soil and gasoline, gave me
a guess at what the swerve of army mule-drawn
wagon must have been.

Fort Leavenworth, itself, is a sleepy little old

city of retired and resident officers and citizens. It
is the only sleepy thing in Kansas. As a fort, it is
not liked by Army men. Since the ending of Indian Wars, chances for promotion are slim. Ambitious men are transferred elsewhere and the fort
sleeps away its drowsy tranquil days. The Great
War brought it again to life when as many as a
hundred thousand men were at times encamped on
the rolling hills and plains. You can see the
abandoned buildings now for the most part occupied by colored families of troopers. The stables
that used to roof and train hundreds and thousands
of the finest army horses in America, are like the
fort—sad relics of glories that have departed. The
few horses yet there are beauties—perfect mounts;
but how few! I was both sorry and glad. Sorry
the day of the most beautiful creatures in the animal world had passed; glad these noble brutes
would no longer be mangled to torture in war but
had been replaced by machines that could not feel,
however much the men driving the machine might
suffer. The men have a vote on war. The horse
hasn't.

It is rather ridiculous to have to set down that
among the soldiers and minor officers, not a man
but one lone sentry and one prison convict could
we find to give us information as to the wall of the
ancient fort. Sherman and Grant—yes—monuments and streets named after them, but we chased
our car round in the futile circles of a kitten after

its tail hunting monuments and streets in memory
of General Leavenworth and Kearny and Miles
and Crooks and Custer, Sheridan, yes, and Colonel
Cody—Buffalo Bill—and a dozen others without
whom the West could never have developed. It
would have been the Great American Desert to
this day. Pacifists or militants, we may hate that
statement or like it; but as a fact of history it has
to stand. Uncivilized people—yes, and some civ-
ilized, too—have to fear first and love second; and
the love usually comes as the growth of reverence
for the justice behind the fear.

I paused in our circling to watch a bunch of
convicts brought in from field work by a detail of
troopers. I looked over the marching line of convicts—with the exception of a dozen, perhaps, de-
serters or insubordinates or sub-morons, who ought
never to have been in the army at all, where they
would have been useless in action, a danger to
themselves and others. They would have collapsed
or gone wild. Some were colored, the majority
white, only a few, I should say, unsafe brutes in
human form—as Parkman called some Indians—
men but not yet with souls. Many were well born,
but from some trick of ancestry or environment—
weaklings mentally or ethically, not to be trusted in
ordinary life, much less in the wild action of ruthless war.

Will old Leavenworth's departed glories ever
return? Indian Wars are forever past and I never

want to see another war mobilizing a hundred thousand men here; nor do I believe another war could. The aeroplanes and submarine explain that.

All the same, Leavenworth is worth the run out. It explains why neither Kansas City nor Omaha could ever have been here. The Missouri Flats are too wide here—eight miles in flood tide. A rail bridge here was for all time an impossibility; but here from 1827 were concentrated eight hundred troopers—the majority mounted with a pack mule for each horseman—besides officers for every unit of one hunded and two hundred men. The flats gave inland expresses pasture and water to prepare to cross to the Platte. The army units were detailed to keep order amid a million warring raiding tribes much more hostile to one another than to the whites. Cholera and sunstroke across the thousand miles of pathless plains patrolled were, down to the 1870's, much more deadly than raiders' arrows. We know now that much of what was called cholera was nothing more than the terrible effects of alkali water with a meat diet and heat to broil one's brains. No white could stand up against day sweats that drenched in a Turkish bath and night chills called "ague" and the constant drainage of reserve strength by enteric disease. Much less could he withstand the drain if he could not resist the temptation to hunt buffalo in the heat of midday, when the buffalo clustered in the shade of the poplars and cottonwoods along stream beds. Hunters' blood up, the troopers gave chase. The herds stampeded for the hot unshaded sand and lava plains. The white rider followed and paid for his folly. Of one group of eight hundred troopers sent west in all the panoply of war to impress the plains Indians during the 1830's, fewer than two hundred came back alive. The dead were buried on the plains where they fell to be devoured by wolves scraping up graves. Only a few were brought back to be interred in some fort.

Telescope your memory back to old General Leavenworth so human, yet a great army man. He is described as a veteran of the 1812 War, but he couldn't have been much of a veteran in years, for he came down in the prime of his powers from Ft. Snelling, St. Paul, to build Leavenworth—on the west bank of the Missouri in 1827-28. He passed Omaha, site of the grave of the famous Black Bird chief buried astride his war horse "to watch the French traders" passing up and down the river. It was Catlin the artist, in the 1830's, who found the skeleton of Indian horse and chief. In his first trip west, Catlin had seen nothing in Indian life— except the tortures in the dances of the Mandan Lodges near modern Bismarck—to condemn. In his next trip, his clean sheet for Indian life had dimmed. He wasn't quite sure the old chief hadn't been "a murderous brute" in spite of courage.

The courage of using poison on enemy chiefs and calling it "mystic medicine" wasn't a brand of cunning liked by white men.

Leavenworth had been built as a sort of breakwater line between the Indian raiders—Cherokees, Shawnees, Tuskaroras, Delawares, south; and Omahas, Pawnees, Crows, Sioux, Blackfeet, north. Six or seven companies had been sent away up the Arkansas Southwest to arrange pow-wows of peace. Fifteen ladies dwelt at Leavenworth. Horseback riding was the great racing sport. Fires in the high dry grass of autumn were the awful danger. The Indians called those sweeps of livid flames "the Spirit of Fire" to create new pasture. The Kansas tribes now numbered about 1560, the Pawnees twelve thousand warriors, the Omahas fifteen hundred.

"Catlin," said Leavenworth, as they came riding back across a thousand miles of heat-scorched plains in August from the Arkansas, "we are getting too old to hunt buffalo—we—" Just then the rise to the crest of a hill showed a herd of the shaggy buffalo moving across the plains in search of water. Leavenworth's horse was off like an arrow on the chase. Leavenworth wanted a nice young yearling calf whose fur was in good form and meat would be tender. That calf was no dunce. He had a rabbit trick or two. He would let Leavenworth come right up where the rifle hot to the touch could be aimed—then he would double

back over his tracks and Leavenworth's horse
would be thrown on its haunches in the sudden stop.
Leavenworth laughed. "I'll have that fellow if I
have to break my neck for it," he yelled. Catlin
himself had been tossed astride a small tree. Catlin
saw Leavenworth's horse down and the general on
hands and knees over its head. "Hurt?" shouted
Catlin running up. "No, but I might have been,"
answered the veteran of Indian Wars; and he
fainted. He died a few hours afterward while
catching up with his troopers. In that summer,
more than a third of the troopers on the trail from
Fort Leavenwoth died.

I listened to the whippoorwills' plaintive ditty,
to the quails' querulous note, to the bob-o-links'
joyous call in the clover fields and thought of the
days in the middle of 1830's when Narcissa Whitman and the dauntless doctor came ferrying across
the Missouri to the whitewashed barracks of Fort
Leavenworth high on the ledge above the flats.
The soldiers must have gasped to see a woman
coming as missionary to the back of beyond in this
perilous land, where the only white women, up to
1830, dwelt inside fort walls. And the missionary
hopes were yet so high, their faith so undiminished
by failure, their zeal so unselfish! Hadn't the Indians asked for missionaries? Didn't they pray for
instruction in the Sacred Book? And the way so
far by steamboat had been so easy, warnings as to
perils ahead seemed devices of some coward devil.

The officers of Leavenworth looked sad; but Narcissa Whitman sang her beautiful hymns and looked at the gorgeous sunsets and smiled. She was divinely happy.

To the everlasting credit of the Daughters of the Revolution be it said, they finally restored the old crenelated wall of the first fort with its slit eyes for rifles to cover and protect ferry and steamboat below. On the flats often a thousand people were in promiscuous encampment—traders, rum runners, missionaries, Overlanders.

Pioneers from the Middle West were very religious and sang "Old Hundred" round the camp fires blinking above the yellow flood of the Missouri. Indians lounged about, stoically observing each party. Voyageurs gambled and sang and fiddled and danced. "Eat—drink—be merry—to-morrow we die." Mormons, when their day came, though their chief jumping-off place was Omaha, were a bit grimmer and more fanatical than the Middle West and New England colonists. The Mormons had been hounded with persecutions; and martyrdom always acts as cement. It hardens into adamant unity. There were always Mexicans to swap saddles and horses and silver jewelry to traders and voyageurs and colonists. A great many wagons had come to grief and the blacksmith's anvil above the ridge rang day and night to mighty blows. There were no lazy men in the camp. The Overland was not a trail for lazy men. House-

wives rinsed out clothing in the river or baked
bread in tin reflectors banked opposite the fire. I
think it was at Leavenworth, Narcissa Whitman's
white hands did the first family washing on the
Trail! Poor delicate hands—they were to know
rougher, harder duty for delicate hands within
three years; and they never flinched, however deep
her hopes sank. Matches were few and bottled
for security against damp. Butter had been packed
in the middle of cornmeal sacks. So had eggs and
sometimes the jars of travel had mixed an omelet
all ready for the bake tin. Ready money was carried in a box or belt but was very sparse. Wages
were from twenty-five cents a day to four dollars
for good guides or as much as five dollars by clever
fellows for each passage across a ferry. These men
had calked their wagon boxes with tallow and
tracts sent out by misguided missionary societies
in far lands, when, "the hell fire" missive was apt
to be mixed with tar and tallow and serve a more
immediate use. Many an Oregon Pioneer from
1843 to 1848 learned his first A B C's from these
"hell fire" tracts and they sent him to bed with such
fright, as a boy, sleeping in the cabin loft above the
grown-ups below, that he would awaken howling
with a nightmare complex of too much pudding
and too much imaginary sulphur.

It was well on in the 1860's before stages were
general as far as Leavenworth and these were so
cramped that knees sat interlocked with knees, and

husky travelers preferred horseback. When you consider that even the fastest stage travel of the 1850's seldom exceeded ninety miles a day and often averaged twenty miles with upsets and broken axles and delays in quicksand fords—the discomforts of such travel can be guessed.

Prices were staggering from Leavenworth to Laramie—$1.50 for a pound of tea or coffee; so settlers contented themselves with kin-i-kin-nick—willow leaves steeped as a tea, which were a good purgative for too heavy a meat diet. Sugar, brown, was twenty-five cents a pound; so the Pioneers had brought maple sugar. Flour was $1.50 a pound; so travelers came to depend more and more on berries and roots dried and pounded to a flour.

The place has come to deal with two very controversial topics as to the Overland Trail. The disputes rage chiefly with study-chair trail markers —not Pioneers, nor the descendants of Pioneers, nor people who, themselves, have followed wild trails.

Can the Overland Trail be set down definitely as running always from here to there, and from this point to that?

How many people were on the Trail each year?

Remember there was first the fur traders' migration West. Then there was the Missionary-Pioneer-Oregon migration. Then there was the gold stampede to California.

Parallel with these was the Mormon movement.
Also the Santa Fé wagon travel. Five distinct migrations paralleling and diverging en route as each
traveled westward. Just to state that fact is to
show the absurdity of the disputes.

In some years there were as many as twenty thousand wagons following a road so dusty the wagons
behind could not see the wagons ahead and many
wagons moved five and eight abreast and, as each
platoon of wagons formed for each day, self-im-
posed regulations compelled the dust-free leaders
of yesterday to fall to rear today. It is nonsense to
imagine the same fords could always be used, or
the same ferries were in service. Fords and ferries
depended on flood tides and dry seasons; and these
varied each week and each day as they do today. I
have been over these routes—all of them—in years
when rail tracks were washed out by a cloudburst
and in the very same season in the next year when
the rails would gladly have paid the loss of a washout to help the scorched crops to increase traffic.
I have been out in the month of June when sixteen-
foot snow banks stopped us in a motor and we had
to diverge to a lower road; and I have been out
in April when you would have paid an extra fare
for a whiff of snow air to lower the temperature.
It has always seemed to me such disputes are a bit
futile. Enough to set down that if you draw a
broad belt from Kansas City and Omaha westward

up the Platte to South Pass, you are on the Overland Trail, the epic road of human history.

Leavenworth is not on the Oregon Trail; but you have to know its position relative to the Overlanders' highway. Else you will not understand the hopeless impossibility of moving troops westward fast enough to avert the awful tragedies of the 1847-49 era. Beyond Leavenworth every Pioneer took his life and law in his own hands; and in each covered wagon were more women and children and babies. One does not know whether to tremble at the temerity or applaud the courage. Perhaps both.

How many people were on the Trail each year? What matters it?

When one Pioneer tells you he was in a band of two hundred and seven people and another tells you he was in a group of forty to fifty, and another tells you he saw five thousand wagons pass Laramie in a day, can such figures be checked up by the census of California or Oregon, when the census was guesswork and no census existed west of the Missouri and these birds of passage in movement across the plains were as varied in numbers as the wild geese winging overhead? As a wise guide of mine once answered in the North, "We don't travel here as the crows and geese travel in an air line. We travel as the sand-bars and head winds compel us." Yet who has ever attempted to check up a census of the wild geese awing for the North?

I say no more. The best one can do is tell the story of various groups on the Trail. Then if you don't take your hat off in reverence to hero Pioneers, and feel the tears choke your throat over the lonely graves, or the blood rush to your head in fury at the brutality of some thugs, both red and white, it is because you have lost the zest of real living. These people lived and died to create the West.

CHAPTER III

OMAHA—"ABOVE THE WATERS"

THERE is no mistaking the appropriateness of the Indian names from now on, "Omaha—Above the Waters," "Nebraska—Shallow Waters," and "the Platte—Flat-Muddy-Bottoms." You realize that whether you go on from Kansas City over the Overland Trail by rail or motor; and Council Bluffs hardly needs its name explained. There, under the self-same oaks where Lewis and Clark spread their awning and met the Indian chiefs of a dozen tribes a hundred years ago, you can park your car below the high bluffs and think about the past and the future of the two cities on the heights above the flats. The rivers, themselves, here, are not wide, but from ledge to ledge where the cities stand, it is about eight miles. As in the Kansas Cities, the dividing state line between Iowa East and Nebraska West is right on the viaduct highway.

It is worth while to pause on this viaduct, too. You can see where the river below has shifted its tortuous course twice in a century—once in recent years, once in what became known as the great Madrid earthquake about a hundred years ago. No city was possible on the flats but it was feasible to find foundations for bridges, though you can see where one bridge planned had to be abandoned, with piers left standing, because engineers could not overcome the quicksand bottoms. It is plain, too, why General Dodge and President Lincoln had to choose this spot for the crossing of the first great transcontinental. Northwest, the Missouri Channel widens to a lake seven miles across. Though in two states with separate civic governments, commercially the two cities may be regarded as one, Omaha with over two hundred and sixty thousand people, Council Bluffs with more than sixty thousand.

Again telescoping the mind back to the old days, you can see why the Astorians, following soon after Lewis and Clark, avoided the great circle of the Missouri as well as the raids of Blackfeet north, and came to grief in the Rocky Mountain passes westward of the Platte. You see why missionary and colonist essayed to cross the plains overland rather than attempt any river route by canoe and rowboat. To have followed the river routes would have been akin to tracing the course of a long wriggling snake. The best air line was directly west.

Be it acknowledged frankly, both cities show signs of having suffered declines—perhaps I should say setbacks—following the War; but as the causes of the setbacks are also the causes of the comebacks, the swing of the pendulum is worth analyzing.

Let it be acknowledged frankly also—Panama is working a silent inevitable revolution in the Middle West. Chicago is not the Middle West. It is the western terminus of the East. Draw a line down equal distances from the Mississippi and the Pacific. The 100th Meridian marks the dividing line. That is the Middle West. Canals have never lastingly helped nor hurt any other section in America. Only where they deepened natural waterways to the ocean have they created new central cities by moving the ocean farther inland; but Panama is more than a canal. It is the shortest portage between two oceans; and ocean transport is cheaper than rail as one to seven. It must always be. There is no track bed to be built. There are no rails to be bought and replaced. There are no ties to be laid and replaced. There are no track crews to go out daily and clean up the cluttered highway. There are no spikes to be driven, no weeds to be sprayed out, no washout to be repaired, no bridges, no fill-ins, no sidings, no stations every few miles, no freight sheds, no round houses, no water tanks, no freight cars to be built, repaired, no tunnels. Compare these with any corresponding costs of ocean transport. The difference totals thousands of dollars a mile in places, millions in sections with long tunnels and long bridges.

Has, then, the Middle West suffered a vital final blow from Panama? By no means. Why not? Because in that Middle West dwell sixty million people, who must always be heavy buyers of all that the factories produce. Because that Middle West is the great producer of all the staples that the whole world eats. Across it must always shuttle the carriers of what is bought and sold. Can freight rates be reduced to meet ocean rates? They cannot. Such rates would throw every carrier in the Middle West into bankruptcy. Can the waterways of the Missouri and the Mississippi be deepened and improved to move the ocean inland as in the case of the St. Lawrence up to Montreal? There is a violent controversy over that right now. The Army engineers say the Missouri and the Mississippi cannot. The civil engineers say these river highways can be improved to become cheap feeders to ocean traffic. In other words—can the Missouri which is the longest water highway in the world be humanly controlled? It is a big job. It would cost as much as Panama and would be worth as much as its cost to the Middle West in a single year. Panama required a century to be conquered. Can the Missouri be conquered in this century? Will Hoover be the Saint George to slay the Dragon Snakes, the Pythons Missouri and Mississippi? Who can answer? Sixty million people buy and sell in the Middle West. Though the Atlantic and Pacific seaboard cities enjoy ad-

vantages no inland centers can, no inland centers
that are the hubs of a wheel turning round such an
empire can be sufferers from a final setback. From
what are these prosperous Atlantic and Pacific
cities prospering? From what the Middle West
buys and sells.

Other causes that came as hard back-kicks from
the Great War are another example in the swing
of the pendulum from low to high. Try to see
clearly here. There is no use doing anything else.
It is a lesson for all time. A great deal of the
Middle West was settled by the thriftiest, hardest-
working type of German settlers in the immigra-
tion movement from 1848 to 1870. In fact, during
the Civil War, St. Louis was known as a "Dutch
town." They did not love their native land less
because they came to America, but they loved the
freedom of America more. I, who am of British
and American ancestry, acknowledge that the
aspersions cast on these people during the War
were unjust. When War Bonds came to be sold,
their thrift enabled them to be eager and ready
cash buyers. War prices had bulged their bank
accounts and the proof of their fealty to Uncle
Sam was that they bought War Bonds eagerly.
But War prices had also sent up new factories for
hides, beef, hogs, flour, sugar; and when bonds
had to be floated to expand these factories, further
proof of the German-American's loyalty was demanded—may I say forced?—to buy the bonds

of these factories. One of these in the beef-pack-
ing industry went into bankruptcy, another went
so close to the bankrupt dead-line that its stock
fell to seven and six from a hundred and reduced
one of the biggest packing fortunes in America to
such a residuum that the public gasped.

With the added pressure of the banks, the Middle West thrifty German-American, to prove his
loyalty, had bought these inflated factory securi-
ties. He had not bought as Americans buy—for
a quick profit. He had bought to hold and lock
up; and when the smash came, he was locked up
all tight in bad losses, in many cases, in total
losses. Now recall, too, that in the inflated period
of the War, even the canny stolid German-American had also lost his head and over-expanded his
holdings of live stock and farm lands. Against
those the banks held his paper.

When the smash in prices came after the War,
fell tragedy, dire tragedy—terrible tragedy, for
those in debt, more terrible for older folk past
fifty and sixty years of age. They could not live
long enough to recover and swing back with the
ascending pendulum of the eternal balances. Those
not in debt were safe. Those in debt were caught
between the blades of two scissors—debts to banks
for live stock and investments, and loss on live
stock hurried to market on a glut of lowered prices
and sold under pressure to pay interest overdue
and overdue instalments on investments. The

banks, themselves, were on no easy street. They
had underwritten those bonds. They had advanced
money on notes to expand factory and farm.
Lands that ought to have been left in pasture had
been plowed up for wheat. Now wheat from
dry farm areas west of the Rockies is one thing and
wheat on the eastern foothills of the Rockies is
quite another. Wheat on the dry farm areas of
the Inland Empire, the country between the Rocky
Mountains and the Cascades Range, grows from
the glacial silt of millions of years. Give it moisture in winter rains or snowfall, and it will hold that
moisture for summer use, but the eastern foot-hills
will not. They have a top humus of thin soil that
grows bunch grass (buffalo grass) forever; but
they haven't a depth of soil to hold moisture. It
runs off to bottom lands, which are rich as the
richest; but to let shallow land revert back to pasture requires from ten to twenty years. The interval is an era of weeds high as barb-wire fences
drifting in terrible tumbling waves of dry seeds
spreading ruin. Then back gradually comes the
grass and back comes the pasture and back comes
the vast herd of cattle or sheep. Both Nebraska
and Wyoming have hinterlands in the Northwest
belt with thousands, yes, millions, of such acres.

Now ride round Omaha and you will read the
whole story in a moving human picture film ticked
off by life's balance wheel. It is a speaking human picture, too; but it ends well; and all's well

GROOVES MADE BY PIONEER WAGON WHEELS IN SOLID ROCK
NEAR SPLIT ROCK, WYOMING

INDEPENDENCE ROCK

KANSAS CITY 1855.

From old engraving, NATHAN GREELEY, Esq., KANSAS CITY TIMES

Courtesy of Kansas City Chamber of Commerce

KANSAS CITY, 1855

that ends well, as Shakespeare says. You see the oozing prosperity of the banking and hotel section, but on the bridges near the packing plants, the prosperity doesn't ooze quite so noisily as it did. Circle round the stock yards. Not gloomy, but still distinctly disturbing—stock yards being ripped up; miles of little houses for workmen, needing paint if not empty; miles of little shops looking lame and moribund if not dead. Something forced these occupants to move away. It was necessity. The Pacific Coast got many of them and gained as the Middle West lost.

But wait a minute! What is happening now? The live stock beginning to come back is rising in price weekly from ten to twenty-four cents a hundred. Those hinterlands are beginning to ship again from Nebraska and Wyoming. I think of one little German burg of perhaps two hundred people, where a gruff old burly fellow, part farmer, part banker, who is now yearly sending to market for himself and his neighbors, a hundred thousand dollars' worth of furs and six times that value in cattle and sheep. "What do the farmers chiefly need?" I asked one taciturn old chap. "To be let alone—to cut out the middleman—cheap water rates if we can get 'em." I have no comment to add to his answer. He hit what is called "a problem" on its head and he hit it with a mallet from annealed experience. Only you must not be surprised if some folks in the Middle West are a little sore on their banking experiences and some politicians perfectly conscientiously a little muddled on remedies.

From the present let us turn to the past long before Lewis and Clark's day.

It will jolt Eastern feeling of aged experience a bit to realize that Nebraska and Wyoming are two of the oldest sections in the United States. As Alfred Sorenson says in his admirable narrative of Omaha: eighty years before the Pilgrims landed on Plymouth Rock, sixty years before Hudson came poking into New York harbor, three years before Shakespeare was born, when Queen Elizabeth of England was yet a toddling baby— Nebraska and Wyoming had been discovered by Coronado with his three hundred Spaniards and eight hundred Indians seeking the Seven Mythical Cities of Indian lore. Proof? Coronado's own record and the fact that an antique Spanish stirrup of that date was dug up on the very streets of Omaha.

We may hate to shatter some illusions here but truth compels it. From paintings and drawings on this Spanish period, one's mental picture is of soldiers clad in mail from helmet to leg greaves and metal boot, with a flag held high aloft and a holy padre with cross upraised in one hand. Far different was the real scene. The soldiers were for the most part ragamuffin convicts wearing little but canvas shirts belted at the waist, broad hats of Indian weave and such foot-gear as would protect from cactus spines. They were—as we know from priest annals—both lawless and evil in all their relations with the Indians; but they were armed, heavily armed with bayonets and pistols and swords. They raided Indian camps for food for themselves and forage for their poor scrubs of starveling horses. This probably explains the perpetual enmity between Spaniards and all Indian tribes. The Indians had at first regarded the Spanish as gods. Too often the gods acted like evil demons of untellable cruelty; and the young Spanish officers could not control their mutinous convict troops.

The Overland Trail is not only the longest in history, but it is one of the oldest.

While Lewis and Clark camped first ten miles below the present cities to send their scouts out to call the tribal chiefs, the council under the tent awning was held a few miles above Omaha on the west bank. If you ask yourself why Lewis and Clark's estimate of the tribes is so much lower in figures than Catlin's, you had better umpire the difference with the estimate of General Grenville Dodge of Union Pacific fame, who knew these tribes better than any man except General Miles. He puts their fighting force in the 1860's at twenty-five thousand, higher than Catlin or Lewis and Clark, and he gives the explanation. He would not touch the construction of the Union

Pacific without an entirely free hand on the railroad in laying the tracks up the best roadbed—the Platte—and adequate protection from the Army. He had had his bitter experience of directing Western affairs from the East during the Civil War; and on this stand he had the full support of Lincoln and Grant and Sherman and Sheridan —who knew the West as he did. He knew the Pawnees were huge fellows, tough as whalebone and ferocious fighters, though they might squat and lounge round frontier towns in rags, acting as beggars and petty pilferers. Every Indian tribe they conquered they absorbed in their own numbers, so they might speak in a dozen dialects and as many distinct languages. This accounts for Lewis and Clark's different names and totals. Dodge had fought them first, but later employed them in the Civil War. That didn't exempt him from their raids. Not in the least. Every tribe from the Upper Missouri to the Kansas was by Dodge's time leagued against the white man's advance—first, because he now knew the white men were divided among themselves; second, because from Lewis and Clark's day, each tribe had been increasing its use of white man firearms and knew its fighting ground as the white scout couldn't. He had learned a lot, too, from the white man —scouting, spying, semaphoring, cutting off from base supplies, weakening first by running off enemy horses—then a pounce on the encircled

enemy marooned on the ocean of prairie as completely as ever crew could be marooned by pirates.
Where he couldn't beat a white force, he maneu-
vered to split it and defeat first one end of it and
then the other. That was Custer's undoing. Once
Custer and Dodge met in a great rail office in the
East. Everybody had had a good dinner and was
feeling pretty "heady." Custer was boasting any
well-trained white soldier finely mounted and
armed could defeat six times as many Indians.
"Custer," said Dodge in his blunt way, "that may
be brave but it is no longer true. It is rash madness. You talk like a fool. The Indian has learned
a lot in a century."

But we are anticipating our story.

Lewis and Clark noted "the sand bars so rolling
we were unable to steer with our oars," "the great
muddy river so rapid" below its oily yellow surface, the hot temperature at midday, the sudden
fall to chill at night, the gobble of wild turkeys
in the high grass of July, the wild oaks and wal-
nuts you see today, the lonely threnody of the
whippoorwill all night, the thick fogs of night
and morning, which acted as such a dangerous
screen for spying Indians, a little river coming
in on the west called Elkhorn from a chief. Please
note that name. You will meet it again presently
in one of the most terrible episodes of the Overland Migration—seldom told. At or near Council
Bluffs, Lewis and Clark camped under oaks, wal-

nut, elms. When the chiefs came together, Lewis
and Clark found the Pawnees had many lodges,
many clans, many tribes—Wolf Pawnees from the
Platte well named; Kites back from the river, so
called because they rode so furiously that their
passing raiders were like hawks pouncing on victims of "extreme ferocity," never yielding in
battle. It was the first week of August the council
was held. The Indians expressed joy because they
"wanted firearms." Of course they did, and you
will learn how they used them for half a century.

About sixteen to twenty miles north of Omaha,
General Henry Atkinson from 1821 to 1828 held
his Fort Atkinson as a sort of breakwater to hold
these Pawnees in check till, the flats proving too
unsafe, the fort had to be moved down to Leavenworth. Atkinson is another of the old soldier
heroes whom Fort Leavenworth has as completely
forgotten as though he had never existed.

Then began to drift past the Bluffs the fur
trade up the Platte because it was shorter than
up the far Northern Missouri from the river route
across to the headwaters of the Snake; and after
the fur traders came the missionaries of the 1830's
and the Pioneers of the 1840's—then the Overland rush to California from 1848, then the
rail era.

In the 1850's, when the Oregon Massacre had
temporarily stopped the Oregon Pioneer rush, the
Mormon migration had been in full flood west.

Kanesville—modern Council Bluffs—was the jumping-off place for the Mormons to the great unknown West. It is said at this period as settlers approached Council Bluffs (then Kanesville) the converging lines of travel to the river, the covered wagons resembled a great flat iron pointing to water front. There were ferries of every variety on the Missouri at this time—flatboats propelled by polesmen, which swirled and whirled like tops to the current; steamers, side-wheelers, which puffed and grunted day and night from side to side of the broad river; wagons calked with tar and tallow, which were unsafe in flood waters of spring; Indian canoes, rowboats, log rafts for single passengers; and the flats below the cliffs on the west side resembled a tent city roofing every sort of frontier character from scoundrel riff-raff to such saints as the Whitmans. Crime was, of course, rampant.

Logan Fontenelle, a fur trader, by marriage had allied himself to the protection of the Pawnees. You will see his portrait in the rotunda of the Fontenelle Hotel in Omaha—a clean, strong, terribly strong face. He was finally killed by fourteen arrows in a battle defending the Pawnees from Northern Sioux. To give you an example of the ferocity of those halcyon days before white men came: an Iowa Indian had killed an Omaha boy by spearing his living body to the ground. The Iowa who did it was drunk. No matter. Fontenelle's Indian wife took an ax, watched her chance when the drunk slept off his torpor, entered the shanty where he slept, plunged the ax in the murderer's head and escaped by jumping through the shanty window.

Five miles out on Elkhorn River, between the site of General Dodge's first cabin and the modern city of Omaha, you will find the name on rail maps commemorating an almost unknown episode. In 1852 the flood tide of Westward Ho was at its height to Utah and California. A brutal blacksmith on his way to California had sworn he would shoot the first Indian he saw just to "have a nick in his gun." He did. His victim was a Pawnee boy. Now when the Mormons began moving across from Kanesville (Council Bluffs) to Omaha (Florence) they had made a treaty with Big Elk for a lease of land during five years till they could move the people gradually westward; and both parties had respected and observed that treaty; but here was a frightful crime unprovoked against the Pawnees. The Mormons did not want to stain their hands by becoming hangmen. Neither did any of the other Pioneers, though crimes later along the Trail compelled them to overcome that reluctance. They handed the white murderer over to the Pawnees for punishment. The Pawnees tied him to a wagon wheel and skinned him alive. For years this gruesome spot was known as Rawhide.

Still graver was the danger to lonely outpost

cabins along the Trail from white man thugs per-
petrating outrages on the Pawnees and the Pawnees' demand for blood atonement falling on these
unprotected families. So great was the danger,
Colonel Dodge moved his family across to Council Bluffs. Buffalo Bill at this time scout, sometimes Pony Express rider to Fort Kearney, moved
his family to Fort Leavenworth. When six thousand Mormons moved across to Florence (Omaha)
to begin their long trek, this suburb of the city
was named after Brigham Young's favorite wife,
a relative of President Cleveland's wife. Mormon
trade was worth two million dollars a year to the
little shops of what is now a beautiful suburb.
Purchases by Overlanders ran at two thousand
dollars a day in Omaha. Lots were selling at
twenty-five dollars each or nothing to people who
would build and improve. Omaha had numbered
only five hundred before the Mormons came. As
emigrants passed westward, the first post-office was
a man's hat. He would come from his shop and
yell the name of the emigrant and hand the letter
out of his hat. Farther along the Trail, a buffalo
skull was marked Post-Office and letters of advance parties were picked out by following relatives. Later still, a wagon box was rigged up with
pigeonholes and set behind the counters of outfitters' shops in whose care letters were left. It was
all very primitive, but it answered.

Of course fur traders with Indian wives resented

the slurs on their families by newcomers and the
story is told of Peter Sarpy challenging a bully
to settle the question on the spot with a duel. The
bully accepted the challenge and onlookers got out
of the way; but as the two duelists left the shop,
Peter turned and shot out the candle. When he
looked for his antagonist to pace off distances, the
fellow had dived in the dark.

By the time Nebraska became a territory, 1854,
a stage ran between the two cities and gaiety began
to intersperse hard living.

To the barn dances came ladies from Fort
Leavenworth, hoops, bustles, fine slippers, with
the officers in full regalia. The old Spanish fandangoes and minuets were stepped off gracefully
as in any ballroom; but on the same floor danced
"mountain men" in thick boots pegged for the
rocks, and in traders' moccasins. The rough floors
were not waxed. They were worse. They were
cottonwood fresh peeled. Now cottonwood fresh
peeled is about as glassy as slippery elm. The
moccasin dancers were all right. They could keep
on the perpendicular, but as the German fiddlers
played faster and faster to the final whirl of the
fandangoes, fiddling so their heads almost bounced
from the beer barrels on which the orchestra sat,
those mountain men came to awful grief. They
sat down expectedly on the slippery planking. It
added to the fun of the unexpected.

The first murder of a white man came from

claim jumping; for titles were to a hundred and sixty acres with "squatters' rights" till survey could be made. Ruffians used to come in, defiant of law, and jump a claim by planting a whisky bottle upside down at the four corners, just as, in stage days, in defiance of law, they would drive their wagons with a whisky bottle on the end of a pole and crossbones drawn on a flag. They proclaimed themselves land pirates and gloried in it. The first time a jumper tried tricks on a squatter's right, he was ducked in the river. Three duckings usually cured the habit. Still, white vagabonds would run off stock and sell it to the Pawnees, or steal firearms from lonely settlement cabins and trade them to the Indians. The first policy was to pay the Indians to arrest the thieves, when the culprit would have his beard or head half shaved and be given thirty-nine lashes on the bare back. Still, no white man wanted the dirty job of flogging a human skunk. So the emigrants hired a Madagascar negro; and it is said he did his job very thoroughly. But the attacks and threats against women alone in cabins while their men were on the trail were a graver crime that had to be stopped. They would enter a cabin whetting their hunting knives against high boots and bid the wife jump to cook a meal, or hand over spare cash, or give up her absent husband's firearms, and then if drunk or emboldened by the woman's fear— worse was likely to follow. Where two black-

guards guilty of this had been thoroughly identi-
fied, the self-called jury pronounced sentence of
death; but no one wanted the dirty job of execut-
ing the sentence, or the memory that if half a
dozen executioners fired simultaneously, no man
would know which bullet caused the death. Again
the frontier carried out law in its own way. The
men weighed about the same. They were not blind-
folded to spare their feelings. Two poles were
erected. A crossbeam connected the tops. The
criminals were placed on props. The drop noose
was fastened to each neck so it would tighten and
strangle—then the prop knocked from their feet.
Each man's weight strangled and broke his partner's neck. Where the bullies had not succeeded
in terrorizing a settler's wife but had been perhaps
cordially received with a pot of lye, the rascals
were given so far to outrun punishment, then a
vigilante committee fired at the racing heels. These
methods were very effective in stopping crimes.
The methods had to be drastic till law could be established and proper courts with military protection set up.

After the gold rush of 1848 set in, as many as
twenty thousand were on the Overland Trail
in a year, with at least eleven thousand men on
horses and families under the tent of the covered
wagon, oxen for beef, cows for milk trailing behind or parallel. When you add these totals to the
Mormon migration and Oregon Pioneers, it mat-

ters little how many reached their destination, how many turned back discouraged, how many perished by the way. It gives a faint idea of what the Overland Trail was in the great epic of a nation.

In 1847, two thousand Mormons were on the trail, some moving with hand carts across the plains. By 1856, the Mormons were on the trail literally in thousands. That treaty with the Pawnees stood them in mighty good stead. By 1847, five thousand Oregon Pioneers were on the Trail, a thousand Californians, though gold had not become the magnet of the stampede that followed in the next few years. Wagons required rough corduroy bridges across some streams and mud holes; from which one Pawnee got a bright new inspiration. He would post himself on the bridge and demand toll to cross. A long rawhide mule whip, or rifle handed out by the wife in the covered wagon usually sent him scampering. Long dresses became Turkish bloomers. Boots were exchanged for the easier moccasin and hats for sun bonnets extemporized from superfluous petticoats to screen the face from the blazing sun and awful powder of cloudy dust.

Storms broke the heat with terrible violence of balls of lightning bouncing over the ground; but what was lightning to a peppering rain of Indian bucks' small shot hitting the tent roof? The rains laid the dust and permitted a good wash of faces and clothing, as well as swelling the dried wagon

frame threatening to rattle apart from sheer sun-
scorch. Repairs could only be made at few and
far intervals, we shall visit as we pass; and I do
not know whether those travelers were wiser whose
pace quickened to the watch word, "Faster—faster
—today," or those who slowed up to avoid break-
downs. All knew they must get across South Pass
before snow blocked the way.

Lincoln was one of the most picturesque figures
in 1859. He had loaned money on a mortgage at
Council Bluffs. He came out to look over the
ground. It was while sitting with his feet on the
railing of the old Pacific House that he dug out
of Dodge, the young surveyor, all the facts for a
route up the Platte, which later materialized in
the Union Pacific. A shaft commemorates his visit
to Council Bluffs, but he was quick to see that the
real Western terminus must be Omaha, and he
enforced that, when he later became president.
One would give a good deal to know his
thoughts as he sat with his long legs braced against
the railing of the old Pacific Hotel, which you
can see to this day. Lincoln was at this time an
exceedingly handsome young man in spite of his
ungainly lank long shambling figure. He was
clean shaved. His hair was thick over his temples, brushed back. His forehead was very white,
his face fuller and healthier in color than a few
years later and quite untrenched by the terrible

lines of care that soon after trenched eyes and forehead with a sculpture of agony. It was really the face of a young prophet. We know that even in the 1850's, he grasped what few in the nation did—that here westward must grow up a new republic to be held in national unity at any cost. He had been an attorney for Eastern railroads and knew they must be projected across the Missouri —again at any cost, though the nation must pay the cost. He knew roads—rail and wagon—must be built and protected by troops.

I have spoken of the Pony Mail Express preceding rails. It deserves more than passing notice. It was one of the most picturesque things on the Trail. It developed some of the finest types of booted and spurred knights known to history; and nearly all have passed to oblivion or died on duty in their boots. Far as I know only one— Buffalo Bill—came down in history and he came by the showman's route. Yet I know sons and daughters of some of those Pony Express riders, who have told me tales of their fathers, who lost a leg or arm by being frozen as they reeled off the dizzy miles in winter blizzard; but—they got the mail through and for that duty received five dollars a day and keep.

The Pony Express was in sections the same old trail the Astorians had followed, the fur traders and the Oregon Pioneers and the California

Argonauts; but its era was short and glorious as a meteor blazing out of the night and back into the dark. "The Boulevards of Steel"—as Miss Pack describes them—took the mail contracts and the telegraph lines, which the Indians first feared as "bad medicine" and then cut down to defeat white man movements, gained much of the Pony Express Mail business; but few episodes in the West are so crammed with thrills—human thrills, too, not "colicky" bull-frog dilations. Just before the Civil War, Fort Kearney, west of Omaha, was counting eight hundred wagons with ten thousand oxen passing a day. How many people were in each wagon is pure guesswork; but the cost and uncertainty of mail post-offices in old plug hats and buffalo skulls and wagon-boxes was no joke. Letters might cost from five dollars to fifty cents from New York to the Pacific Coast. They might require six months in transit or a year. It was a joke that as many of the Western Territories were organized, their representatives in Washington might not receive mail from constituents till the term had expired.

The Pony Express began in 1860. It averaged two hundred and fifty miles a day! Look at these figures. Alexander the Great's express riders over the best roads the East ever knew made ninety miles a day and President Washington's Army Express did well to make twenty. Stage lines and covered wagons were already on the Trail when

AERIAL VIEW OF BUSINESS DISTRICT, KANSAS CITY, MISSOURI, SHOWING NEW AVIATION FIELD IN UPPER RIGHT

INDEPENDENCE ROCK, SHOWING AUTOGRAPHS OF DESERT
TRAVELERS AND MODERN DESECRATION

WAGON TRAIN MOVING DOWN ECHO CANYON, BRINGING SUP-
PLIES TO THE BUILDERS OF THE UNION PACIFIC

the Pony Express began. Miss Pack says, forty thousand emigrants were on the Trail by 1849; and those figures are nearer the truth than the ridiculous estimates of from twelve hundred to five thousand a year. One firm's freight teams numbered six thousand wagons and seventy-five thousand oxen. Of course, the Eastern senators and congressmen ridiculed the possibility of the new fast Pony Express, but a government expenditure of two millions a year for mails did ultimately beat into Eastern heads that something must be done to connect Pacific and Atlantic to handle mails faster and cheaper. The outlay involved by the private firm undertaking the Pony Express was enormous. Cool-headed, light-weight young fellows were picked for the riders from the Missouri to the Pacific. Hardy, lean fast horses—crossbred from best plains cayuses and domestic racing strains—were selected—our typical fine broncho, at two hundred dollars to four hundred each. Almost two hundred changing stations with four hundred helpers and eighty riders were placed at these stations. Spectators came out to cheer the riders at each way house, and one of the first races was made in nine days and twenty-three hours from the Missouri to Sacramento. Each rider's division was limited to seventy-five miles. Saddle, bridle, saddle bags, could not exceed thirteen pounds and the mail was limited to twenty pounds a runner. Riders could not exceed one hundred and thirty-five pounds weight. Arms were two revolvers and a sheathed knife. A buckskin coat, trousers tucked in high boots and a slouch hat were the picturesque costume. The mail was tied in water-proof bags. Each rider had to take oath, *"I . . . , do hereby swear, before the Great and Living God, that during my engagement, and while I am an employe of Russell, Majors & Waddell, I will under no circumstances, use profane language; that I will drink no intoxicating liquors; that I will not quarrel or fight with any other employe of the firm, and that in every respect, I will conduct myself honestly, be faithful to my duties and so direct all my acts as to win the confidence of my employers. So help me God."*

Often all that the emigrants saw was a flashing horseman riding at mad speed through the dust, who waved his hat, vanished and perhaps at the next turn of the trail ran into a peppering shot of Indian bucks' raid, which he dodged by sheer speed or ducking down on the far side of his horse. Into the night, out of the night, through winter blizzard and summer heat he rode.

Though Fort Leavenworth was the army destination of much eastbound mail, owing to growing commercial requirements, Kansas City and Omaha received and sent the bulk of the mail; and it is at these points and on the Pacific Coast, you will find the best traditions of the Pony Express service.

One night as I paused at one of the great Air

Mail stations across the continent, where a hail-storm had stalled many of the young air pilots, I watched the skirts of the gale sweeping the snowy peaks in dusky majesty. I thought of Narcissa Whitman with her high dreams of a beautiful service—how she used to sing in her lovely soprano voice the hymns of her childhood home to the rough campers at nightfall; how she used to quell their wild lawless passions with memories of a childhood almost fading from their memories; how she must have watched just such sunsets amid storms and blood-red clouds; how the blaze of translucent light in the West must have seemed a paved path of consecrated glory straight to God. As I watched, the sun was setting in the blaze of a gold shield to the far West. The young aviators charting a new trail through the skies were singing lustily in rooms all down the corridor. They were not chanting Old Hundred either, but they were chanting the timeless chant of youth's high endeavor to new trails, to new eras in human progress. Of youth's quest there is no toll. I glanced down the head-lines of the evening paper in my lap—six dead that day among the air pilots. Yet the reckless daring of the Pony Express conquered one difficulty long ago in the 1860's. Without the recklessness of youth, where would we troglodytes of earth be today? Where Snake Indians and Bannock Indians were—in our caves of life, of soul, of foreshortened vision. The sun was sinking. Darkness was falling in a pansy blue curtain over the snowy peaks, but before the day's curtain had fallen over the darkening valleys, the setting sun sent a shot of light that created against the receding storm that rainbow of eternal hope for the next day; and sure enough, the next day dawn, these air birds were off in their blue-winged beautiful aeroplanes. Was it symbolic of today and tomorrow—I asked.

And again as the Mexican says—*Quien sabe?*

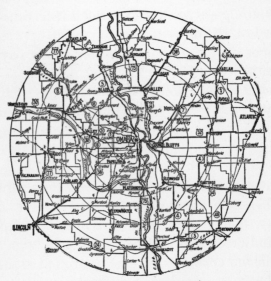

METROPOLITAN OMAHA

CHAPTER IV

"At Last We Are Off"—Fort Kearney

WHETHER from Omaha, Leavenworth or Kansas City, the direction of all Overlanders was up the Platte. Whether one party traveled along the north bank of the Platte and another along the south bank of the Platte and yet another took the short cut—the diameter of the circle—across the Big and Little Blue Rivers, at last all were off.

Hopes were sky-high. They were the hopes of an eternal youth—hearts young as long as they cherished hopes. Very few of the Overlanders at first were over forty-five. It took well on towards Fort Kearney—two hundred miles as the Platte looped among the sands, one hundred and eighty-six by modern rail or by motor—before confusion on the Trail shook down to some semblance of self-regulated order. In this shaking down process, there were heart burnings. One of the most ludicrous was as to pet dogs. Old home dogs were in the covered caravans or trotted along beside the horsemen; but at night when the wagons formed a circle round the campers and hobbled horses and pasturing cows and oxen, the men said the barking of the dogs betrayed the camping place to spying Pawnee raiders; for bark these dogs would in defiant chorus to the challenging howl of the wolves—whether wretched little mangy coyotes or big timber wolves still common among the brushwood lining the stream beds. The women said, "no," when asleep in camp, these dogs acted as dependable sentinels against foes, snakes, "varmint," by which they meant prowling coyotes, porcupines, badger, skunks "loaded for bear," anything that could scratch under tent skirts and steal ham or bacon or pemmican bags. I hardly need to explain what "loaded for bear" meant. It meant a little skunk could shoot a big bear into quick retreat. The dispute as usual, when humans do not scratch irritation to a running deeper wound, settled itself in the case of the dogs scampering off after the wolves or Indian mongrels, and ending their earthly race in an Indian stew pot. A more ludicrous dog episode comes later in the story, when we reach Laramie.

Guides more or less dependable were picked up among the fur traders from the jumping-off place; but the guides were subject to orders from the leaders of each Overland Party; and a great many self-appointed leaders strutting with an untried confidence came to grief against the supreme test —Facts. By the time the Platte was reached, they were either eager to give place to better men, or sulked off with their own particular groups; and these groups, finding that such "blind leaders of

the blind" either ditched them in a ford, or bogged
them in quicksands, or made camp beside alkali
water, dropped off to the bands with better leaders.
Scouts proceeded ten to fifteen miles ahead of the
marching caravans. These were to watch for Indians. They used spy-glasses, or else recognized
the tell-tale signs of Indians on the ramp—unshod
cayuse tracks in the mud and sand, little marks
stuck up or nicked in brushwood, waste refuse of
recently abandoned night camps. These scouts
also had the imperative duty of picking good
camping places, not too exposed to raid, flood or
dust storms; close to good drinking water for man
and beast. Behind the scouts rode the best frontiersmen to pick up such fresh game as they could
—rabbit, buffalo, antelope, prairie chicken, ducks
in myriad flocks quacking on the flood waters of
April and May. Then followed the caravan
wagons in line and as the migration grew greater
with each year abreast in procession of five and
six trails—a moving army five hundred miles long
when the Overland Trail was at its zenith. It was
usual to have a horseman with rifle over shoulder
riding abreast of each four or sixteen wagons, and
his wife often had an extra loaded gun in the
tented caravan to hand out in case the guard had
not time to reload when attacked. She, too, could
use that gun and frequently drove the team.

A milk cow plodding behind was another feature in the picturesque procession. The horse or

mule group was called "the wagon column"; the stock or oxen behind, the "cow column"; but old bossy with the milk was needed nearer than the "cow column." She could be used at once on camping and housewives didn't want her stampeded in a buffalo run or Indian raid.

Perhaps the very hardest duty was the night sentry's to guard the stock. He slept out close to his own stock. Doesn't convey much meaning, that phrase "slept out"—does it? What it meant was he stuck a piece of oilcloth over the barrel of his gun—then he slept with both ears alert for restlessness among his herds. When a storm broke in the terrific suddenness of that region, he covered himself as best he could with "slicker coat" or canvas, and often came in to breakfast soaked to the skin or with his high boots filled with water. When the heat of midday changed to the raw foggy chill of night, or a ramping whining peevish wind from the north, he huddled up close back to back with his snoring cow or ox.

So gay were the spirits of youth on setting out, each night camp witnessed mouth organs and flutes and concertinas playing an old-fashioned dance where lovers laughed at hardships, told each other why the Man in the Moon smiled, and exchanged vows often ratified on the Trail if a parson could be found to tie the holy knot of a life partnership. Why not laugh and be glad? Wasn't there a pot of fortune at the end of the Rainbow Trail? Yes, there was; but it was at the end of the Trail; and for some the grave lay between them and the end; and for others, the Rainbow of Hope spanned twenty to forty years before hope could be realized. Perhaps it is a good thing they did not foreknow that, or the surplus of hopes would not have been ample enough for the sight draft on reserves. Very few had even a hundred dollars cash on their person. They had expended all cash on stock and supplies—such useless cumbering supplies too—cupboards, cook-stoves, bedroom furniture, parlor organs, what-nots, flour that molded in the damp, feather beds to ease sleep in the wagons but requiring too much space. Before the Platte was reached, much of this useless baggage was being discarded to lighten loads at boggy fords or permit faster pace, to keep ahead and avoid dust of teams to the fore. The discard was good for the marchers but bad for the pilfering Pawnees. It kept them hounding the Trail like the coyotes; and in the past fifty years—as Grenville Dodge said in the 1860's—the Pawnees had learned a lot. They had learned how to shoot. They had learned how to semaphore. They, too, had spy-glasses bought from traders—spy-glasses of longer range than their own wonderful vision, or that of "Long Eyes" Dodge, himself. Many an old harmless looking chief would sit on a hill semaphoring by glass or tin mirror or smoke signal young bucks on the raid, whom he querulously complained he could not control. You will get some examples of this as we reach Fort Kearney. Hancock tells how in 1845, still on the Blues, Indians had stolen "quite a number of our cattle" and "a bell-cow" —good signaling for a prowling thief—was found full of arrows, and what was mistaken for game in a tree top proved to be "a buck" spy, who scampered. At the ferry across the Little Blue were "more wolves" than ever he had seen and the night echoed with "their yells as if all the wolves for a thousand miles had congregated for our benefit." He calls them "traveling musicians" just as my own guides in the Far North used to call them "our string band." On the Platte, "fifty miles out," smoke signals were descried and horses were "missed." That night, his group camped "without fire." The Indians were Sioux, probably buffalo hunting; for the big beasts went lumbering past in their yearly trek north and had to be kept off the wagon circle by an "incessant firing of guns." He saw the devilish ingenuity of the wolf packs, too. Where the old buffaloes could not keep up with the herds, the wolves "would gnaw their hamstrings" and begin their feast on the living, but lamed victims. It was on the north side of the first Platte ford that four horses and twenty-five cattle were run off. At a halt to wash clothes and repair wagons, a white scout was found lifeless, naked, scalped.

Incredible as it seems, babies were born in the

marching caravan. One does not know whether to deplore or admire the rashness of fortune seekers, who took such chances on the Trail. Sometimes, the mother and child survived. Sometimes, they didn't and left little families to go on, a half-orphaned brood, to be mothered by others in the caravans. When such births occurred, a strange hush fell on the night camp. When Dr. Whitman led the Overlanders in the great rush of 1843, he was an Angel of Help to mothers and children.

By the time the Platte was being followed, few had energy left for the gay dances, or singing of Old Hundred, or camp fire religious meetings. All were tumbling to bed utterly exhausted each night. The Platte seemed so muddy many travelers used to clear spring drinking water made a terrible mistake. They persisted in digging shallow holes, where the water filtered through the sand and seemed clearer; but water not drawn from deeper artesian sources was apt to be impregnated with alkali sediment. The effects of alkali water were known to the fur traders and mountain men but not to the Middle Westerners, and the usual symptoms of cholera became apparent next day—griping cramps, stomachs that reacted to food in pains and enforced stop to recover. The muddy water of the Platte draining from the mountains westward was less harmful.

The program for each day was much the same for all groups in the caravans. Night watches sniffed whiffs of coffee and camp fires and roused their stiffened limbs to the oxen's slow lift and uncurling of his stiffer foot-sore legs. A trumpet blew "Up—" at 5 A.M. and the call "grub —get ready," "roll out," "rise," went from tent to tent. Animals were sorted out and rounded up. Breakfast was served 6 to 7, and the teamsters expected to have beasts yoked or harnessed according to oxen or horses by 7. As a horse would go lame, an ox was often hitched to team with mule or horse; but where the latter didn't object to the partnership by vigorous kicks, the ox often did by pitching. Patience accomplished more than profanity, though I think it is Meeker records that once a patient Quaker counseled, "If thee has to say the word to make him go, let out the word." Twenty miles a day was the aim—often surpassed on a good road, often delayed by rain and mud and breakdown.

Camp time at night varied in the long daylight with the best camp spot found and the condition of the teams; but it was usually from 5 to 6. It also varied as cholera took its death toll and from sixteen to twenty graves had sometimes to be dug in a day and stamped and rendered secure from the wolves. Some heroism occurred in these death scenes from which the curtain of dull records can never be rolled. The scenes were too sacred and heart breaking. Some groups were so loyal they would not leave a companion's family undefended and stayed on at their own peril to the end and in many such cases, the rest, the change from alkali water with heavy meat diet to pure cow milk worked such a swift cure, that the invalid could be hoisted to a feather bed under the wagon roof and was presently back on horseback. When heartlessly left to die by frightened panicky comrades, these same comrades went on to their own death from the same real causes of the disease. By 8 P.M., supper was over and the call, "All's Well," by the watchman sent the spent day travelers to that deep dreamless sleep in which they garnered strength for the morrow.

It was in the great migration of 1852, a few miles along a transcontinental survey there occurred the pathetic death of Rebecca Winters, August 15. Hoof tracks had packed the arch of the sunken grave, but someone had stuck up a broken iron wagon tire with the name and date scratched on and when the railway surveyors came along and found that grave, they diverted their line to leave the brave mother's resting place in peace, a perpetual monument for all time to the mothers of the Pioneers. The lonely grave is fenced today. It lies not far from Scott's Bluffs, much farther westward but a monument to the heroism of the epic Trail.

Jesse Applegate's account of the Trail in 1843 has been quoted so often, it has become a classic. It can never be quoted too often. He was a little lad of nine when he went over the Trail in 1843, and an old man of eighty when he recounted his memories. When a boy drowsed in the tented wagon and sometimes ran or rode afield to the terror of his mother, critics can easily find lapses of memory as to events or points on the road; but for the main, it remains one of the best pen pictures we have:

"It is 4:00 o'clock A.M.: the sentinels on duty have discharged their rifles—the signal that the hours of sleep are over —and every wagon and tent is pouring forth its night tenants, and slow kindling smokes begin lazily to rise and float away in the morning air. Sixty men start from the corral, spreading as they move through the vast herd of cattle and horses that make a semi-circle around the encampment, the most distant perhaps two miles away.

"The herders pass the extreme verge and carefully examine for the trails beyond to see that none of the animals have strayed or been stolen during the night. This morning no trails lead beyond the outside animals in sight and by five o'clock the herders begin to contract the great moving circle, and the well-trained animals move slowly towards camp, clipping here and there a thistle or a tempting bunch of grass on the way. In about an hour five thousand animals are close up to the encampment, and the teamsters are busy selecting their teams and driving them inside the corral to be yoked. The corral is a circle one hundred yards deep formed with wagons connected strongly with each other; the wagon in the rear being connected with the wagon in front by its tongue and ox chains. It is a strong barrier that the most vicious ox cannot break, and in case of attack from the Sioux would be no contemptible intrenchment.

"From 6:00 to 7:00 o'clock is the busy time: breakfast is

to be eaten, the tents struck, the wagons loaded and the teams yoked and brought up in readiness to be attached to their respective wagons. All know when, at 7:00 o'clock, the signal to march sounds, that those not ready to take their places in the line of march must fall into the dusty rear for the day. There are sixty wagons. They have been divided into fifteen divisions or platoons of four wagons each, and each platoon is entitled to lead in its turn. The leading platoon today will be the rear one tomorrow, and will bring up the rear, unless some teamster, through indolence or negligence, has lost his place in the line, and is condemned to that uncomfortable post. It is within ten minutes of 7:00; the corral, but now a strong barricade, is everywhere broken, the teams being attached to the wagons. The women and children have taken their places in them. The pilot (a borderer who has passed his life on the verge of civilization, and has been chosen to his post of leader from his knowledge of the savage and his experience in travel through roadless wastes) stands ready, in the midst of his pioneers and aids, to mount and lead the way. Ten or fifteen young men, not today on duty, form another cluster. They are ready to start on a buffalo hunt, are well mounted and well armed, as they need to be, for the unfriendly Sioux has driven the buffalo out of the Platte and the hunters must ride fifteen or twenty miles to find them. The cow drivers are hastening as they get ready, to the rear of their charge, to collect and prepare them for the day's march.

"It is on the stroke of 7:00; the rush to and fro, the cracking of whips, the loud command to oxen and what seemed to be inextricable confusion of the last ten minutes has ceased. Fortunately everyone has been found and every teamster is at his post. The clear notes of a trumpet sound in the front; the pilot and his guards mount their horses; the leading divisions of the wagons move out of the encampment and take up the line of march; the rest fall into their places with the precision of clock work, until the spot so lately full of life sinks back into that solitude that seems to reign over the broad plain and rushing river as the caravan draws its lazy length toward the distant El Dorado.

"The pilot by measuring the ground and timing the speed of the horses, has determined the rate of each, so as to enable him to select the nooning place as nearly as the requisite grass and water can be had at the end of five hours' travel of the wagons. Today, the ground being favorable, little time has been lost in preparing for the road, so that he and his pioneers are at the nooning place an hour in advance of the wagons, which time is spent in preparing convenient watering places for the wagons and digging little wells near the bank of the Platte. As the teams are not unyoked, but simply turned loose from the wagons, a corral is not formed at noon, but the wagons are drawn up in columns, four abreast, the leading wagon of each platoon on the left, the platoons being formed with that in view. This brings friends together at noon as well as at night.

"Today an extra session of the council is being held to settle a dispute that does not admit of delay, between a proprietor and a young man who has undertaken to do a man's service on the journey for bed and board. Many such cases exist and much interest is taken in the manner to which the high court from which there is no appeal, will define the rights of each party in such engagements. The council was a high court in the most exalted sense. It was a senate composed of the ablest and most respected fathers of the emigration. It exercised both legislative and judicial powers and its laws and decisions proved equal and worthy of the high trust reposed in it.

"It is now one o'clock; the bugle has sounded and the caravan has resumed its westward journey. It is in the same order; but the evening is far less animated than the morning march. A drowsiness has apparently fallen on man and beast; the teamsters drop asleep on their perches and the words of command are now addressed to the slowly creeping oxen in the

Courtesy Union Pacific Historical Museum

VIEW OF OMAHA, 1868

A. Phimister Proctor, Sculptor

"PIONEER MOTHER"

"THE SCOUT"

In Penn Valley Park, Kansas City, Missouri

soft tenor of women or the piping treble of children, while the snores of the teamsters make a droning accompaniment. . . .

"The sun is now getting low in the west and at length the painstaking pilot is standing ready to conduct the train in the circle which he has previously measured and marked out, which is to form the invariable fortification for the night. The leading wagons follow him so nearly around the circle that but a wagon length separates them. Each wagon follows in its track, the rear closing on the front, until its tongue and ox chains will perfectly reach from one to the other; and so accurate (is) the measure and perfect the practice that the hindmost wagon of the train always precisely closes the gateway. As each wagon is brought into position it is dropped from the team (the teams being inside the circle), the team is unyoked and the yoke and chains are used to connect the wagon strongly with that in its front. Within ten minutes from the time the leading wagon halted, the barricade is formed, the teams unyoked and driven out to pasture. Everyone is busy preparing fires . . . to cook the evening meal, pitching tents and otherwise preparing for the night. . . . The watches begin at 8:00 o'clock P.M. and end at 4:00 A.M.

"The evening meal is just over, and the corral now free from the intrusion of cattle or horses, groups of children are scattered over it. The latter are taking a game of romps; 'the wee toddling things' are being taught the great achievement that distinguishes man from the lower animals. Before a tent near the river a violin makes lively music, and some youths and maidens have improvised a dance upon the green; in another quarter a flute gives its mellow and melancholy notes to the still night air, which, as they float away over the quiet river, seem a lament for the past rather than a hope for the future. It has been a prosperous day; more than twenty miles have been accomplished of the great journey. The encampment is a good one; one of the causes that threatened much future delay (a childbirth case) has just been removed by the skill and energy of that 'good angel' of the emigrants, Doctor Whitman, and it has lifted a load from the hearts of the elders. Many of these are assembled around the good doctor at the tent of the pilot (which is his home for the time being) and are giving grave attention to his wise and energetic counsel. The careworn pilot sits aloof, quietly smoking his pipe, for he knows the brave doctor is 'strengthening his hands.'

"But time passes; the watch is set for the night; the council of old men has been broken up, and each has returned to his own quarter; the flute has whispered its last lament to the deepening night; the violin is silent, and the dancers have dispersed; enamored youth have whispered a tender 'good night' in the ear of blushing maidens, or stolen a kiss from the lips of some future bride—for Cupid here, as elsewhere, has been busy bringing together congenial hearts, and among these simple people he alone is consulted in forming the marriage tie. Even the doctor and the pilot have finished their confidential interview and have separated for the night. All is hushed and repose from the fatigues of the day, save the vigilant guard and the wakeful leader, who still has cares upon his mind that forbid sleep. He hears the ten o'clock relief taking post, and the 'all well' report of the returned guard; the night deepens, yet he seeks not the needed repose . . . the last care of the day being removed, and the last duty performed, he, too, seeks the rest that will enable him to go through the same routine tomorrow."

Next to the buffalo stampedes, the Overlanders dreaded the floods and the storms of rain and tornadoes of wind preceding the storm. Tent pegs were torn from the dry sands. Tents on wagons almost tipped to the blast of the hurricane and like the animals, the campers learned not to lose heads in confusion, but to close up ranks, turn backs to winds and hang fast to tent ropes till the storm passed. These torrential drenches didn't last but added to the difficulties of all fords.

It was the Gold Rush from 1848 to 1860 brought the scamps on the Trail, as it was the Rail Era of the 1860's brought "Hell on Wheels" of which fuller details will presently be told. Though there was no law, there was no mob law.

Fort Kearney, the first army post on the Trail, was really established like Leavenworth to act as a boundary between marauding Indians north and south, especially to protect trails up towards Montana. It was an outer patrol for Indian Territory. Why it was not exterminated in the few years of its existence, is one of the heroic annals of the Army never told and passed on to oblivion, ungrateful as it is unpardonable.

Look out on it as it is today—a beautiful little city with banks and tree-sheltered homes and warehouses and wheat and stock sidings—the typical little hub of a farm-wheel on whose prosperous turns depends the prosperity of bank and finances. Only four miles distant from modern Kearney is the site of Fort Kearney—the difference in spelling need not be emphasized, it occurs along all sections of the Trail. What a haven was that old fort to tired travelers for rest and repairs! Hardly a frontiersman of the period—Joe Meek, Jim Bridger, Buffalo Bill, all the rest, did not pause here. It was a stage coach stop, a pony express relay, a city of refuge for all comers. It was not easy to hold these Indians in leash.

Here occurred two of the most terrible battles in all frontier history—the Fetterman Massacre and the Wagon-Box Fight. They do not concern the Oregon Trail, but as they do bear on the trails that forked north from the Platte, passers-by may care to recall who opened these highways for them and at what cost. Jim Bridger had been employed here as a guide in the 1860's. It was Bridger advised all teamsters and all mule wranglers for the Army to park wagons in a natural wall of protection from Indian fire. He became the watch dog of the Army. Alas that they did not heed his warnings! He told the command that Indian spies were behind every sage clump till officers thought old Jim had Indians on the brain. Still, as many as seven soldiers a day had been buried as Fort Kearney was being built—buried as victims of Indian spies prowling under wolf robes, among the real wolves haunting the slaughter house out from the fort walls. That ought to have been warning, but it wasn't. Then Bridger would point to the semaphore flash of tin mirrors. Bah! Only sunlight on a sharp stone! Would Indians be over there howling where the wolf pack could be heard running? No, but the wolf howl might be an Indian howl as signal. Bah! The old chap had Indian howl in his ears. "Nay, you fool," Bridger had retorted to Fetterman, himself, "wolf howls have no echo. Spy howls have." "Bridger," Fetterman had retorted hotly, "you are crazy." "No, you are," said the old guide.

Colonel Fetterman and eighty-one men had been sent out to protect a mule train with timber for logs. He went out improperly equipped. The soldier horsemen on their skittish horses were clumsy riders compared to Indians, who could ride bareback and duck as they fired with guns or arrows and zigzag and mix up to avert slower aim from the soldiers. The soldiers had a habit of dismounting to take slow, sure aim.

That very morning two Cheyenne spies had been sent to Kearney on some faked errand. They hung round the Fort gates listening, lounging idly here and there; but they must have semaphored Red Cloud outside. They knew Fetterman had gone to the Pine Woods seven miles away, gay as a schoolboy poking a hornets' nest for fun. It was winter. The Indians rushed the troopers and then feigned a retreat that drew Fetterman in pellmell pursuit to a hornets' nest. He and his company disappeared over a ridge. The Fort heard quick desperate firing, file firing followed by a sickening, awful, prolonged, dead silence. Lieutenant Ten Eyck with fifty-four men hurried in the direction whence had resounded the battle. Eighty-one mutilated bodies lay on the hillside, slain by raiding Sioux on the 21st of December, 1866. Not a soul escaped to tell the tale of the last man's shot. Of course, the Sioux captured the battalions' guns and bullets; and old Red Cloud retreating in a whirl with his warriors, must have smiled his sinister smile at white man rashness in running into well laid traps; but punishment fell quick and dire. The Sioux, drunk with victory and three thousand strong, grew rash. The fort's wagon-boxes for wood were of thick tough fiber. Major Powell, who went out to help to escort the wood detail in the next year, formed fortifications out of his wagon-boxes by setting them on their sides and having a relay of extra rifles behind each sharpshooter. These were stacked upright, three and four for each man. No pausing to take slow, sure aim in this battle! It was rapid-fire work, the swiftest the Indians had ever experienced. Never dreaming he could not repeat his victory over eighty-one men, now in August, 1867, against thirty whites, Red Cloud hurled his warriors down and led the whirling charge in person. But more troops had come from Laramie during the winter. These were armed with Springfield repeaters. The August day had been fearfully hot. Red Cloud's warriors shot fire arrows inside the Wagon-Box Fort till the ground smoked and the grass caught fire. Not knowing other rifles stood stacked ready at hand, Red Cloud now charged his full force of three thousand at the encircled whites. The rifles were hot to the touch. The dry grass flamed up but died down almost as quickly because the hillock under it was bare. The fire arrows came flaming in to hit the dust inside the square, but the sharpshooters behind the wagon-boxes, now on sides with floors of iron, broke Red Cloud's arrow showers and the bullets coming from shelter of the lined boxes picked off the zig-zag warriors dodging as they charged to jump inside the wall defense. The Indian hated to leave traces of the disaster and paused to rescue and drag off his wounded and dead comrades. He, too, fell, till the charge stopped, paused, fled. Powell lost only three men, the Sioux 1,137. If that victory had been followed up instantly, it would have averted fearful massacres in a few years to the north; but the Army heads in Washington did not understand.

Was it any wonder that Indians burned Fort Kearney to the ground? Its memory is one of the most heroic in the West. The Wagon-Box Fight can be compared only to Dollard's fearful fight at the Long Sault on the Ottawa to defend the infant colony of Montreal from massacre, almost two centuries earlier. Only Dollard's fight has been immortalized. The Wagon-Box Fight is hardly known outside certain Western States.

CHAPTER V

From Kearney to Laramie and Beyond

THE next three-hundred-mile jump from Kearney to Laramie is the most dramatic on the epic Trail; and—except for certain spotlights—the least known. Along this section, all prongs begin to fork to their different destinations, southwest to Santa Fé, direct west to Salt Lake and California, north to Montana, northwest to Snake River and Oregon; but the spotlights flash through the gradual obscurity of oblivion like the rays of a powerful searchlight illuminating the past, fading in darkness of a film screen, and like the film screen these spotlights recall comedy and tragedy following one another so swiftly that, unless you keep the high lights clear, the mental picture is apt to become a blur.

For instance—take Julesburg where the South Platte was frequently followed instead of the North Platte, which comes in here. The Union Pacific had to follow the bee line west in as nearly a direct route as the terrain permitted. Rocky ground, quicksands, rolling but high foot-hills might compel divergence, later to be straightened and shortened as tunnels and rip-rock piers and cut-offs could replace long curves round bad obstructions to the straight line; but General Dodge knew his first duty was to push the Union Pacific forward with all speed to earn the land grant given to his line by the Federal Government; and Julesburg was one of the points at which he had to concentrate.

Dodge detested that designation of his advancing rail construction, which the roughs had given it—"Hell on Wheels." "Hell on Wheels" meant the tent town, which just preceded his own construction gangs handled with the order and precision of a military march. Telegraph, pony express, stage line now connected the outside world with this wilderness of the West. He disliked the lurid news going to the outer world of the wild lawlessness in these tent towns, which jumped just ahead of his construction gangs and sat down to demoralize Indians and white men with bad whisky, gamblers, strumpets, and too frequently ended in free-for-all fights and murders. Town lot claim-jumpers gambling on the chances for a future city created great trouble. Dodge was sick and impatient of such gentry hovering over his rail line like vultures. They would set up stakes to land which he needed for shops and "defy all creation" or send out complaints to Congress that left Dodge hot under his collar. The brothers Casement were two of his most trusted construction engineers. Dodge had wired ahead for Jack Casement to clean these gangs of ruff-scuff out from

Julesburg before he came with his army of builders. Jack, himself, had a thousand men and a hundred teams working under him. They were former "soldiers, mule skinners, Mexicans, Irish, bush-whackers, convicts"—inflammable stuff to turn loose in such a tent town as "Hell on Wheels." The rough element had been growing bolder at each jump of the rail line westward from Kearney, from North Platte and here was Julesburg literally in possession of the roughs, the worst of all.

Three weeks later, Dodge arrived at Julesburg.

"Got the gamblers cleaned out?" he asked Casement.

"You bet, General!"

"Where are they now?"

"Out in the graveyard."

No details given.

Or take another episode equally illuminating. It's a dog story, too. The Indian dearly loves pomp. Gold medals, gold braid, soldier uniform, all the regalia of power through force, impressed his imagination as the old fur trade heads well knew. In pow-wows, peace or war, the Indian chiefs do not fail to impress their own warriors with such insignia of leadership. The chief might be as poor as a church mouse, but he always had his show costume of spotless buckskin in white or tan worked in colors of dyed porcupine quills; and he loaded himself with silver, necklets and bracelets and anklets and bells down his trouser leg seams, from eagle-feathered head dresses to beaded moccasins. Now every Army Indian fighter knew this feeling of the Indians and in pow-wows came with the full panoply of power and show. The Indians, not to be surpassed by white brothers, usually opened proceedings by a great feast of buffalo humps, buffalo tongues, antelope spare ribs, bear steaks, and their Army guests had to partake of the feast or give deep offense. The Indian etiquette was—eat or burst. The great stew pot was placed in the center of a buckskin table cloth laid on the ground and round this grouped his white men guests—always safe under Indian code of honor, as long as they were his guests.

Dodge was making a survey of all Indian affairs for Washington. Indian affairs were not in good condition during this era. All tribes were against white men. Still, Dodge had been able to employ fine bands of Pawnee scouts from the Indians. An old French guide rallied chiefs to meet the Army men at Laramie. The feast was celebrated in an Indian council-house—tent, of course. The Army had supplied light wines and canned goods, but the Indians, not to be outdone, had catered the soup stew; and it was tasty stew, too, seasoned with sage and such berries as only good squaw cooks knew. Wooden spoons were used on Army tin plates. The air at Laramie is ozone. It is apt to give a ravenous appetite. Everyone was eating heartily till Dodge himself turned over on his plate—a paw.

"What is it?" he asked the French interpreter.

"Bow-wow: pup," answered the Frenchman, jerking with his thumb over his shoulder, where other Indian pups could be seen following the dog packs lying in the sun.

Three of the big Army generals famous in history "got up quickly, ran from the council-house and returned in about twenty minutes" looking about as cheerful as a landlubber who has been contemplating the depths of the sea after a squall; but the most fastidious of the officers had to stick it out, or offend their Indian hosts. One of these officers was so badly smitten over the beautiful half Sioux daughter of the French interpreter that Dodge had to break off the love affair by hurrying the officers to other scenes. I do not know whether this episode should go in comedy or tragedy; for as the handsome officer rode away, the beautiful girl stood outside the fort gate with her head down to hide her eyes and the officer, himself, could not restrain his tears; but the wisdom of Dodge's level head was already self-evident on the sun-dried plains. Smoke signals were on every horizon and the plains ablaze with prairie fires to block white progress. With Mormon hand carts creaking westward at the rate of six thousand a year, and Oregon Pioneers' caravans in streams of forty-five hundred, and Californians tumbling in a stampede at twenty thousand—the Indians read the signs clearly and plainly as the white men. They were banding now for the last great fights extending over twenty years.

Nearly a quarter of a century earlier and one of the most famous of all councils with the Indians was Frémont's, held at Laramie, in 1842. Frémont was making a survey of affairs from the East westward as Wilkes was from the West eastward for the authorities of Army and Navy in Washington. Frémont had followed the usual route from Kansas River across and up the Platte. He had encountered the usual experiences of the period by army and Overland Caravans. Kit Carson was his guide and seasoned frontiersman as he was, he, too, had suffered the ailments from heat, meat diet, and alkali water. The same raids went on at that early date between Pawnees and neighboring tribes as from days preceding the coming of any white men—one of the unexplained enigmas of Indian life: why races with hunting ground, more than enough hunting ground for all tribes or ten times their number, devoted themselves to only one vocation, killing one another like wolves. "Half devoured before he was dead," on July 4, they found one poor old buffalo bull. Twenty wolves in a pack had run this old fellow down. As the French guides say—wild life had always and has yet much more in it than "le petee-cat-ee-cheesm."

Frémont, too, noticed "the hoodoo" of Chimney Rock—three hundred feet high—one of the great landmarks beyond Kearney, visible for many miles to all Overlanders. You can see many such in the Bad Lands of the Dakotas today. In that day the resemblance of all these conglomerates of sand and stone left by ancient seas to fantom cities of a spirit world, made them peculiarly good camping places safe from prowling Indian raiders. Wind and rain have since worn Chimney Rock down to a distintegrating pinnacle destined to disappear in a few years.

There were wild buffalo hunts going up the Platte in one of which they met Jim Bridger of later fame. Jim spun his best yarns and told of the Sioux far south as the Sweetwater at Independence Rock, trying to catch some Snake River Indians, who had a rendezvous with traders there. War parties were everywhere. Kit Carson deemed it wise before going on to make his will. When Indians met Carson at Laramie, they gave Frémont the usual feast from "a litter of fat young puppies." Though his stomach heaved, Frémont cleared his plate.

"Our young men are bad," declared the Indian chiefs. "They will fire upon you." They had "no control over the young men." Frémont saw through the crafty motives and made one of the most spirited answers ever heard in the Laramie Council House:

" 'You say you love the whites; why have you killed so many already this spring? You say you love the whites, and are full of many expressions of friendship to us; but you are not willing to undergo the fatigue of a few days' ride to save our lives. We do not believe what you have said, and will not listen to you. Whatever a chief among us tells his soldiers to do, is done. We are the soldiers of the great chief, your father. He has told us to come here and see this country and all the Indians, his children. Why should we not go? Before we came we heard that you had killed his people and ceased to be his children; but we came among you peacefully, holding out our hands. Now we find that the stories we heard are not lies, and that you are no longer his friends and children. *We have thrown away our bodies, and will not turn back.* When you told us that your young men would kill us, you did not know that our hearts were strong, and you did not see the rifles which my young men carry in their hands. We are few, and you are many, and may kill us all; but there will be much crying in your villages, for many of your young men will stay behind, and forget to return with your warriors from the mountains. Do you think that our great chief will let his soldiers die, and forget to cover their graves? Before the snows melt again, his warriors will sweep away your villages as the fire does the prairie in the autumn. See! I have pulled down my *white houses,* and my people are ready; when the sun is ten paces higher, we shall be on the march. If you have anything to tell us, you will say it soon.' I broke up the conference, as I could do nothing with these people; and being resolved to proceed, nothing was to be gained by delay. Accompanied by our hospitable friends, we returned to the camp. We had mounted our horses, and our parting salutations had been exchanged, when one of the chiefs (the Bull's Tail) arrived to tell me that they had determined to send a young man with us; and if I would point out the place of our evening camp, he should join us there. 'The young man is poor,' said

he; 'he has no horse, and expects you to give him one.' I
described to him the place where I intended to encamp, and,
shaking hands, in a few minutes we were among the hills, and
this last habitation of whites shut out from our view."

It was July 31, when Frémont went up to the
Sweetwater to Independence Rock and a few miles
further on to Devil's Gate. By August 8, he was
at South Pass.

Soon you will pass the point where the Big
Muddy comes in near Casper. Says Grace
Hebard—one of the highest authorities on this
section of the Trail:

"Near the center of the Big Muddy field, a few feet south
of the Oregon Trail, is a lonely grave, covered with stones and
marked by a rough headstone on which is rudely chiseled the
name and date of death, of a little girl, Ada Magill, a member
of the party of Ezra Meeker, who passed this way en route
to Oregon more than fifty-six years ago. The party camped
for the night on the bank of the North Platte. The child was
taken ill, died, and was buried by the edge of the trail. Stones
were heaped on the grave and a rude fence erected about it
to keep off wolves and coyotes. The fence long ago disappeared, but the stones remain. Nearby is a red stone marker,
an official Oregon Trail post. Hundreds of automobiles pass
over this highway every day en route to Yellowstone Park.
For more than half a century canvas-covered wagons, headed
westward, crossed the rich oil sands of the Big Muddy, the
owners little realizing that there were riches under their feet
as well as at the far end of the trail. Over this lonely grave
the noonday sun beats down, and not one in a thousand of those
who pass by know of its existence. The snow covers it with

a mantle of white in winter. In spring the winds whisper, and the birds sing above it. And in the watches of the night the stars keep vigil over this tiny God's acre in a treeless land."

Scott's Bluffs, Independence Rock, Devil's Gate, Split Rock, were other great landmarks on the Oregon Pioneer's Trail. They, too, stand just as they have stood for centuries westward of Casper and Fetterman. Casper is the modern spelling of that son of an officer in Colorado who died here at the verge of his manhood. Split Rock comes west of Devil's Gate. Scott's Bluffs takes its name from a trader found dead on the plains. It is not known whether he was deserted by comrades in the early 1830's or died of starvation under the Bluffs. Only two miles away lies that lonely grave of Rebecca Winters, of 1852.

All these names explain themselves. Only one remains lost again—Laramie, both the old fort three miles to the south and the new fort to the north. All we know is Laramie took its name from "Old Jacques Laramie," a fur trader, who had drifted up from St. Louis or across from Quebec and at some time made Laramie his camping ground. The new fort was built both to protect the pony express and the tie choppers of the Union Pacific in 1866-69 and it was shifted from the old site because it was now apparent that Dodge had found a better opening through the Rockies than South Pass, to which he gave the name of his friend—Sherman. The old fort lay

on the south side of the North Platte just where
Laramie River came in and it was the camping
ground of all plains Indians raiding north and
south as well as the site for countless pow-wows
with white men.   It dated back to the fur adventures of the St. Louis traders—Fitzpatrick, Sub-
lette, Jim Bridger, Fontenelle.   From 1848-49
about the time Stephen Kearny died, it was bought
by the Federal Government for an army post.
Kearny, Leavenworth, Frémont, Miles, Sherman,
Sheridan—all the big men of the American Army
had here met the Indians.   Into its spacious corral
had "crept the immigrant trains," says Miss
Hebard, to repair "creaking sun-warped wagon
wheels, buy fresh provisions, shoe oxen and horses
and for the first time in these three hundred miles
sleep secure from Indian raid."   The lumber to
build Laramie had been freighted from Leavenworth.   No mistaking the site today.   A monument fourteen feet high marks it.

To compare the Laramie of the past with the
Laramie of the present is to repeat Rip Van
Winkle's experience.   You rub your eyes.   Here
is a university city of three thousand people, with
several professors whose names are international
for scholarship.   Here is a city of beautiful little
homes ensconced in flower beds with a bloom rival-
ing the gold of dawn or the red of sunset.   The
university has been built without one cent of taxa-

tion against the state, solely from oil royalties. Here is a rail center that might be one of the trimmest stations out from the suburbs of New York or Boston. Here are ("palatial" is, I believe, the over-used word) luxury trains that are really not "Hell on Wheels" but the most comfortable well equipped small hotels on wheels. Was it only sixty years ago that Dodge's Army officer ducked from an Indian pow-wow to interview pup meat? You may have fresh berries from Colorado and fresh cantaloup from Arizona and fresh peas from nearer gardens and fresh trout on your menu. And over all is an atmosphere translucent as heaven's own rays.

Independence Rock was "like a great rock in a weary land." It was Father De Smet gave it the appropriate name "the Register of the Desert," where early and late travelers had chiseled their names, and Overlanders had scratched the date of campers' deaths and, sorry to relate, later passers-by have blurbed over the sacred old landmark their own names in great blots of tar black obscuring the early sacred records. It stands a gray granite pile somewhat the shape of a giant scaled tortoise. It is more than a third of a mile long and fifty or sixty feet high but, owing to the flat plains, seems much higher. The Sweetwater circles along its south side. Now, the Sweetwater is not very sweet to those who know mountain streams. Indeed, it is as many an Overlander described it—distinctly insipid, a tasteless amber stream, but compared to the muddy Platte or alkali pools, it was nectar to the travelers; and between it and Independence Rock was space for roadway and camp. It was up the Sweetwater the caravans had to follow to reach South Pass and get across the mountains to the headwaters of the Snake, and it was at this very section of the Overland Trail, the railroad had to diverge to a better bee line pass; so that the next three hundred miles of the Trail though opened by good roads lie deserted, less traversed than from 1830 to 1866. You can see the Trail in all its primitive loneliness there.

It was Frémont in 1842 put Independence Rock on the world map. Here is his account of it:

"August 23, (1842,) yesterday evening we reached our encampment at Rock Independence, where I took some astronomical observations. Here, not unmindful of the custom of early travelers and explorers in our country, I engraved on this rock of the far West a symbol of the Christian faith. Among the thickly engraved names I made on the hard granite the impression of a large cross, which I covered with a black preparation of India rubber, well calculated to resist the influences of the wind and rain. It stands amidst the names of many who have long since found their way to the grave, and for whom the huge rock is a giant gravestone.

"One George Weymouth was sent out to Maine by the Earl of Southampton, Lord Arundel and others, and in the narrative of their discoveries he says: 'The next day we ascended in our pinnacle that part of the river which lies more to the westward, carrying with us a cross—a thing never omitted by any Christian traveler—which we erected at the ultimate end of our route.' This was in the year 1605; and in 1842, I obeyed the feeling of early travelers, and I left the impression of the cross deeply engraved on the vast rock a thousand miles beyond the Mississippi, to which discoverers have given the national name of Rock Independence."

Devil's Gate, about six miles from Independence Rock, like all the other Devil epithets in the Rockies from Colorado to Alberta is the usual narrow rift between two precipices cut by the boiling waters of a prehistoric era in a plunging canyon. It is four hundred feet deep, barely three hundred feet from top to top, a chasm where ripples today the Sweetwater from a valley that was a paradise of peace and pasture and surcease from plains' raiders. Into this reposeful paradise crept the Satan of all Gardens of Eden—not the Snake River Indians, who at first were remarkably friendly to the whites, but the Satan of white man crime. Ezra Meeker tells the story. A murder had been committed for purposes of robbery. The guilty man had a family of four children and a wife; but the jury of twelve men had found him guilty and crime had to be stopped on the Trail. At sunset he was publicly hanged before all campers. A driver was appointed to care for the family, well rid of the brute, for the rest of the journey. Many campers kept their children in the covered wagon till the execution was over. Wagon tongues were braced up, a pole spanned across, and a team rope did the rest. It was an unwritten law that the name of an executioner should never be told.

But joy, too, came back to the travelers resting on the Sweetwater. The gaunt spent oxen and horses wallowed girth deep in pasture and drank their fill. The mouth-organs and old violins and concertinas again tuned up. There was now no peril in kindling good camp fires with such brushwood as grew or floated down on the Sweetwater or could be made from buffalo chips (dried offal) collected by boys on the plains for night fires. Trout leaped nightly at midget flies and old fishlines were hauled out. Not a bleaching skeleton of man or beast reminded one of the cruelty of the scorched plains. Today, the brushwood is beginning to grow again; but by 1856, it was becoming terribly scarce.

Split Rock was a narrower defile than Devil's Gate—through a cleavage in a precipice a thousand feet high.

By the time the second great jump from Kearney to Laramie had been passed, the race westward had become a scramble to get across the Rockies and Blue Mountains before the snows of October, before, too, the chill nights of September on the uplands, for clothing was now in shreds. Here was a family of children deserted by parents and left to die. They were adopted and mothered by some Pioneer. The new-made graves were appalling in frequency—from six to twenty-one each day, seventy-five in one stretch of a hundred miles. Both the north and south banks of the Platte registered these terrible totals; and the sadness is that many of the deaths were not from the cholera so feared as a contagion or infection, but from the alkali water, meat diet and bad or scant food. Fear of cholera had become almost a panic and mounted to a brutal panic among the selfish. It perhaps accounted for deserted wives and children. Still the opal snowy summit of the Rockies shone like a beacon luring to the West.

Take a roll call now roughly from Kearney to the Sweetwater. You need not trouble yourself very greatly with tables of distances, for estimates varied with almost every group of Overlanders, though, if you must have hitching posts and road marks in your mind, Chimney Rock was one hundred and fifty miles from the Forks of the Platte, Scott's Bluffs twenty miles from the Chimney, Laramie sixty miles from the Bluffs, Independence Rock about two hundred from Laramie, Devil's Gate and Split Rock and the Sweetwater eight hundred miles from the start at the Kansas Cities. Which had not its comedy and tragedy and heroism unsurpassed in history?

Yet Americans complain their western annals lack the fragrance of romance and adventure in the Old World. Such comment provokes tears or laughter. It is time we dragged these shadowy figures of the past from the deepening dark of forgetfulness.

We have left them too long to the maps and study-chair man, and both have confused and wearied us with a multiplicity of names and dates and check-ups which obscure the human element. What does it matter that modern Laramie was once Fort Saunders and old Laramie shifted its site two or three times; that the boy Caspar spelled his name in one way and the town Casper changed *a* to *e;* that Philips Kearny didn't sign an *e* to his name and modern Kearney has one; that Jim Bridger had a ferry east of Fetterman and a fort southwest of South Pass; that we wish to goodness there hadn't been one Independence down at Kansas City and another Independence Rock out in the foot-hills; whether Jacques Laramie spelled his name Laramee or La Rame; whether Frémont was really a discoverer or only an explorer following the other men's trails; whether Jim Bridger was right in thinking all Indians treacherous (he married a succession of Indian wives himself), or Catlin was right in thinking all Indian life superior to white man's (he didn't marry an Indian wife and perhaps had not had Jim's intimate first-hand experience); whether Ashley, Bonneville, or Whitman was first to use wheels across the Rockies; whether there were sixty fords on the Platte or sixty-one; why in the world fur

trader and traveler and railroad named half the
beauty spots through the mountains after the
Devil; why they all named South Pass a pass when
it isn't a pass at all but a climb so gradual to a
summit, you hardly know you are crossing a divide; whether Steve Meek was cousin or brother
of Joe (Joe wasn't proud of him)? What we
want to know is what all these heroic humans did
out on the Trail and how they did it, and when
you know that you are fairly convinced whatever
their faults, you would not have done half so well
out on the Trail and might in places have turned
back, beaten, defeated, a failure.

CHAPTER VI

LEGENDS OF SOUTH PASS

LONG since you have forgotten, as the Over-landers forgot, the sweet clover meadows scented with the nectar of white and red and pink bloom where the big bumble bees make more of a merry din than honey, and the gorgeous butterflies surpass, like the lily, Solomon in all his glory with their velvet cloaks woven of pansy petals in blue and yellow and gold and pass their days or nights to perish on some humming birds' needle beak. Humming birds are to this day in myriads above these clover fields of the Kansas and the Platte. You have seen the wheat heading out with odor elusive at dawn or ripe tops in full blaze of midday sun. The motor or steel rail has hastened through the pasture lands where the fat herds are knee-deep in long grass of the bottom lands or wallowing in the Platte fighting the fly pests of midday. You will have passed in two days what took your ancestors from twenty-five to forty days.

Then come the foot-hills scant of grass, in places still cactus and sage brush, but the bleating of the lambs, the woolly backs of sheep cropping the short grass, with the tent-covered chuck wagons somewhere on the offing, tell you these lands are not so desolate as they seem. The station stops and stock-yards and sugar factories and little towns trim as gardens tell the same story. There is no more that Great American Desert of Red Buttes and fantastic sandstone chimney "hoo-doos" and dust fine as flour or small pebbles whipped to a pepper of sand-hail as the wind chants its sad old refrain, plaintive and peevish, or tuned to fiercer mood of hurricane, when you can see the lightning flash in livid flame as fire arrows from the Thunder God of all Indian tribes. He was just as real a Thunder God as to the ancient Hebrews who chanted of the flashes of lightning as the arrows of an Upper Power.

Then you become aware the opal clouds to the west are not all moving. Some stand majestically still, not clouds at all, but the Shining Mountains of the Rockies, called in the North Big Horns from the big horn sheep; Holy Cross down on the Colorado Border from the banks of snow lying in great crevices of rocks dyed in a blood-red sunset; or Wind River Range, or Lone Pine Tops, or Porcupine from resemblances that need no explanation. On the crest of the foot-hills now begin to appear fringed edges of sharp green—the pines like porcupines with "their backs up"; but they are green. You are passing from the gray world of the Desert to the green world of the mountains. The ascent has been so gradual you hardly noticed it unless sharp ears discerned that motor or rail engine was beating faster and harder with an occasional grunt as if the climb demanded more breath. Unless you have a distinctly bad heart, you need not be alarmed if you, too, breathe a little faster. It will do you good. It will clear out every vestige of dead air from lazy lungs and send fresh oxygen cleaning up poisons in lungs and blood; and like the engine, you will demand more fuel. You begin to have an appetite with the zest of edge to it. Air and appetite begin to give you pep. You want to step lively when you take a promenade at some station stop, or stretch your legs when you pause to refuel your car at a filling service shop. Better at such filling station have the mechanic look over tires and axles and knocking nuts and brakes and gears. The roads are excellent—good as the best in the East, broader at all sharp curves, posted with warnings and advice and directions and not so crowded with speed maniacs as in thickly peopled centers. Notwithstanding more perilous motor roads through the mountains than in the East, fewer accidents occur to motors in a month than in New York State in a day. The driver in the mountains dare not be irresponsible. It is his own neck he is risking, not some other person's.

Take your map out now. Put the prong of a compass down on either South Pass—now little used—or Sherman Pass, the traveled road. Swing the leg of the compass round down to Colorado and Utah, up through Wyoming and the Yellowstone and Montana, across westward through East Oregon and Idaho—you are in a Robin Hood arena of romantic colorful adventure in which the difficulty is not what to see but what you have not time to see.

There are three different eras of the past here and they blend in one another like the films of moving pictures—the rail builders' era, the settlers and missionary caravans, the fur traders'. I omit the cowboy period. It was really a brief picturesque interval between rail builders and modern life and is rapidly fading on the film of epic creating events. The cowboy is still in the hinterlands of Western Nebraska and Wyoming; but he is not the fantastic swash-buckler of "shootin' tongs" and saloon and "neck tie" lynching parties. He is a sharp stockman in daily radio contact with world markets and weather warnings as to drought, heat, blizzard. If he is not utterly thoughtless, he can forefend himself against risks and loss; but woe to him if he takes risks. Explanations do not avail with drought and blizzard. Neither will political slogans. The squarest-headed old fellows I have ever known in the West have taken such risks of blizzard warnings to be found frozen to death over a foot-hill not two miles from their ranch house, one with the poor, hitched horses buried in the drift beside him. If he had turned them loose, instinct would have guided him home, but jerking reins hither and thither, he lost sense of direction himself and death took its toll. Others contemptuous of these new-fangled fol-de-rols have ignored signs of drought and a glutted over-supplied market, sending prices down, and had to slaughter sheep or lambs to save their flocks from starvation on scant pasture. Such have run blindly into a stone wall of ruin. Against these stand the opposite class—the man who can read the signs of his own times. I give you only one example. He was a young rancher—one of the youngest of the big sheep men. He had garnered experience from the school of hard knocks and bad example of older relatives, who had been ruined in similar climatic and market catastrophes. Too busy out on his ranch to pay much attention to politics—though his ancestors had been governors and senators from his own state—when he read the signs of drought from the dry springs, he rented uplands near a supply of snow water. As the scorching heat dried the grass to burnt brown paper, he moved his flocks up and up to cooler levels. Then he pledged all he owned to buy lambs and lambs and lambs of the best breed for meat and wool as the price fell to two-thirds of normal. He bought at three dollars a head what he knew would soon sell at ten to twelve dollars. He knew in a country that does not grow a fraction of all the wool needed, lambs must later go back up in price as the freak-

ish weather and markets drained all surplus in
the market over-supplied in rush sales to avert
starvation. From the worst year in the sheep industry he emerged with a million clear. If you
stop off in the sheep country and knock up against
sheep men, you will hear these stories first hand.

One keeps one's perspective best in this no-
man's-land round South Pass by telescoping back
from the present. Without the steel rail, the stockman could never have had world markets. Dodge,
the construction engineer of the Union Pacific, had
seen that ascending South Pass, he could not keep
a short bee line westward and follow the Sweetwater where it came rippling and boiling through
the mountains. He must get through those mountains. Colorado passes were too far south to meet
the requirements of the Washington Government.
Motor out to the Cabin Rest House named as a
memorial to Dodge. It is only a little over an
hour's run. You will see the setting of the whole
picture. Dodge was in conference with Washington officials down at Laramie, when—says Perkins,
his biographer:

"A rider, with foaming horse, dashed up to the post with
the news that the Percy T. Brown engineering party, engaged
in the difficult work of making locations across the Great
Divide had been severely beaten by the Sioux, and Brown had
been killed. Then Dodge heard the story. Brown and thirteen men, beset by a powerful band of three hundred Sioux
Indians, fortified themselves on an elevation in the Great

Basin and fought from noon until night, when their foes, for reasons unknown, withdrew. Brown, badly wounded, begged his men to leave him, but they refused, made a litter of their carbines, and carried him twelve miles to a stage station, where he died within an hour."

A bit heroic with a dying man—wasn't it?

"General Gibbons was not surprised at the attack and told Dodge that building the road from Fort Saunders—Laramie— to Bridger's Pass south would constitute the gravest problem.

"One of the government commissioners, having talked to several members of another engineering party, wanted Dodge to halt all work for six months, awaiting stronger military organizations. But his reply was to place other engineering parties in the field."

"If we stop now we may never get started again," he wrote to Oliver Ames, his backer financially. He knew if he paused, enemies in Congress would assail the whole project and the road would fail to win its subsidy in land. Without such subsidy in land, who would buy the railroad bonds and keep the cash coming along to hasten construction?

"I'll push this road on to Salt Lake in another year or surrender my own scalp to the Indians," wrote Dodge. Again a type of courage along the Overland Trail.

"Gibbons gave him another company and Dodge pushed on west to strengthen his badly disorganized engineering parties all along the line. At Rattlesnake Pass he discovered coal and

FREIGHTING TRAIN KNOWN AS "BULL OF THE WOODS"
From a photograph taken on Main Street, Nebraska City

OX TRAIN FORDING A STREAM

OVERLAND WAGON TRAIN WITH OXEN

REMAINS OF WALL OF OLD FORT LEAVENWORTH

FIRST COURT HOUSE OF JACKSON COUNTY, BUILT, 1827

later sank a mine, which was the first that ever supplied the Union Pacific along its own route. On reaching the North Platte he found it to be swollen from heavy mountain snows. He ordered it to be forded, but two of the young officers who attempted it were swept back to their starting-point, and the remainder of his escort refused to budge.

"Dodge jumped on his own horse, 'Rocky Mountain,' and plunged into the stream, calling on his entire command to follow. It proved to be a desperate undertaking and three of his men had narrow escapes from drowning.

"If you are going to help me build the Union Pacific through this country, you've got to learn to swim horses across more rivers than this one," the chief engineer shouted to his struggling followers.

"West of the North Platte, they rode into a barren country; night came and the command had been without water for several hours. No water in this area entailed suffering to man and beast that cannot be told. Quite by accident, Dodge and Rawlins came upon a spring that gushed out of a wall of solid rock. Grant's chief of staff, dusty and weary, knelt and drank deeply.

" 'It is too beautiful for words, Dodge,' he said.

"Dodge stood for a moment in deep thought and then replied: 'Rawlins, we will name this spring after you.'

"And this is how Rawlins, early a division point on the Union Pacific, got its name.

"The next day they came upon the Percy Brown engineering party, strongly reenforced it, started to work and then pushed toward the great divide. At their feet was a vast basin. Dodge lifted powerful glasses and looked in every direction.

" 'I see some teams down there,' he told Rawlins, who stood by his side. 'Must be white men—perhaps returning emigrants.'

"He plunged down the basin, followed by his escort, and an hour later came upon one of his own engineering parties—

the one headed by Charles Bates that had been ordered to
survey the Green River back to the east to meet Brown. Bates
and his men were in bad condition, without water and with
swollen tongues. But they were at work, running a true line,
for they were the kind of men who made the Union Pacific
possible."

Dodge tells the story in several addresses. It
is more graphic as the living actor's always is.

"One of the parties which was trying to work west from
the North Platte had found the maps of the country mislead-
ing. Endeavoring to find the summit of the continental divide,
this party had dropped into a great basin. Percy T. Brown,
the chief of the party, finding himself in an unknown country
entirely different in character from what had been expected,
took eight of his escort and started to explore the region.
When near the center of what is now known as the Red Desert
he was attacked by three hundred Sioux Indians working south
to the Bridger Pass stage road coming from the Sweetwater.
Brown took measures to defend himself, occupying, after a
severe contest with the Indians for its possession, a small hill,
and fighting from 12 o'clock noon until toward midnight, when
he was shot through the abdomen. He then ordered the soldiers to leave him and save themselves, but they refused and
allowed the Indians to get hold of the stock, after which the
redskins withdrew. The soldiers then made a litter of their
carbines and packed Brown upon it fifteen miles through the
sagebrush to Laclere station, near Bridger Pass. Their laborious efforts to save him were made in vain, however, for
Brown died at the station.

"Upon an examination of this country we discovered that the
divide of the continent had let down from the Wind River
Mountains on the north to Medicine Bow, the beginning of the
main Rocky Mountains on the south from an elevation of

thirteen thousand feet to one of seven thousand into an open plain, and that the divide was in reality a great basin about eighty miles across in its widest part east and west and a hundred to a hundred and fifty miles northwest and southwest in its longest part. The streams running into it sink, leaving a red soil over the entire basin, from which it receives the name of Red Desert. The Union Pacific Railway crossed the Red Desert near its southern limit between the stations of Creston and Tipton, a distance of about thirty-four miles.

"In the basin we found and rescued the party headed by Thomas F. Bates, which was coming from Green River east. When I reached what is now Creston, I discovered Bates and his party. They had been in the wildest part of the basin for nearly a week without water, and were almost exhausted. When we discovered them they had abandoned the line and were taking a course due east by the compass, running for water. At first we thought them Indians, but on looking through my glasses I saw that they had teams with them. We went to their relief at once and saved them. They were in a deplorable condition from thirst.

"After reaching the west rim of the Red Desert you immediately drop into the valley of Bitter Creek, the waters of which flow into the Pacific. The crossing of the continental divide by the Union Pacific is thus by way of an open prairie of comparatively low elevation, about seven thousand feet instead of a mountain range. The work of building the road there was unexpectedly light and it almost seems that nature made this great opening in the Rocky Mountains expressly for the passage of a transcontinental railway."

This is only one episode from the dramatic rail era.

The Dodge Memorial Cabin affords a fine meal and room for one night. Stay and see the clouds light

to jasper at dawn and float away in banners of an
aerial army as the sun rises. At nightfall, you
will see the shy game creatures come out to water
pools and hear from the young guards on duty
stories of life at an altitude of nine thousand feet
above mundane cares. You cannot motor to Casper so early as May. There may be sixteen feet
of snow by this road; but you can go by lower
roads or by steel rail and read another later modern
story of oil. It isn't a story I can give here for
reasons you will appreciate on the spot. In fact,
it is the red hot end of a red hot poker—perhaps
I should say of a tea pot spout. It is both a ludicrous and sad story. Oil, like gold, is a will-o'-the
wisp. It is like Dickens' boy—"you look and there
he is. Then you look and there he isn't." Casper
was once and may yet again be a great producing
center. No one knows when a well is going to
come in, sending hopes sky high as its own first
gush. Also no one knows when it is going to go
out. Casper is yet a great shipping center for oil.

From the Dodge Cabin, too, on a clear day you
can see Frémont's Peak, where the explorer in the
1840's almost broke his neck in as adventurous perils climbing the great sharp peak named after him
as ever Lewis and Clark or the Astorians knew in
their wanderings through the mountain wilderness
to find a way to the Pacific. However the political
controversy raging round Frémont's name may
write him down or up in a final verdict, it has

seemed to me he has never received his full due as
a great explorer here.

Of South Pass, Frémont says:

"About six miles from our encampment brought us to the
summit. The ascent had been so gradual, that, with all the
intimate knowledge possessed by Carson, who had made this
country his home for seventeen years, we were obliged to watch
very closely to find the place at which we had reached the
culminating point. This was below two low hills, rising on
either hand fifty or sixty feet. When I looked back at them,
from the foot of the immediate slope on the western plain,
their summits appeared to be about one hundred and twenty
feet above. From the impression on my mind at this time, and
subsequently on our return, I should compare the elevation
which we surmounted immediately at the Pass, to the ascent
of the Capitol Hill from the avenue at Washington. Approaching it from the mouth of the Sweetwater, a sandy plain,
one hundred and twenty miles long, conducts by a gradual and
regular ascent, to the summit, about seven thousand feet above
the sea; and the traveler without being reminded of any
change by toilsome ascents, suddenly finds himself on the waters
which flow to the Pacific Ocean. By the route we had traveled,
the distance from Fort Laramie is three hundred and twenty
miles, or nine hundred and fifty from the mouth of the Kansas."

It was the month of August.

"All the mountain peaks are gleaming like silver. Though
these mountains are not the Alps, they have their own character of grandeur and magnificence, and will doubtless find pens
and pencils to do them justice.

"Our arrangements for the ascent [of Frémont's Peak] were
rapidly completed. We were in a hostile country, which
rendered the greatest vigilance and circumspection necessary.

The pass at the north end of the mountain was generally infested by Blackfeet; and immediately opposite was one of their forts, on the edge of a little thicket, two or three hundred feet from our encampment. We were posted in a grove of beech, on the margin of the lake, and a few hundred feet long with a narrow prairillon on the inner side, bordered by the rocky ridge. In the upper end of this grove we cleared a circular space about forty feet in diameter and, with the felled timber and interwoven branches, surrounded it with a breastwork five feet in height. A gap was left for a gate on the inner side, by which the animals were to be driven in and secured, while the men slept around the little circle. It was half hidden by the foliage; and garrisoned by twelve resolute men, who could have set at defiance any band of savages which might chance to discover them in the interval of our absence. Fifteen of the best mules, with fourteen men, were selected for the mountain party. Our provisions consisted of dried meat for two days, with our little stock of coffee and some macaroni. In addition to the barometer and a thermometer, I took with me a sextant and spy-glass, and we had, of course, our compasses. In charge of the camp I left Bernier, one of my most trustworthy men, who possessed the most determined courage.

"We left the camp, fifteen in number, well armed, of course, and mounted on our best mules. A pack animal carried our provisions, with a coffee pot and kettle, and three or four tin cups. Every man had a blanket strapped over his saddle, to serve for his bed, and the instruments were carried by turns on their backs. We entered directly on rough and rocky ground; and just after crossing the ridge, had the good fortune to shoot an antelope. We heard the roar, and we had a glimpse of a waterfall as we rode along; and crossing in our way two fine streams, tributary to the Colorado, in about two hours' ride we reached the top of the first row or range of the mountains. Here, again, a view of the most romantic beauty met our eyes. It seemed as if, from the vast expanse of uninteresting prairie we had passed over, Nature had collected all her beauties together in one chosen place. We were overlooking a deep valley, which was entirely occupied by three lakes, and from the brink the surrounding ridges rose precipitously five hundred and a thousand feet, covered with the dark green of the balsam pine, relieved on the border of the lake with the light foliage of the aspen. They all communicated with each other; and the green of the waters, common to mountain lakes of great depth, showed that it would be impossible to cross them. The surprise manifested by our guides when these impassable obstacles suddenly barred our progress, proved that they were among the hidden treasures of the place, unknown even to the wandering trappers of the region. Descending the hill, we proceeded to make our way along the margin to the southern extremity. A narrow strip of angular fragments of rock sometimes afforded a rough pathway for our mules, but generally we rode along the shelving side, occasionally scrambling up, at a considerable risk of tumbling back into the lake.

"We had reached a very elevated point, and in the valley below, and among the hills, were a number of lakes at different levels; some, two or three hundred feet above others, with which they communicated by foaming torrents. Even to our great height, the roar of the cataracts came up, and we could see them leaping down in lines of snowy foam. From this scene of busy waters, we turned abruptly into the stillness of a forest, where we rode among the open bolls of the pines, over a lawn of verdant grass, having strikingly the air of cultivated grounds. This led us, after a time, among masses of rock which had no vegetable earth but in hollows and crevices, though still the pine forest continued. Toward evening, we reached a defile, or rather a hole in the mountains, entirely shut in by dark pine-covered rocks.

"Our table service was rather scant; and we held the meat

in our hands, and clean rocks made good plates, on which we spread our macaroni. Among all the strange places on which we had occasion to encamp during our long journey, none have left so vivid an impression on my mind as the camp of this evening. The disorder of the masses which surrounded us; the little hole through which we saw the stars overhead; the dark pines where we slept; and the rocks lit up with the glow of our fires, made a night picture of very great beauty.

"Sometimes we were forced, by an occasional difficult pass, to pick our way on a narrow ledge along the side of the defile, and the mules were frequently on their knees; but these obstructions were rare, and we journeyed on in the sweet morning air, delighted at our good fortune in having found such a beautiful entrance to the mountains. This road continued for about three miles, when we suddenly reached its termination in one of the grand views, which, at every turn, meet the traveler in this magnificent region. Here the defile up which we had traveled, opened out into a small lawn, where, in a little lake, the stream had its source.

"It is not by the splendor of far-off views, which have lent such a glory to the Alps, that these impress the mind; but by a gigantic disorder of enormous masses, and a savage sublimity of naked rock in wonderful contrast with innumerable green spots of a rich floral beauty, shut up in their stern recesses. Their wildness seems well suited to the character of the people who inhabit the country.

"I determined to leave our animals here, and make the rest of our way on foot. The peak appeared so near, that there was no doubt of our returning before night; and a few men were left in charge of the mules, with our provisions and blankets. We took with us nothing but our arms and instruments, and as the day had become warm, the greater part left our coats. Having made an early dinner, we started again. We were soon involved in the most ragged precipices, nearing the central chain very slowly, and rising but little. The first ridge hid a succession of others; and when, with great fatigue and difficulty, we had climbed up five hundred feet, it was but to make an equal descent on the other side; all these intervening places were filled with small deep lakes, which met the eye in every direction, descending from one level to another, sometimes under bridges formed by huge fragments of granite, beneath which was heard the roar of the water. These constantly obstructed our path, forcing us to make long detours; frequently obliged to retrace our steps, and frequently falling among the rocks. Maxwell was precipitated toward the face of a precipice, and saved himself from going over by throwing himself flat on the ground. We clambered on, always expecting, with every ridge that we crossed, to reach the foot of the peaks, and always disappointed, until about four o'clock, when, pretty well worn out, we reached the shore of a little lake, in which there was a rocky island.

"On the northern side of the lake was a bank of ice, or rather snow covered with a crust of ice. Carson had been guide into the mountains, and, agreeably to his advice, we left this little valley, and took back to the ridges again; which we found extremely broken, and where we were again involved among precipices. Here were ice-fields; among which we were all dispersed, seeking each the best path to ascend the peak. Mr. Preuss attempted to walk along the upper edge of one of these fields, which sloped away at an angle of about twenty degrees; but his feet slipped from under him, and he went plunging down the plane. A few hundred feet below, at the bottom, were some fragments of sharp rock on which he landed; and though he turned a couple of somersets, fortunately received no injury beyond a few bruises.

"Having divested ourselves of every unnecessary encumbrance, we commenced the ascent. This time, like experienced travelers, we did not press ourselves, but climbed leisurely, sitting down as soon as we found breath beginning to fail. At intervals, we reached places where a number of springs gushed from the rocks, and about eighteen hundred feet above the lakes came to the snow line. From this point our progress was uninterrupted climbing. Hitherto, I had worn a pair of thick moccasins, with soles of parflêche; but here I put on a light thin pair, which I had brought for the purpose, as now the use of our toes became necessary to a further advance. I availed myself of a sort of comb of the mountain, which stood against the wall like a buttress, and which the wind and the solar radiation, joined to the steepness of the smooth rock, had kept almost entirely free from snow. Up this I made my way rapidly. Our cautious method of advancing in the outset had spared my strength: and with the exception of a slight disposition to headache, I felt no remains of yesterday's illness. In a few minutes we reached a point where the buttress was overhanging and there was no other way of surmounting the difficulty than by passing around one side of it, which was the face of a vertical precipice of several hundred feet.

"Putting hands and feet in the crevices between the blocks, I succeeded in getting over it, and, when I reached the top, found my companions in a small valley below. Descending to them we continued climbing and in a short time reached the crest. I sprang upon the summit, and another step would have precipitated me into an immense snow-field five hundred feet below. To the edge of this field was a sheer icy precipice; and then, with a gradual fall, the field sloped off for about a mile until it struck the foot of another lower ridge. I stood on a narrow crest, about three feet in width, with an inclination of about 20° N. 51° E. As soon as I had gratified the first feelings of curiosity, I descended, and each man ascended in his turn; for I would only allow one at a time to mount the unstable and precarious slab, which it seemed a breath would hurl into the abyss below. We mounted the barometer in the snow of the summit, and fixing a ramrod in a crevice, unfurled the national flag, to wave in the breeze where never flag waved before. During our morning's ascent, we had met no sign of animal life, except a small bird having the appearance of a sparrow. A stillness the most profound and a terrible solitude forced themselves constantly on the mind as the great feature of the place. Here, on the summit, where the stillness was absolute, unbroken by any sound, and the solitude complete, we thought ourselves beyond the region of animated life; but while we were sitting on the rock, a solitary bee (bromus, the humble bee) came winging his flight from the eastern valley, and lit on the knee of one of the men.

"We had climbed the loftiest peak of the Rocky Mountains, and looked down upon the snow a thousand feet below, and, standing where never human foot had stood before, felt the exultation of first explorers. It was about two o'clock when we left the summit; and when we reached the bottom, the sun had already sunk behind the wall, and the day was drawing to a close. It would have been pleasant to have lingered here and on the summit longer; but we hurried away as rapidly as the ground would permit, for it was an object to regain our party as soon as possible, not knowing what accident the next hour might bring forth."

It would be hard to find in the pages of Lewis and Clark or the Astorians, more dramatic adventures than these.

Between Dodge's Memorial Cabin and Frémont's Peak lies another romantic area. Remember this was the old fighting ground between the Indians of the mountains and the tribes of the plains and as heat sent the buffalo to the uplands, like the sheep, for better pasture, Sioux and Crow hunters used to clash here in bloody raids. Even as late as the 1840's and 1850's, Overlanders witnessed vast herds of buffalo round and in South

Pass. Here was the old home of little Sacajawea, Lewis and Clark's Indian guide, wife of Charbonneau, and it was her presence that obtained guides from her own people for Lewis and Clark to go down the Snake River to the Columbia. She had been captured years previously by plains tribes and now recognized her own brother among the Snake Indians spying furtively and suspiciously on Lewis and Clark, who had come west by the Three Forks of the Missouri. You will recall how in the middle of the first pow-pow held by white men and Snakes, she had interrupted by falling on the neck of the young Snake chief, her own brother. One can guess how her reassurances dispelled the Snakes' fears of white men and told them how to beat their plains' foes by obtaining the white man's arms. For manhood, womanhood, childhood heroism, was ever trail like this one in all the world? Later down Snake River Canyon far to the north, you will cross the trail of another little girl Indian wife—Holy Rainbow, wife of that useless scamp, Pierre Dorion, who led the Astorians such a mad chase it almost wrecked the Astorian Overlanders. Useless scamps the Dorions were as you will learn, when you go down the Snake to Walla Walla—trouble makers, gamblers, cowards in emergency and treacherous friends in trial. But South Pass gave little worry to the Overland Pioneers. It was so much easier than they had anticipated.

Jim Bridger, one of the most famous of the mountain men, both as guide for all comers and friend with the Indians of whom he married several wives as others had died or gone back to tepee life, but who hated the Indian type of treacherous warfare, had a profitable ferry down on the Platte; but he had a wise old head on young shoulders in the 1830's and a wiser head in the 1840's, when Jim looked sixty, but was only in his forties. Wind and weather had trenched his face with deep lines. Indian perils had given him almost a diplomatic cunning, but he masked his hate to foes and was always fair to Indians and whites alike. Unless some rich tourist hunter of whom he guided many, pestered him with fool questions, his word was true, though he could spin wild yarns to people with no sense. It left Jim mad as a hornet, however, to have people down the Missouri at St. Louis laugh at his first reports of Yellowstone Park having "boiling springs" that gushed in regular explosions of mud and water, or rock crystals like diamonds, or hot water that boiled eggs. We know now those reports were true of Yellowstone Park, but it left Jim hot to hear the sneers and he often paid the sneers back in the slang vernacular of the day by such impossible features that they could only be described as "skunk loaded for bear."

Was Jim the discoverer of South Pass and the Yellowstone? I do not know. Neither does anyone else. If he wasn't in the Yellowstone as soon

as Colter whose report of the Park gave its first
name—Colter's Hell—he was soon after; for he
had drifted to this region in his boyhood. It was
really Father De Smet who in the 1850's confirmed
the first reports of both men. One thing, however,
Jim did know and he learned it as early as 1830
when barely out of his teens—wagons could be
used through South Pass.

There was really a natural wagon road between
the headwaters of the North Platte and the headwaters of the South Snake. That is established in
his biography by Cecil Alter through a letter to
the United States Secretary of War. Jim had been
a guide for General Ashley, and Ashley in 1830
had sent eighty men with "10 wagons, 5 mules,
2 dearborn democratic double buck-boards with
one mule each, 4 oxen and a milk cow" as far as
South Pass to take in provisions and bring out
furs from the great fur rendezvous up at the Three
Tetons. The fur rendezvous were known as
Pierre's Hole West of the Tetons, and Jackson's East.
Jim knew about those wagons, though the traders
didn't blazon the fact to rivals; and now early in
1840, Jim knew more and grew wise. Emigrants
were coming—they were coming in hordes. The
Whitman missionary party had a wagon though it
did not fare well down Snake River. Jim figured,
as a rail builder for the Santa Fé did later at Topeka, that if he could build a cut-off fort near
South Pass affording rest place for all Overland-

ers he would do a big business as blacksmith, repairing wagons and shoeing beasts, and he would
do a big business selling supplies to both Indians
and whites; so he built him a fort southwest of
the Pass where the snow was not so deep, the spring
earlier, the water pure, the trout always many,
the buffalo frequent. While he hied him hither
and yon as hunter, trader, guide, he left his partner—a Spanish gentleman of the old school—to
keep the books and do the trading and the two
were presently reaping a fortune, which became
a target for envy and later a cause of ruin, of which
more anon.

The fort has been described in almost every year
of its existence. It was built of pickets daubed
over with adobé mud, which baked to stone in the
sun. There were usually about twenty-five to fifty
Indian tents round outside the walls. Goats and
cows for milk made up the stock with ponies countless as Jim needed them or traded firearms for
better stock from the Indians. Inside the walls
were two or three cabins for the owners and their
families. To rich tourist hunters, the fort seemed
mean: to the Overlanders—a palace of plenty and
safety in desert of want. Roofs were adobé—un-
kempt as to appearance, but heat and cold proof.
The cabins were forty feet long with adobé floors.
The gate was of strongest timber, arrow and bullet
proof. When at the rendezvous North, Jim had
met the Whitman missionary party and sent his

little daughter to Walla Walla to be educated by them; but when disaster befell Walla Walla, Jim sent his other children down to St. Louis under Père De Smet to be educated in the Indian Catholic seminaries.

Legends countless cling to Jim Bridger's name round South Pass. He had really come on South Pass from the west. He and a trader were making a circuit from the Yellowstone and Missouri across the mountains when hostile raiding bands made it unsafe to return the way they had come and following some clue from Indians, Jim had worked South and got through East by South Pass to the Platte. It was really a circuit of about a thousand miles, but it saved sixty thousand dollars' worth of furs a year from risk of raid; and there were other ways for rival traders to beat each other in the game than to cut one another's throats. The wildest yarns of the wildest West can never surpass truth here. The Hudson's Bay traders came down to the Three Tetons and South Pass by the Columbia and Snake River. The Missouri traders came up by the Platte and Three Forks. The Hudson's Bay Company paid only one dollar for a beaver skin; but they carried the Indians on long time credit and advanced supplies a year ahead in food and firearms. The Americans paid five dollars a pelt, but gave no advances in food and firearms.

Only for medicinal purposes or in fearful emergencies did the Hudson's Bay men use whisky.

Always whisky was used by the Missouri traders, though it endangered their scalps. Often early winter storms caught both rivals camped in the same passes and blocked by quite impassable snow. Once the Missouri men caught Peter Skene Ogden from the Hudson's Bays on Columbia River with a cache of sixty thousand dollars' worth of finest pelts. No, they didn't fight. Nor did the St. Louis crowd rifle little Pete's cache of furs; but they got them. Whisky and the Indians did that and at the higher St. Louis prices that year's cargo was worth a quarter-million. Pete's daily journal for that trip is a lament from the depths, and curses on the head of his foes to make the welkin ring. He vowed him vengeance and he got it the very next year. Again rivals were blocked by the snows in the Tetons. The Americans had no snow-shoes to get out and no provisions to stay. Pete had both, and the squaws, who followed his horse brigades, supplied more and more snow-shoes. Pete got all the St. Louis men's furs that year and he got them at less than one dollar, where they had paid five. Pete went back to the Columbia chuckling. The Americans didn't.

It was up at the rendezvous Dr. Whitman cut a Blackfoot arrowhead from Jim Bridger's shoulder in 1835. Dr. Parker and Dr. Whitman had gone West with the St. Louis fur traders to survey the new mission field. Kit Carson and Jim Bridger were both present in Jackson's Hole. "I gave each of the hunters a few tracts for their lonely hours," records Parker. The tracts proved useful, but not as the good man expected; for hardly a mountain man could read the alphabet; and few of the brigade trappers spoke any language but a sort of French patois mixed with English and Indian dialect.

In 1929, these famous fur trade rendezvous of a century ago in the Teton Mountains were dedicated with bronze plaques placed on the peak of Teton Mountain. The region was set aside by Congress as the Grand Teton National Park. Lodges for tourists now stand where once gathered in wild disorder plains and mountain tribes, traders and fur brigades to rob one another or be pillaged by raiding Indians. Where Old Hundred was sung by the first missionaries, or chansons of Quebec by the French trappers in 1828-1839, the Star Spangled Banner sung by Wyoming University rang out in 1929; and Old Glory floated to the breeze, unfurled by Dr. Grace Hebard. It is rather beautiful to know that Camp Brown here "was named for Captain Frederick H. Brown who was killed in Wyoming on December 21, 1866, in the Fetterman massacre in Sheridan county. A fort was established in 1869. In 1873 the name was changed to Fort Washakie. On March 30, 1909, the last United States troops marched out after Lieutenant McCain had taken down the colors."

Bridger discovered coal near his fort and used it in his cabin fireplaces. He deplored the Indian waste of buffalo meat, using only the tallow and tenderloin and hump, though they might starve before spring.

Bridger was guide westward for many a Mormon party and had housed and fed many a nameless wanderer in the hand cart migration, but fell out with them when, as the Mormons prospered round Salt Lake, the Ute Indians became terrible plunderers. Next to the Apaches of the South, they had the reputation of being the meanest and cruelest of the mountain tribes. They were merciless to women and children. They were huge insolent fellows and are to this day not an easy tribe to control. This is easily explained. They can exist on lands where white men perish from thirst and hunger. They were really in the West what the wildest Arabs are in the East; and the wildest Arabs to this day remain unconquered by any foe.

The Mormons wanted Jim to stop selling firearms to Indians. Jim didn't take orders from any man. It may be guessed that his answer was not diplomatic. Anyway he gave up his fort and it was taken over by the Mormons. No use going over old details of the quarrel. They are apart from the Overland Trail. Jim escaped to the mountains and got his prior possessions registered with the Washington authorities. When after a stormy era between Mormon possession and Washington Army possession, Jim put in a claim for his possessions, the settlement of that claim was deferred, year after year till the old scout's real services had been forgotten and the claim was shaved to six thousand dollars and paid. Jim had returned to Kansas City, where he died in 1881, almost blind, but game, erect, and a good rider to the last. A monument was erected to him in 1904 and there his grave lies in the city he saw grow from muddy flats to a great metropolitan center. Not one book but many could be written on his life.

THE DEVELOPMENT OF THE OVERLAND TRAIL

PART II

DOWN SNAKE RIVER CANYON TO THE COLUMBIA RIVER

LEWIS AND CLARK (1804-1806)

Their explorations up Three Forks and the Missouri were extended into the Nez Percés country in 1805 and their return trip over the trail was made in 1806.

ASTORIANS AND MISSOURI FUR TRADERS (1811-1840)

Astorians made the terrible passage of Snake River Canyon between September 26, 1811, and New Year's Day, 1812; they rested on the Umatilla and reached the Columbia River January 21st. The rendezvous of the fur traders at Pierre's Hole, Jackson's Hole, and Henry's House, became stations for rest and repair of gear. Fort Hall and Boisé grew from American and British posts in the fur war. After the Hudson's Bay Company and the Northwest Company of Montreal united in 1820, Peter Skene Ogden commanded their formidable forces until the trade lost its supremacy.

PIONEERS AND MISSIONARIES (1836-1856)

Gradually as its use increased the trail was made more serviceable. Jim Bridger knew in the early thirties that it was possible to get wagons across the Tetons. Bonneville may have been the first to do it in 1832 or 1834. Dr. Whitman's wagon lasted only so far as Boisé in 1836.

By 1843 wagon caravans were in full parade. Hancock describes fording the wagon trains in 1845. Meeker tells of calking wagon boxes for ferrying in 1852. At its best the passage was exhausting and from being a pausing place for caravans to rest and make repairs grew Walla Walla.

MILITARY OCCUPATION (1827 to present)

Under the supervision of the army were conducted the Stevens' Survey, Wilkes' Survey with his unfavorable report, Frémont's discoveries, all of which with Governor Stevens' Indian Treaties had a great bearing upon the future of the Inland Empire from the Rockies westward.

RAIL PIONEERS (1856-1893)

Though Dodge of Union Pacific fame was forced to find a more practical way of crossing the Rockies than the South Pass, his contribution to the trail was great. Proven possibility called into operation the Northern Pacific and Great Northern, the Oregon Short Line. And today the automobile is giving to the old trail a new lease of life.

CHAPTER VII

ON TO THE NORTH DOWN SNAKE RIVER CANYON

JUST as round South Pass, three highways diverge away from the main Overland Trail, the Californian, the Mormon, the Taos-New Mexico; so on to the North down Snake River Canyon, two older trails, Lewis and Clark's and the Astorians', now run directly into the Oregon Pioneers' Trail. Lewis and Clark were driven south to cross the Rockies by the hostility of Blackfeet raiders. You will find that fact duly commemorated by such rail stations as Blackfoot, marking the crossing over from sources of the Upper Missouri to sources of the Upper Snake; or by such motor highways as connect southern Montana with northern Wyoming and the great Yellowstone National Park to which you can branch off whether eastbound or westbound. The roads are good as the best in any part of the United States with hotel accommodation in which there is a bathroom attached to every bedroom. This fact you will appreciate in the heat and dust of midsummer, when, if wise, you will do the most of your traveling early in the morning or late in the afternoon, and time your rests in the hot midday as all travelers in the South have learned to do. It is by ignoring such simple common sense many travelers subject themselves to unnecessary physical discomfort. It doesn't matter much on the train; for there you have an electric fan and oil engine free of coal dust, and the rail schedules have worked their time-tables out so that the most comfortable trains on through lines pass the hot spots during the night.

Let us take a look at the spotlights on the main highway beyond South Pass before we telescope back to the heroic past. Here's Pocatello, where Wyeth—poor visionary from New England—thought to beat the fur traders from St. Louis and from Hudson's Bay by building his Fort Hall to catch the Snake River Indians in trade instead of permitting them to go on down the Snake to Fort Walla Walla, whence all furs went down the Columbia to the English traders at the Hudson's Bay Company's Fort—Vancouver, Washington. The theory was all right but it didn't jibe with hard facts. The furs were of the best quality from the beaver meadows and tree-sheltered ravines— silky, of good depth and beauty from the severe winter cold; and the profits were enormous in barter so far from base of supplies on the Columbia or on the Missouri; but this region was not a good rendezvous for the mountain Indians. It was too near the plains raiders, north and south, Crows who swooped in through the passes like hawks,

Utes who came up from modern Utah on horses stolen from the Spaniards and fought like demons, yes, on the way even of Sioux and Blackfeet from the north, who had to raid south to get horses every summer and to take scalps, which they prized as trophies in war even more highly than the horses, which they rode like centaurs and threw aside with the cruelty and abandon of all war. Besides, the very remoteness which assured big profits assumed a fearful cost in transporting supplies, which swamped profits. One is loath to set down in definite figures either the losses, financially or in human life, which Wyeth suffered. Certainly we know Wyeth lost two-thirds of all he and his New England backers invested in his venture and his loss of men was not far from two hundred out of fewer than three hundred. He was glad to sell out Fort Hall to his rivals, the Hudson's Bay Company; and there a Captain Grant took charge. You will meet him retired a few years later up off Puget Sound. He always befriended travelers but he would not sell supplies to rivals and he had to charge for his supplies a figure that brought on his head the curses of many an Overlander who would have perished without them; but one of the things the Hudson's Bay Company would not tolerate in white man or Indian was an unpaid debt. Did the Indian dodge his debt for firearms? Till he did pay, he was bartered no more. Did the passing colonist dodge his debt and curse the British Company? That man got no more advances and the trader was dismissed. Since the Hudson's Bay Company controlled all advances from Fort Hall to Fort Vancouver on the Columbia opposite the Willamette, that delinquent didn't find himself scotfree on reaching Oregon. By 1870, both sites of the old forts had been shifted slightly and today the oldest sites close to the water have been submerged by the backwater of dams built to create electric power.

Now look round Pocatello, near old Fort Hall, a central city in the Southern belt of Idaho. What do you see? A shipping hub for fruit, grain, sheep, hogs. No wonder Joe Meek and Jim Bridger said on seeing Ashley's first wagons in 1830 and the missionary wagon of the Whitman's in the same ten years—"There goes the beginning of the end to the fur trade." Less wonder they sent their children to be educated for a new era. Every valley here on the rich bottom land of streams coming down from the snows of the mountains is now a cluster of prosperous farm homes.

Only a few hours farther down Snake River nestles Boisé, site of the next fort established by the traders to cut supplies from Wyeth at Fort Hall and catch the Snake River Indians at a point less perilous to them from other raiders and almost in a bee line from the great rendezvous of Jackson's Hole East and Pierre's Hole West under the shadow of the Three Tetons, which you saw from

Frémont's Peak, or from the mountains out from Laramie. Chimes rang out the hour from the beautiful little Spanish rail station at Boisé as the train passed at sunset—rang out the hours as the wagon "creaked out" the hours of an earlier day. Again prosperous homes nestling in valleys where once roamed Indians who starved in the winter and slaughtered both man and beast in summer, and spent the autumn guzzling on a surplus of plenty and the springs starving and invoking the gods for an early break-up of ice and the coming of the life-saving fish. Why didn't they hoard in summer plenty against starvation in winter? Simply because an Indian is an Indian with less thrift as to forefending want than a pine tree squirrel, which hoards its nuts for use against famine.

Nor need you break your neck to find American Falls and Twin Falls as the early pathfinders did in disaster to their frail canoes. Lovely little cities are beginning to cluster round each water-power center; and when I add that community churches, theaters, speaking movies, are already at all these centers, I do not need to play prophet and predict that these little cities will be big cities in your lifetime and mine. They have a water-power supply that never runs dry and can be used like the water-power of the Coast Cascades over and over for irrigation pumps, factory, rail power. Go and see them and use your head. The water boils in a fall that must easily be two hundred feet high before it leaps in early spring and summer thaw; and at the lowest can never fall less than thirty feet, which explains the amazing differences given by all old trail finders. Both rail and motor highway pass close enough for the white foam to splash you. But alas, as you go on down the canyon, you will see, too, the reason for the suffering of the early pioneers. Where you first strike the Snake west of South Pass region, it is crystal clear as the sky and glad as nymphs of Grecian waterfalls in ancient lore. It leaps, it races, it sings aloud, it plunges over waterfalls in a wild abandon of boiling foam and dashes on over rocky snag or through deep canyon past arid sandy foothill or down between precipice walls, but there are countless places—you can see them as you ride—where the water bed is from two hundred feet to ninety feet below the top of the banks. That is not far to notch steps down in a spiral trail on the face of the bluffs if the bank is not sheer vertical. You will see where stockmen today have cut such safe descents down to watering places for cattle and sheep; but it is another story where the bank is perpendicular in a rock. There is where the old trail finders came to woe. By frail canoe, they were wrecked. By land trail, along the crest of the bank, they perished from thirst, while they heard and saw far below their reach the wild waters. You will learn presently, where the Snake takes a great curve north, that its canyons have

defied rail construction to this day. Tunnels must
be too long to pay for costs, rock blasting too risky
for track beds; so passes through these Blue Mountains became an awful battle through snows at
sky line and heat below; and the Blue Mountains
are two thousand feet higher than South Pass.
The rail lines have beaten the terrible grades by
taking a short cut across the great Snake Curve
to the Columbia westward, or Walla Walla eastward. You must do the same thing by motor road.
The Blue Mountains need no explanation of their
name. The atmosphere hangs in a blue curtain
between the rugged, ragged peaks. But Idaho does
need an explanation of its name. It is not named
after some sweetheart. Its name is most poetic. It
means "El-dah-how"—Snake dialect for "Sun
Marching Down the Mountains" to the west.
White men mangled this to Id-a-ho.

But do not run away with the wrong idea that
because these banks of the Snake are so forbidding
to human habitation, the lands on each side are
uninhabitable. They are not. Dry farming on the
arid lands has produced the heaviest wheat yields
in all America, yields from sixty to eighty bushels
an acre according to season; and irrigation farming
in the valley bottoms has done as well. Dry farming in the Inland Empire today yields from eight
to twelve per cent of the total wheat crop in the
United States, which explains why grain lands of
the Inter Mountain region sell at a hundred dol-

lars an acre and pay their costs in a few years. I think of farms bought in the slump after the War at that price, which paid for themselves in three years. As I write I pick up a report on sales for six months of 1929—raw lands at fifty-five dollars an acre, two thousand farms sold in a half year. The buyers of these farms are not fools but they have to know a highly specialized job.

Now let us go back to the earliest trail finders, Lewis and Clark. They had been pushed south over the Three Forks. They had bestrode the headsprings of the Missouri—a hunter standing with one leg on one side of the Divide and one leg on the other. Then the mountain ozone had set their feet dancing as it set many an Overlander's in the mountain passes. Then the Snake branch wigwams were found far different from the buckskin tepee peaks of the Platte Indian. There are several rail stations along East Oregon and South Idaho lines named after old Lewis and Clark men, who had the colic from too much starvation, then a sudden fill of food. I'll not cumber memory with their names—you'll find them in every rail timecard. The Lewis and Clark trail from the Missouri came finally into the Oregon Trail up in North Idaho.

Come now to the Astorians of 1811. They had not gone up the Platte in the first place. They had followed the Upper Missouri, but like Lewis and Clark came with their guide, Pierre Dorion, through the rendezvous of the Tetons across to the Henry branch of the Snake, between what is now an Indian Reserve south of Pendleton and north of Boisé. This had drawn them far south of their expectations to strike a branch of the Snake, where stood the abandoned cabins of some trader, which later became known as Henry's House. It was just under the shadow of those famous Three Tetons; so they headed away from the cabins north. Just here, get those Dorions untangled. They are badly mixed in old annals and you will meet them again and again in tragedy and nearly always in treachery. The first Pierre was an interpreter for Lewis and Clark, used up the Missouri but sent back. The second Pierre, his son, was guide for the Astorians, and his little wife—Holy Rainbow— was the heroic figure. The pity is her son did not perish when the grumbling, undependable skulking Pierre the second did; for he was one of the traitors who brought destruction on the missions of Walla Walla. Likewise, though the Astorians did not follow the Platte westward, they did on the return overland three years later and described it in detail to that Grand Island Ford, famous in all Overlanders' wanderings.

Pierre second, when drunk, was notorious for abuse of his wife and two children, but did yield the use of a horse to his little wife before the birth of a third child who died a few days afterward on the trail. Coming out on the Snake from

the Three Tetons on September 26, 1811, if the
Astorians had obeyed their first impulse and beaten
their way at terrible speed down the most tumultuous rivers they had yet seen, past Idaho Falls, American Falls, Twin Falls, Glen's Ferry, they would
have escaped the fearful suffering that almost
wrecked their bands of sixty men or more; but the
Snake River Indians told them plainly the river
could not be run by canoe. It was "a mad river."
The Canadian voyageurs became gloomy. Wild
snow-storms began to fall in October. Horses
wading the head waters of the Snake were up to
girths in icy currents. The river was in full flood
of rain and snow was a hundred yards wide; so they
built canoes. The canoes were poorly constructed
in haste—raw wood that split, undried thongs in
place of close-fitted boards or tarred seams of bark,
and weak saplings for oars and paddles instead
of strong ash. One of the partners—Miller—
became so despondent and morose he dropped out
and remained to trap with hunters for the winter
in the mountains. He probably reckoned on his
rifle supplying food for four, where forty to sixty
men might come to starvation or cannibalism. The
canoes built on the spot were launched down the
Snake on the 18th of October and the tired voyageurs bounced gleefully forward; for the river
was doing the work and river navigation they
knew. They could see the Three Tetons or Pilot

Courtesy of Yakima Chamber of Commerce

A CROSS SECTION OF THE YAKIMA VALLEY, TAKEN DUE WEST OF YAKIMA

Courtesy of Northern Pacific Railroad

THE FAMOUS INLAND EMPIRE HIGHWAY KNOWN AS THE YAKIMA-ELLENS-
BERG CANYON ROAD

Knobs to the east and knew this river must lead
ultimately to the Columbia.

A week's travel disillusioned such hopes. They
came to a fall described as two hundred to thirty
feet vertical. Was it Twin Falls or American
Falls? Heads have been broken over the dispute.
I do not know and I do not think anyone can know;
for the water was at high flood and that must have
lessened the sheer drop. Of course, they tried to
portage the canoes past these rapids but cactus
spines stabbed their naked feet and canoes held by
tump lines to the margin where the men on the
rope ran along on the crest of the cliff swamped
to the wild rush of waters. Crooks, the bravest of
the partners, sitting in one canoe, struck a rock.
The canoe was cleft from stem to stern and five
men plunged in boiling seething floods. One of the
best paddlers perished. Gloom deepened. Three
scouts went along the north bank and three along
the south bank to report conditions ahead. Both
parties came back hopeless, dejected, mutinous.
The river ran for forty miles—wild waters, which
no canoe could weather—especially down stream,
more dangerous than up current; for the rush carried to watery death before the frail paddles could
stem and side-sweep in-shore. The voyageurs
simply refused to go on. Yet, they could not go
back. Snow barred the mountain passes and they
had exactly five days' supply of food. The leading
partners—Hunt, Crooks, McLellan—now did

what seemed to them the wisest thing. We know now it was not wise. Better have held together under a tight hand as Lewis and Clark had than disperse to death under no leadership; but the Astorians were nervously apprehensive of cannibalism among men now going insane from fear. Lewis and Clark had military power over their men and had drilled them for a winter before leaving St. Louis. The Astorian leaders hadn't. They broke their men into three groups—McLellan to follow the Snake as close as he could; Crooks to try to find his way back up the Snake to those abandoned cabins later known as Henry's Fort; McKenzie, a veteran trader of Montreal, to try and take the short cut across the bend on the Snake as the rail lines do today. Hunt, head of the Astorians, had thirty-one men left on his helpless hands with Dorion, the little Holy Rainbow and the two children.

The first thing was to cache all needless baggage and beaver pelts. This was done in the usual fashion, by digging a hole, burying all wrapped in buckskin or burlap, then covering with stones and turf, then tramping down the winter snows to wipe out all smell that might lure hungry wolf to scratch below. A cache in trees overhead was impracticable because of marauding war raiders. The next blast to flickering hopes was the return of Crooks from tramping back up the Snake. The way to any fort on the back trail was already utterly blocked. Of course, it was. It was now October. Trapped between going on and going back, they called the whole section the Devil's Scuttle Hole. How far had they yet to go? A thousand miles. Fortunately they didn't know that. Napoleon always said keep your avenue of retreat open, and your forward course will take care of itself. Cæsar said—burn your ships behind you and you have to go on. Hunt's ships were burned behind him. For a thousand miles, he now had forty pounds of corn, twenty of grease, five of canned soups, and five pounds of dried meats. Estimate that for each man. Hunt and Dorion with eighteen men were following the northeast meanderings of the Snake, Crooks and the others the southwest bank.

For twenty-eight miles, Hunt's party on the North could not get down to the river for drinking water. When they met a Snake River family, they bartered for some salmon and a puppy dog and there were no squeamish qualms as among the Army officers at Laramie. Farther along fifty miles, more dogs and more salmon were bought in barter. By the middle of November, they saw the great mountains which slanted northwestward and crowded the Snake into these impassable canyons. Here the thirst of the men became so unendurable they gashed their own wrists to drink their blood. Rain in little puddles stopped that delirious madness so near to cannibalism that disgraced one party

of Californian Overlanders years later. Men so
delirious can only be described as fevered to insanity. It was right in the midst of these hardships Dorion's wife gave birth to that third child.

December came on with rains but the climate
was less severe west of the Rockies and game more
frequent, though Indian trail after trail often sent
all marchers floundering through snow to mid-
waist and a horse had to be killed at night camp
before food could be supplied. Even the horse
hide was treasured for future soups.

It was on the morning of December 6, that they
saw Crooks and one man on the west bank of the
river signaling desperately for food. Hunt at once
rafted a float of horse hide and sapling poles and
with Guardipie—of a family famous in Western
Indian lore—got across to the rescue of Crooks.
Crooks had wasted to a skeleton. The men now
began to desert Hunt daily either to break away
to the Snake camps, or put up wigwams and trust
to their rifles for food. It was well these deser-
tions did occur, for Crooks was too weak to walk
and too ill to hold himself on a horse. It is supposed these most terrible hardships were encountered between what is now Boisé and the Three
Tetons. It was a clear case of men not only being
lost, but losing their nerve; and such leadership is
worse than being lost or losing nerve. It loses the
confidence of followers. The procession of de-
sponding Overlanders, now became a lawless muti-

nous mob. It is terrible to have to set that fact down; but it is the truth. Only one other such migration across the Overland Trail can be likened to it—the California gold rush; and it did end, in one case, in the very cannibalism which the Astorian leaders feared. John Day, the best Kentucky marksman of all the hunters, was now almost delirious, but faithful as a dog to Crooks. His name is now commemorated on a river west of the Umatilla. Hunt pressed on, leaving Day and Crooks. Pistols in trade hired Indian guides. You recall Hunt had come on by the northeast bank. By Christmas, ice was running in patches on the Snake, but an Indian ferry got Hunt across to the west side and Christmas Eve, he said good-by to a river which the voyageurs called "the mad river enraged"—not a very literal translation, but the literal was a curse. The Indian guides undertook to follow that cut across country which Pendleton marks today. I cannot find there was any Christmas celebration. When I crossed through Pendleton in May, I looked out on such fields of grain as I had not seen anywhere from Lancaster County, Pennsylvania. I had slept in a little hotel with a bath off my room for a hot plunge on arrival at midnight and at dawn I entered a dining-room where food was served second to no hotel in New York. How many of the guests hurrying as I was to catch the next bus or train west to Portland, or northeast to Walla Walla and

Spokane, paused to think of those first pathfinders?

Hunt rested his men for New Year's Day, 1812, and, of course, the Canadian voyageurs danced and sang and ate dog meat bartered from the Snakes and Nez Percés, to their fill. To the infinite joy of all, the climate became more genial each mile westward and the gladness could not be expressed by the human tongue when there spread below the wanderers the green valleys of the Walla Walla with herds of thousands of horses in pastures deep on the stream banks below. Kettles, axes, white men guns told Hunt he was now within trading distance of the Columbia and Pacific—as the river wound in and out closer to five hundred miles than four hundred. It was necessary to rest his footsore men. Exactly where was the rest camp? On the Umatilla. That is as near as anyone can say. Water was high. Beaver were in plenty. The Indians reported that the other Astorians who had gone by the short cut from the bend in the Snake had already preceded Hunt. On January 21st, the Umatilla emerged in the broad waters of the Columbia, greeted with hilarious shout. Over two thousand miles the Astorians had traveled from leaving St. Louis. Over three thousand they traversed before reaching the Pacific.

Before going on down the Columbia, let us dispose of Dorion and his pathetic little Holy Rainbow wife. Between the Blue Mountains and the Umatilla he had dropped out from Hunt either as

trapper or because his services down the Columbia
were useless. Crooks and his faithful John Day
were rescued in March of 1812 by an eastbound
brigade of Astorians. The Walla Walla Indians
had treated both well, but farther down the Columbia the evil Pirate Indians took a fancy to their
rifles, when both men were stripped and set adrift.
Poor Day died within a year quite insane. Those
caches hidden on the banks of the Snake were
found by the same eastbound Astorians rifled by
the Indians and ravening wolves; but on going
east heading for the Blue Mountains almost two
years later, near the outlet of the Walla Walla,
some Astorians heard a woman's call to them in
broken French. There on the banks was Pierre
Dorion's wife and her two children, now about
five and seven years old. The third had died.
Pierre had gone five days up the Snake trapping,
leaving his wife in camp. One of her husband's
comrades stumbled into her camp with word
Pierre had been murdered. She caught two
beaver, gathered her clothing and food in a parflêche bag, tied all to a saddle, threw the wounded
man across one horse and with her two children
mounted the other and fled north. The trapper
died the first night out. She pushed on at dawn.
In a week she was on the Walla Walla. She built
a bark wigwam, killed her two horses for food,
smoked their flesh and lived through that winter.
In spring, she set out for the Columbia and came

to it where the Walla Walla joined. It was there
the eastbound Astorians found her; and there the
curtain must ring down on one of the most heroic
Indian girls in history.

How fared it with the Oregon Pioneers along
Snake River Canyon?

Jesse Applegate gives very full details on the
great migration of 1843. Perhaps the novelty of
excitement on the Platte had worn off. Perhaps
scant fare had worn the little chap's exuberant
energy off the edge. His wise mother may have
been keeping him under cover of the tented wagon
along this perilous section; or the more awful experience suffered by a boy aged nine on the Columbia may have effaced much he saw and heard along
the Snake. There were no buffalo chips to be
picked up and bagged for fuel by the boys along
the Snake. Game was very scarce by autumn and
it no longer lured off the trail as it had on the
Platte. He remembered and described the peaks
—Three Tetons—between the Snake and the Yellowstone. He recalls the sage brush, the grease-
wood—all now brittle from the heat of midsummer
along the stream beds. There was now always a
big pistol in his mother's belt and she frequently
handled the reins of the teams. Captain Grant
was in charge at Fort Hall for the Hudson's Bay
Company and nothing but kindness was received
from the Englishmen. The Fort was adobé plas-
ter. Salmon Falls sounded in a roar like distant

thunder. They were the first big falls the little inland lad had ever seen; and dried salmon hung in lines about the fort and every Indian camp like small clothes on a washing day. The Snake Indians shocked the youngster by moving round the Fort stark naked, except for the loin cloth tied in a "gee" from hips to front waist line or the scant skirt of buckskin belted round the squaws' waists, which were hardly waists in the white man's understanding of that word but rather fatty protuberances, produced—though he didn't know that —by alternations of gorging feast and colicky hunger. The blue—blue wild waters so different from the tawny flow of Missouri and Platte—gave him a sense of living in a new world. He found the oily bears' meat at Boisé nauseous. The river at Boisé was a hundred yards wide and one man was drowned. The Indian graves gave him a terrible scare. The bodies were boxed or trussed in buckskin and left in slatted graveyards, where pots and kettles and bows and arrows and lumps of decayed food were supposed to assist the departed on the trail to the Happy Hunting Grounds. The boy got the first big fright on the trail by sneaking out to one of these and encountering a real living ghost that sent him scampering back to camp to have an awful nightmare and fit of repentance for disobeying orders not to stray out. Just when he was, with youngster curiosity, examining those graves and perhaps taking a fancy to some of those

bows and arrows, a gnome-like horrible apparition
rose wailing from the graves. It had long tangled
hair overhanging eyes and face. The skin was that
of a long dead mummy; and the thing was living.
It rose and came stumbling after him with long
clawy thin arms. Did he wait? He did not. One
does not need to add that the ghost was some poor
half-blind old Indian out to wail nightly at the
graves. These half-blind and often utterly deaf
old Indians have a sense of *feel,* which I have
often witnessed myself. Being sightless and deaf,
you may approach within ten feet, when they begin
to stumble and roll in your direction. Shift your
line of approach to avoid collision, and they shift
their line of approach and come lumbering on at
you. One of the most comical and pathetic scenes
I ever witnessed chanced to me on the Desert of
Arizona with a half-blind old Indian albino. My
companion on that trip didn't like Indians. She
was a descendant of the old Spanish slave holders.
And she liked smallpox less; and there had been
a great deal of it the preceding winter. The Indians had thrust corpses down deep crevices of the
rocks and the sunlight had pretty well disinfected
the air of filth. Still we wanted to see the camp
and yet not get in too close contact with the Indians. We met the old albino waddling in our
direction. We shifted. He shifted. I put her on
the side away from him. He lolled over to her
side. He seemed to feel her nervousness till we

both had to laugh and to avoid collision let him
come head on, then quickly sidestepped and proceeded on our way.

Little Applegate's experience cured him of exploring Indian graves as I think ours did us of
exploring at too close range an Indian camp. Two
or three memories stood out clear with the boy;
he fell from the wagon, there was a man implicated
in a murder for which he was later hanged. The
Umatilla Mountains were to the west and the Blue
to the east, and the Cayuse Indians were terrible
horse thieves. The oxen had sore necks from the
friction of the yokes, and hoofs of oxen and horses
were brittle, cracked and worn.

The south bank of the Snake was favored from
Fort Hall to Boisé. The Snake had to be crossed
twice between the forts. The Whitman wagon
proved a terrible nuisance in 1836 on the steep
grades. It upset twice in one day. Its axle trees,
warped by the heat, snapped. At Fort Hall, it was
left or two wheels taken off. At Boisé it disappeared from history. As many as thirty wagons
were left at Fort Hall in these years, or sold for
provisions. Boisé, with its blue waters and safe
adobé walls, was a great place for the tired wives
to uncramp limbs from the wagons and wash out
the clothing almost stiff from dust and sweat. By
1843, wagon caravans were in full parade.

Hancock coming in 1845 doesn't say much about
the Snake, but what he does say is to the point:

"Upon our return to camp we ascertained a number of the enemy's shot had penetrated our wagon beds, fortunately doing no other damage, although the families had taken refuge in the wagons during the skirmish.

"The next day we arrived at the crossing of Snake River, when two men of the company forded it for the purpose of hunting on the other side, and did not return that night; in the morning four men went in search of them, and found blood and the traces of something being dragged in the ground; they followed this and found the body of one of these men divested of its scalp, clothing, gun, etc. After looking around and making the most diligent search for the other and seeing no traces of him, they concluded that he had shared a similar fate, and burying the comrade already found as best they could, returned to camp. We now made preparations for crossing the river, which was very rapid and deep, and perhaps two hundred yards wide; the crossing was effected by propping up the wagon beds above the reach of the water and having three men on horseback by the team of the first wagon, to which all the others were all chained each to the preceding one, and with a man on horseback to keep the teams straight, we reached the opposite bank safely, though some of the smaller cattle were forced to swim. Continuing our travels peacefully for three or four days we reached Fort Boisé, where we had to recross Snake River, and here we encamped and remained a day.

"We drove along for several days without being molested by Indians, though frequently seeing them, until we arrived at an exceedingly rough mountainous place, where we had to establish our road as we went, over a country never traveled perhaps by human beings, save the trapper in pursuit of game or roving savages. Sometimes for the distance of many miles the entire surface of the country was covered with medium sized stone or boulder, just large enough to make it difficult to travel over them; the only way the teams behind could distinguish the route was by the bruised and broken boulders occasioned by the wheels of the front wagon passing over them, and the blood from the feet of our poor animals that suffered almost beyond endurance, for in many instances they would lie down and suffer any kind of punishment in preference to rising, and frequently we were obliged to leave them lying upon the rocks, where nothing could be obtained for them to eat.

"Finally crossing this range of mountains, the route became better, being comparatively relieved of these miserable stones so destructive to our teams, although destitute of water! In the hope of reaching water we were now obliged to urge our exhausted animals forward, and in this effort drove all night when we could. One night thirty of our cows left us, and we did not know but that they were stolen by the Indians, although we had seen nor heard nothing of them since penetrating this miserable country, which seemed almost impervious to the savages even."

Meeker tells the same story of "thirst almost maddening" on Snake River:

"Just below lower Salmon Falls the dilemma confronted us to either cross the river or starve our teams on the trip down the river on the south bank.

"The emigration of 1843 had forded the river lower down at a point later known as Glenn's Ferry. It was extremely hazardous at that time. Frémont, crossing at the same time, narrowly escaped losing his famous gun and then got out his boats. Subsequent changes in the channel and the formation of a new island made it imperative to seek some other method of crossing.

"Some emigrants had calked three wagon-beds and lashed them together, and were crossing, but would not help others across for less than three to five dollars a wagon, the party swimming their own stock. If others could cross in wagon-beds, why could I not do likewise? And without much ado all the old clothing that could possibly be spared was marshaled, tar buckets ransacked, old chisels and broken knives hunted up, and a veritable boat repairing and calking campaign inaugurated, and shortly the wagon-box rode placidly, even if not gracefully on the turbid waters of the formidable river. It had been my fortune to be the strongest physically of any of our little party now reduced to four men, though I would cheerfully accept a second place mentally. My boyhood pranks of playing with logs or old leaky skiffs in the waters of White River now served me well, for I could row a boat even if I had never taken lessons as an athlete. My first venture across the Snake River was with the wagon gear run over the wagon-box, the whole being gradually worked out into deep water. The load was so heavy that a very small margin was left to prevent the water from breaking over the sides, and some actually did, as light ripples on the surface struck the 'Mary Jane,' as we had christened (without wine) the 'craft' as she was launched. However, I got over safely, but after that took lighter loads and really enjoyed the novelty of the work and the change from the intolerable dust to the atmosphere of the water.

"Some were so infatuated with the idea of floating on the water as to be easily persuaded by an unprincipled trader at the lower crossing to dispose of their teams for a song, and embark in their wagon-beds for a voyage down the river. It is needless to say that these persons (of whom there were a goodly number) lost everything they had and some their lives, the survivors, after incredible hardships, reaching the road again to become objects of charity while separated entirely from friends. I knew one survivor, who yet lives in our State, who was out seven days without food other than a scant supply of berries and vegetable growth and 'a few crickets, but not many,' as it was too laborious to catch them.

"We had not finished crossing when tempting offers came

from others to cross them, but all our party said, 'No, we must travel.'

"But what about the lower crossing? Those who had crossed over the river must somehow get back. It was less than a hundred and fifty miles to where we were again to cross to the south side (left bank) of the river. I could walk that in four days, while it would take our teams ten. Could I go on ahead, procure a wagon-box, and start a ferry of my own? The thought prompted an affirmative answer at once: so with a little food and a small blanket the trip to the lower crossing was made. It may be ludicrous, but it is true, that the most I remember about that trip, is the jackrabbits—such swarms of them I had never seen before as I traveled down the Boisé Valley, and never expect to see again.

"The trip was made in safety, but conditions were different. At the lower crossing, as I have already said, some were disposing of their teams and starting to float down the river; some were fording, a perilous undertaking, but most of them succeeded who tried, and besides a trader, whose name I have forgotten, had an established ferry near the old Fort Boisé. I soon obtained a wagon-bed, and was at work during all the daylight hours, (no eight-hour-a-day there) crossing people till the teams came up (and for several days after), and left the river with a hundred and ten dollars in my pocket, all of which was gone before I arrived in Portland, save two dollars and seventy-five cents."

When Meeker came back half a century afterward, he got such a welcome in his monument-marking expedition as only Northeast Oregon and South Idaho could give him. Baker City, Pendleton, Boisé, Pocatello, Twin Falls—all celebrated with a whoop. Why? These are not places given to artificial whoops. Because only the people of

these centers fully realized what the Pioneer caravans had overcome or how much present prosperity
was indebted to those heroic, tireless advance couriers of civilization.

DESCHUTES RIVER CANYON, CENTRAL OREGON

Photo by Frank Palmer, Spokane

SITE OF OLD SPOKANE HOUSE, A SHORT DISTANCE FROM THE CITY OF SPOKANE

THE DEVELOPMENT OF THE OVERLAND TRAIL

PART III

DOWN THE COLUMBIA RIVER TO THE PACIFIC

LEWIS AND CLARK (1804-1806)
Reached the Walla Walla River where it joins the Columbia and found friendly Nez Percés camping there in 1805.

ASTORIANS (1811-1813)

THE NORTH-WEST COMPANY OF MONTREAL FUR TRADERS (1811-1820)

HUDSON'S BAY COMPANY (1821-1843)
These three great contestants for the wealth of furs in the country between the Rockies all claimed the territory. David Thompson made a wild dash from Montreal in 1811, across Lake Superior, up the Saskatchewan, and over the Rockies only to find that the Astorians held prior occupation by just two months. In 1813 the Astorians were taken over by the British; in 1820 the Montreal and Hudson's Bay Companies united; and from 1824 to 1840 their great factor Dr. John McLoughlin ruled from Fort Vancouver.

PIONEERS AND MISSIONARIES (1835-1856)
The Lees' Methodist mission was on the Willamette not far from Fort Vancouver; Dr. Whitman's was among the Cayuse on the Walla Walla; H. H. Spalding's with the Nez Percés on the Lapwai. All favored colonization; many who came out upon the slopes of the Blue Mountains

from the dangers of the Snake River Canyon were content to settle. And the thousands of caravans pausing to rest, repair and refit soon drew together at one place and another the beginnings of the cities which today are the supply centers of a wide territory, supplied themselves by boats from Portland. Portland's first cabin was built in 1843; by 1850 it was a thriving town, and in that year dispatched its first brig in the China trade.

RAIL PIONEERS (1870 to 1893 and 1922)

As soon as the Rockies were crossed the railroads came in, Northern Pacific, Great Northern, Chicago, Milwaukee & St. Paul, Oregon Short Line and others. And where the Overland Trail had reached farthest they built up the coast cities—Portland, Seattle, Tacoma, Olympia, etc.

CHAPTER VIII

WALLA WALLA, THE HALFWAY HOUSE IN THE GREAT BEND OF THE SNAKE

WHEN, on the Oregon Trail, you finally emerge from the Snake River County and Blue Mountains to Walla Walla, you are in the heart of more romantic heroism than in all the Highlands of Scotland or Switzerland. For an outsider to keep his bearings, it is a puzzling topography. Snake River Canyons, of such heart-break to all travelers, from Lewis and Clark and the Astorians to modern Overlanders, take a great bend south to north and north to south again where the wild white galloping water horses of the canyons plunge in the final leap to lose themselves in the broad Columbia. A little off the center of this circle lies Walla Walla—the pausing place in the march to the Columbia for almost a hundred years.

It has shifted its site twice during the century. The first fort was a mere trading post built with log pickets and slab warehouses, just where the Walla Walla joins Columbia River, really known as Nez Percés Fort at first. It was called Nez Percé from the Indians who centered there from Lewis and Clark's day. This was burned in 1841 and rebuilt of adobé with two stout bastions, the lower story housing ample supply of ammunition and bayonets stacked for instant action, the upper floor loop-holed for gun barrels to rake each of two walls. This was not because the Nez Percés were hostile. They were not. It was because in a very dry climate earth walls were safer than wood; and no ruffian renegade could set them on fire if he chanced to be in an angry mood. The modern Walla Walla is twenty-five to twenty-nine miles east of the old site.

The plains afforded abundant pasture for horses and oxen exhausted by the traverse of the Blue Mountains and their desert of rocks to the south and worse desert of sands to the north. Always Walla Walla had abundance of food for man— mountain game for the hunters, salmon for the fisherman, roots and berries that could be pounded into flour for pancakes and dried fruit pastries— all of which foreshadowed the modern growth of great wheat areas and fruit farms, prune plums, apples, cherries, peaches, berries of every variety. After the awful alkali waters of the Plains and the still more tantalizing waters of the Snake Canyon, where from high above the precipice walls man and beast could see the whirling blue streams below but no path to go down to them till men fainted from thirst or went mad like poor John Day—who has left his name to Day River—and cattle and horses lay down on the trail with tongues lolling out, Walla Walla was a Paradise, a Garden of Eden, a blood refuge city between the raiding Snakes to the south and the friendly Nez Percés to the north.

First, some explanation as to all the tribes and clans in this area. Rings from the nose in the days before white men came were only used on rare occasions. The Nez Percés did not pierce their nostrils as the gay gallants did down on the Coast. The wrong name seems to have been given because white men first saw slaves taken in war from Coast tribes and these Coast tribes used rings from the nose—rings pierced through the nose like earrings —hence the name Nez Percés, "pierced noses." The Flatheads did not flatten heads. The name came from Coast slaves whom first traders saw among the mountain people. The Pen d'Oreilles did not stretch their ears to long lobes—another Coast fashion; but the young girls did braid their hair in hard bobs over the ears. The Cayuses were not a tribe at all but rather a clan named from the magnificent herds of horses raided—amazing to re-late—from Spanish settlements more than a thousand miles south. The Umatillas were not a tribe but a clan on the river of the same name. Whether the Snakes took their name from their method of hidden ambushed warfare as the Sioux did, or from the fact this country was overrun with the worst type of rattlesnakes in the mountains, I do not know; nor is there any final opinion. Snake

River was first known as Shosh-on-ee—Indian word for "inland." All were friendly to the whites till the great migration over the Oregon Trail, when the Indians, stirred up by educated half-breeds who belonged to neither race and became mischief makers for both, began to whisper that the immigrants were coming to destroy the red man's hunting ground and drive him from the land.

Again a word as to these raids for horses. There is nothing else like them in history, even the Iroquois rushes across the St. Lawrence to the Great Lakes, where canoe tribes fled in terror; or the inundations of Mongolian Desert warriors to the Plains of Mesopotamia. Before these thousand mile raids through canyons and deserts, the best of the young warriors were put through a health clinic not greatly different from modern methods. They were subjected to such a course of training as only the strongest, toughest, youngest could stand. They had to fast and purge more or less for forty days. The purging came from fish oils and vegetable diets—this for kidneys and intestinal tract; but the treatment did not stop with this. They were "stomach pumped" and "stomach pounded" to surpass a modern specialist. A little willow switch with lesser little willow tender shoots was poked down their throats and swabbed round till each stomach did what any normal stomach would do—threw off all stagnant juices and

bile and began working furiously on its own account. Then they were given a Turkish bath. A
tepee was constructed—skins laid on skins till
vapor proof, red-hot stones thrown in pots or
baskets of water till every pore was oozing sweat
and skin obstructions in rivulets from head to heel.
The medicine man then threw in a shell scraper
and helped to scrape the skin clear of all hard
tissue and dust and filth from scalp to foot sole.
Often every muscle was massaged and stretched
and counter stretched till the patient would have
groaned, had he dared; which he didn't. Then
with nought of clothing but a loin cloth, the young
warriors lifted the tent flap and took a flying leap
into the nearest ice-cold water they could reach.
The reactionary shock on high geared nerves or
stiff muscles doesn't need to be told. Like the
stomach, they came alive to natural functions; and
many a white trader taking the same drastic
treatment—if he survived—found himself free of
rheumatism and stomach woes for the rest of his
life. From this treatment to the departure for
the raid, the young warriors prepared their best
weapons and toughest ponies for the thousand-mile
ride. They could reef in their belts against hunger. They could withstand the bad effects of bad
water, sleepless nights in mountain cold or desert
heat. As for death, they were fatalists and feared
nought but the captivity of slavery.

With all the odds in the Indians' favor, two or

three questions must occur to the traveler's mind.

When so friendly at first to the whites, why were these tribes always such thieves, petty pilferers from chief to slave? Because, outside his own tribe, the Indian did not regard taking over people's property as theft. Under his tent roof, yes, the white man guest was secure from theft, if not from fleas and worse vermin and an Indian girl wife wished on him. There many a trader fell either a victim to the worst in himself, or for prudential reasons to bind the tribe's protection married a warrior's daughter. The offspring from the former became the mischief making half-breeds of later era. From the latter sprang some of the very best families in the West today.

With such abundance of food for man and beast, why did these Indians so often—almost yearly— come to starvation? Because the Indian could not or would not forefend against possible future want. When he had a big salmon run, or big game hunt, he sat him down and gorged to his fill; and all the clan sat them down and gorged on his doormat with him. Came a season of prolonged cold when the salmon were tardy ascending the Columbia, or the game slow in emerging from the fifteen-foot drifts in the Blue Mountains, and every "parflêche"—skin bag of dried food—was ripped open and shared till all were hungry or relieved by the thaw. As no family was permitted to save food if others less thrifty were hungry, there was no incentive to lay up store in the present against want in the future.

With such factors in favor of perfect health, why did the Indian fall so ready a victim to filth diseases like tuberculosis and influenza from bad air, or measles and chicken-pox and smallpox from contagion? Because in changing his camp every season under primitive conditions, lung germs were destroyed by sunlight; but when tents were exchanged for log houses, bad air did its fatal work. As to the other filth diseases, if you consider the Indian remedies you will readily understand how in fever cases, they were absolutely fatal. The plunge in ice-water for fever and influenza is an instance. Similar treatment for smallpox was suicide. Before white man living became a factor at all, Wilkes out in the 1840's says smallpox, chicken-pox, measles, had swept away in one devastating blast four-fifths of these tribes; not fewer than fifty thousand all told; and when they began to recur with the coming of the immigrants from 1839 to 1847, fear became a frantic frenzy, a racial hatred, bloody blind brute massacre.

Coming through the Main Ridge of the Rockies every traveler along the old Overland Trail must have received a rude shock as to the difference between mountain maps and mountain facts. On maps, the mountains resemble the great back-bone of a fish with spurs to east and west and between the spurs marked "Pass"; but alas, the Pass was not a simple game trail widened for horsemen, then widened again for wagons, then built up for motor and train. It was often a climb over the back-bone at three thousand to seven thousand feet altitude; and the climb until rails bored tunnels was a switchback and corkscrew up one side and down another; and such spur ridges as the Blue Mountains, not high as mountain passes average, seldom above four thousand feet, the main Blue Mountains not much higher than nine thousand feet, had themselves, bad canyon passes to be traversed. Blue and shimmering and shining in the distance, veiled in filtered mist by day and star-pricked luminous mystery at night, with often a glare of rose-pink sheet-lightning from cumulous opal clouds, the Blue Mountains were a treacherous arid barrier to all travelers who tried to avoid the great northern bend of Snake River and cut across its diameter to the Columbia. By day the racing torrents iridescent as rainbows and shouting with the gladness of disimprisoned waters make a music sweet to the ears of the strong: but when the sun drops behind the opaline sky-line and the waters begin to rush in an ominous hush and the long shadows to etch in melancholy, there is something oily in the coiling canyons as the loops of a monster python. Add to the hushed rush the sharp crescendo dismal howl of the wolf packs, perhaps the scream of a wild cat, the lonely echoing whistle of a mountain marmot, the sigh

like a lost soul of the night winds; and these canyons demand stout hearts to resist the engulfing
depression. Trappers never went out alone. They
went in pairs. Indians went in bands; and where
camp ashes of Indian bands were found, trappers
took turn sitting back to rock or tree on guard
while comrade slept. Where both slept they, too
often, slept the sleep of death.

These were the natural features which alike compelled Indian tribe, fur trader, immigrant, to steer
for Walla Walla as the great halfway house from
what is now Southern Idaho and Northeast Oregon to Southeast Washington. Walla Walla lay
1776 miles from the Overlanders' jumping off into
the Unknown back at Kansas City.

Somewhere in this great Walla Walla area
Lewis and Clark met the friendly chief Twisted
Hair, who kept their horses and gave them guides
on to the Columbia. Here later the divided Astorians wandering along each side of the Snake
River Canyon were rescued from starvation,
clothed, fed and sent on, again to be stripped naked
and set adrift till Day lost his reason and Crooks,
the leader, became an emaciated ghost skeleton.
Here, too, as has been already told, Pierre Dorion,
son of Lewis and Clark's old guide, was scalped
and slain by the Snakes, leaving his little Sioux
wife and two children to escape to cover as they
best could till rescued by an eastbound brigade of
Astorians. You will meet the third Dorion de-

scendant presently. Like too many half-breeds, he embodied the most treacherous features of both races.

After the Astorians, bag, baggage and brigades, were taken over by the great English Hudson's Bay Company, Peter Pambrum, the chief trader at Walla Walla, became the good Samaritan to all stranded Overlanders and helped them to go on down to the Columbia. When he could, he housed them under his own roof. When there were women, he gave them all the comforts the fort permitted in the corner bastions. When the immigrants came in hungry hordes of thousands in the forties, Peter and his successor—McKinlay— let them camp inside the palisaded walls; and if the Indians gradually becoming impudent offered insult to the ragged barefoot starving colonists, Pete was the first to give them a good thrashing and kick them from the fort gates. Indians realized what that meant—unless they behaved, no more trade, no more bullets for raids on Blackfeet and Snakes. Once when a belligerent rabble refused to be ejected and began hacking the palisades down, McKinlay on the instant rolled out a big keg of powder, knocked its head in with an ax and stooped with a flaming torch. The rabble warriors didn't wait. They scampered and the Hudson's Bay man, smiling grimly, rolled the powder keg under the counter. When Bonneville, the gay French adventurer, came here to set up rival trade in the early 1830's, Peter would not sell a pint of liquor to him, nor help him in trade, but he took him in with that feudal hospitality for which the Hudson's Bay Company was famous and was the good host he always proved to the needy. Bonneville was undoubtedly the first man to get wagons or a small cannon trundled on wheels across the Tetons and up in part, if not to Walla Walla, at least close to it by 1832 or 1834.

Here came Uncle Joe Meek in the early 1840's to leave his little girl Helen Marr named from one of Scott's heroines to be educated in the Whitman Mission, five miles from the modern city, or twenty-five miles from the Columbia, where the old Fort stood. Here came Jim Bridger to leave his little Mary Ann at the same school. Here in the middle of the 1850's came Uncle Ezra Meeker, who has probably done more to restore Oregon Trail to the memories of the present generation than anyone since that Trail was a world-famous caravan road.

There is a point here to be remembered; else you cannot understand the tragedy that crashed a bolt from the blue. The fur trader used these rough high-handed methods because they were his only defense in a lawless era in a lawless land; but the Indian was no fool. Especially was the educated half-breed, with the worst of both races too often in his veins, no fool. With the coming of the colonists, he knew the power of the Great

Tyee—McLoughlin of Fort Vancouver—was waning. No more was the Great Tyee's word law. When some of the first missionaries had their ears boxed, or were knocked down by impudent young bucks, or saw wives insulted, they, too, had the aggressors well flogged; but Dr. Whitman, the greatest of all the missionaries, never favored such retaliation. He depended more on slow education and his skill as a physician to hold the Indian's friendship; and so it did till the colonists came in yearly tidal floods; and this brings in the climax in Walla Walla's heroism, which left it for all time a sacred shrine in American history.

Take as the most striking example of the difference between fur traders' tactics and colonists', an occurrence in the migration of 1843, when the Applegates arrived with their two families. They camped not at the mission but at the Hudson's Bay Fort, where McKinlay happened to be in charge. Their tents were outside the walls. McKinlay was kind to a degree to all these Kentucky and Missouri frontiersmen; but an ugly little episode occurred—nothing in itself but an irritation that might have ended seriously if McKinlay had not intervened. There was an educated Indian boy with hair cut short like the whites—Ellis—who strutted about with the vanity common to youth a little superior to its environment; but he happened to be the son of a Nez Percé chief. Now some of the frontier boys of the same age were very insolent to the Indians. They didn't like the Indians prying round the caravan tents with the same curiosity that led the little whites to gape round the Indian tepees. The whites and the Indians began swapping possessions, boy fashion, back and forward. The white boys were famished for real food, fresh roots, berries, fish. The Indians were keen for the bits of iron, nails, bullets, small shot, powder canisters, jack knives, which boys world over jam in pockets. Unfortunately, the pant leg pockets and bagging blouses of the young frontiersmen had suffered in the long journey. There were holes in the bottom of the pockets. Munching the sweet roots, which tasted like sweet potatoes, the whites began jamming pockets and the holes in the pockets began letting marble-like little roots down the pant leg. Not lacking a sense of humor, the Indian urchins began scrambling to grab and run off with the overflow from pockets. One big boor of a white boy with heavy boots let out a kick at a bending Indian, that sent the little fellow head over heels. In a second there was a pitched battle on between the two groups of boys. Sticks and stones were hurled first, then arrows began to fly. The whites' charge and the counter charge were becoming serious. The Missouri boys scampered for the fort yard. The Nez Percés pursued. A bigger white boy grabbed a long cinch strap with iron at one end and began walloping

right and left, till McKinlay came and ordered
the battle stopped at once.

The Indians withdrew sulky. That night, they
began to saunter round the caravan camp with
weapons under their blankets. McKinlay ordered
the campers to move in and sleep that night behind
the fort walls. Gates were closed at sundown.
This episode was known as the Potato Battle. The
collision seemed to be forgotten, but the Indian
never forgets. The campers were two weeks building boats and rafts to go on down the Columbia.
The cattle were branded H. B. C. to protect them
from Indian raid and left to pasture and come on
across country westward at slower pace.

McKinlay, himself, picked an Indian pilot to
guide the boats. I want you to remember that.
It comes in the story later. He was supposed to
be an utterly dependable Indian.

Take a look round modern Walla Walla, a beautiful little city of twenty thousand to twenty-five
thousand people fairly oozing with prosperity—
fine banks, fine stores, fine clubs, fine hotels, one
named after Whitman, a large college, also named
after Whitman, two or three large hospitals, the
usual public schools resembling small universities,
and hosts of homes amid a riot of gardens in
bloom. Apple blossom season had just passed the
last time I was there. The scented petals were still
raining their fragrance over the streets. A hail
storm had swept down from the Blue Mountains

with the suddenness that so often caught the Over-landers, but instead of ox carts turning tails to storm came a scurry of motor cars through the streets and down from the sky another kind of flurry—aeroplanes interrupted in an annual race. And was this the section where Indians and white boys had an ugly scrap only in 1843? Motor round the country out from the city and you learn the source of the prosperity. Fruit, yes; truck gardens, yes; but primarily dry-farm wheat in such oceans as you do not see elsewhere. Prairie wheat fields are like a comparatively quiescent yellow sea. The sea may roll in wind but the roll is in waves not billows, not seas mountain high. Here the plains of the Walla Walla recede in foot-hills that are billows, billows mountain high; and over the billows wave the fields of dry-farm wheat. You wonder where the farmhouses are. Down on the "draws" and stream beds where there is water suppy; not very pretentious farmhouses either, because the yield is so great here that in a good year the wheat farmer after preparing his fields to absorb the winter moisture can very frequently hie him to the cities to pass the short winter till the furbishing of machinery for the new crop calls him out again to his fields. It is not a hard life and cannot be a very isolated life; for motor and rail highway connect with city and town; but it is a life lonely for the young. On a prairie farm, you can at least glimpse your neighbor's chimney like a smoke stack or steamer funnel at sea. You can see the train worming in the distances under a swirl of smoke from station to station; but here these high foot-hills cut off view; and I found my young boy and girl neighbors in the car where I sat—especially those just out of some city college —eager to leave the farm and "get a job in town." Yet the ranch house had a motor, a radio, a telephone, and these youngsters were only three generations away from the Pioneers. What did they want to do? Did they want to sell the farm? Oh— no—they wanted to keep the ranch; she was "a sure shot all right"; but they wanted to be where they could see more life before they settled down.

And so the old memory of the old homestead far back in our youth gives place to a new type—the homestead as a temporary camping place. Is it a good or bad portent? I do not know, for here is Walla Walla—type of countless little cities—the rallying center for a new community life. We cannot go back. We have to go forward; and as forward led them to a new broader Destiny, so I must believe it is leading us. If I were writing a letter instead of a book, I should add, a P. S.— Among boys and girls, old and young, I did not see one grouchy, discontented, resentful face; but remember it is a sunny clime; and where the sun shines, the heart sings.

CHAPTER IX

WALLA WALLA—THE SHRINE OF THE WEST

WHEN you drive over the famous Oregon Trail today and come north between the Blue Mountains and Snake River, on the worst spots—hairpin turns, sharp ups and downs —you have a highway broad enough for two cars to pass or meet. Where the precipice edge is steep, you have a heavy white log railing to fore-fend against a swerve sideways. On lower levels, where you haven't a paved highway, you have a broad dirt road.

Go back to 1852 when Uncle Ezra Meeker went west with his wife and child in a band of one hundred and forty-eight people using thirty wagons. When I first saw Mr. Meeker coming up Broadway, New York, with an ox team hitched to a covered wagon, I paused as the crowds on Broadway paused to gape and stare and wonder what new press trick was this. Later, I realized that the wonderful, aged pioneer of the Trail, who died in 1928, only two years off the century mark, had adopted without a cent of financial support from anyone this method of recalling from utter oblivion and indifference the heroism of the first noble adventurers, who had made a great empire trail from East to West.

When Ezra Meeker came West in 1852, the clouds of dust were so dense the driver of a team could not be seen by the family back under the browned tent of the covered wagon; yet by 1852, what with the rush of gold seekers to California and the Mexican War, the Oregon Fever was beginning to subside to about twelve thousand people a year over the Trail, though there were often 500 wagons in one continuous line. In all, they had ferried or forded over sixty river crossings. Down precipices were only game trails steep as stairs, for nimble feet. How did the immigrant caravan manage these river canyons? They killed worn-out oxen. They braided and twisted the strips of hide in ropes and cables. They used short trees as snubbing posts and warping piles. Then they let down the wagons from the top, the people and the stock scrabbling, sliding, tumbling down the game trail as they could. When you recall that many of the people were now barefoot or reduced to one moccasin, and many of the rocks and pebbles sharp as knives, it is not surprising old settlers describe the Oregon Trail as "baptized in blood" from end to end. They could have added also "baptized in fire," the flaming torchlight of their own quenchless ardor. Without that spirit, Oregon Trail would never have been conquered. Food supplies were down to a third normal. He

tells of his wife giving food to two boys who had
had nothing but grasshoppers to eat for forty
hours. He gives the deaths on the trail that year
as five thousand. Fortunately, a relief party from
Portland—then a village of over a thousand—
saved the oncoming hosts from more deaths by
slow starvation. Yet, it was really a race with
famine to get through to the Columbia before
snows blocked the mountains; but when the caravans came down on the west slope of the Blue
Mountains, the plains of the Walla Walla were a
scene of enchantment, food for man and beast,
herds of Indian ponies in thousands belly-deep in
pasture. The glimmering night fires of skin tepees
blinked through the blue autumn haze, with that
tang of camp smoke sweet as frankincense to the
nostrils of hungry tired travelers. Then it was
not cold on the west side of the Rockies and the
moon was a glorious huge gold wheel, not the cold
sickle of steel it seemed from the high passes like
a death scythe. Surely after all the terrible trials,
this was the Promised Land of their hopes.
Though only five years after the massacre of the
Whitman Mission, the graves of the victims were
already grass-grown.

Go farther back to the great migration of 1845,
when the Oregon Fever was at its height before the
Mission Massacre had focused national attention on
the Pacific Slope. What caused the Oregon Fever
from 1837 to 1856? Chiefly the restlessness result-

ing from hard times. There was a panic in 1837 and forewarnings of the panic of 1857. Farm prices for the Middle West had dropped, farm lands there could be sold to incoming hordes of German settlers at $5 to $25 an acre. Oregon offered 640 acres of land to every adult man, 320 to his wife, 160 to every child. Why try in the Middle West to meet paper money debts in gold, when produce hardly paid the expense of labor and by selling your farm you could set out for Oregon with the cash and get a fresh start on from 640 to 1,000 acres with a little capital? Then, there was the climate. Mission propaganda had spread to the very Atlantic the truth not over-drawn that west of the Rockies lay a realm never hot in summer and never cold in winter. Workers didn't have to fight nor race the climate. Good times or hard times, a worker could live and live well, debt free, though he might not see a dime of coined cash in a year. There were fish, there was game, there was soil of such a richness, producing returns in fruit, or grain, in fodder for stock as neither the East nor Middle West could yield. Then, there was best timber to be had for the tak-ing right at your door; no need to sled lumber in over the snows in winter. All a man needed were brawn and industry and thrift; and conscience knew, many a worker had used all three in the East and Middle West only to find himself bogged with little to show for toil but the land, which he could sell; so he pitched comfort to the winds, joined the covered wagon caravans and set out, little reckoning the cost to be paid in crossing the Rockies, circumventing the canyons, fighting the Indian raiders in a lawless land beyond military protection.

The migration of 1845 was undoubtedly the greatest till rails came in the 1860's. What the total migration was is not known, but certainly three thousand in one band and six thousand in another, and many another little independent group. Every party had its guide. Joe Meek was one of the best. Jim Bridger was another. Steve Meek, a relative traveling on Joe's reputation, was one of the worst. He meant well but good intentions did not pave the Oregon Trail; and poor Steve found himself in danger of lynching, as Hancock tells.

Samuel Hancock came with the party of two hundred in forty wagons from Independence, Missouri, in 1845. All along the Snake, "the howling of the wolf packs made night hideous" and stock that strayed from the encircling corral of fenced wagons was found "hamstrung"—the hind leg tendons snapped by the wolves. The Snake River Indians were much more hostile in 1845 than later. At night bullets of raiders came pattering against tented wagons. One day two young boys had been sent ahead to spy out the best places to ford Snake River. Their bodies were found scalped, stripped,

mutilated. The caravan did not tarry to find a
better ford. The river was two hundred yards
wide, very rapid and very deep; and the trail down
terribly steep. Beds were attached to tent roofs;
this to avoid waters coming over wagon-boxes.
Three men on horseback started across the river.
Each of the forty wagons was chained to the others
in line, so none could be carried away by the swirl
of white angry rushing torrent. The turbulent
shout of the waters drowned human voice. Then
every team was urged by the riders down to stream
bed and under whip and spur had to plunge in.
The forty wagons were rafted across. If one shy-
ing horse lost courage and turned turtle, the pull
of the team ahead brought him head up and heels
down and he was dragged across, half drowned.
Strenuous courage. One can imagine the thumping of timid hearts, young and old, and inarticulate
prayers in the wagons; but all crossed in safety.

After the safe passage of such frightful perils,
it was not unusual for the various religious denom-
inations to group together at night and sing their
highly emotional inspiring hymns in the most emotional missionary period the century witnessed.
Old Hundred, The Lord is my Shepherd or some
other Psalm, would be roared out in joyous ac-
claim of triumph; but by the time Snake River
Canyon was reached, the danger of Indian raid
and the race against winter snows sent the most
of the caravan to camp, too exhausted and filled

with dread about the morrow even for their in-
spiriting chants of faith in their Promised Land.
Yet they had really traveled farther towards their
Promised Land in six months than the children
of Israel did in forty years.

Thirty cows were lost in this section to raiding
Indians. Steve Meek, the poor guide, who had
made an awful mess of trying a short cut to avoid
the Big Bend of Snake River, now joined the party
with his band and there were a hundred and fifty
wagons. Steve had failed to find a safe short cut
across the big bend of the Snake Canyon to the
Des Chutes on the Columbia; and settlers and
stock had almost perished from hunger and thirst.
The men came back ready to rope Steve on a lynch
scaffold. Only cool heads averted the crime
against a guide with the best of intentions but no
knowledge of the trail, which could be followed
in safety in the rainy season but was death in
drought. Pasture was becoming terribly short,
human food scarcer and scarcer, and for seven
days Meek was in such peril of lynching he had
to hide under bedding of a tented wagon. Five
months the travelers had been on the trail. Shots
from the scouts ahead signaled "water." Big frontiersmen sprang back on their teams with tears
coursing down dusty cheeks. Those tears revealed
much. No whimper in peril but pent up relief
when the danger was passed. The women and
children clapped their hands. The caravans went

ahead with an exultant shout. Here cows lost from former caravans were rounded up from watering place. Arrows sticking in flanks told what had stampeded the preceding caravan. Forward down the Snake, the Indians became more friendly, but each morning a few oxen were found shot by arrows from some ambushed irresponsible Indian buck, who wanted free beef. He considered it his right. Hadn't he shot free beef (buffalo) all his life from boyhood?

There had been deaths in the wagons each day along the Snake but the march never paused for a death. Burial was at night with a few weeping friends round the grave—no coffins, the body wrapped in buckskin and laid tenderly in the friendly earth, with the stone pile above. If people had paused to cherish grief, they would have perished. Yet I cannot find the record of a single suicide in all this awful year on the Trail. Self-pity there was none. At one place in a canyon, the water was a hundred and fifty feet below the Trail. Ropes were lowered. A man was let down. He passed up enough water for drinking and cooking, but none for the stock, whose neighing and bellowing that night betrayed a camping place, though fires were quickly smothered not to attract Indian arrow.

The two combined parties were now trying to come out by the Des Chutes River to the Columbia. They would have fared better by the long way round through Walla Walla. One night they came to a river too rapid for the chain wagon device. Chained teams might drag each other down. An Indian with a rope in his mouth swan across. The stream was so wild the immigrants had another rope crossed under his shoulders so they could save him if the current proved too strong. He reached the far side. His squaw wife plunged in and repeated the feat. Her name is lost to history. Then a chain was rigged across the river and attached to this, the wagon-boxes were ferried sidling to the far shore. Ferry men know how a swift current will do this provided the cable does not snap. Opposite the mouth of the Des Chutes was the Methodist Mission, under the Waller family this year. How the Wallers fed at least four hundred people too hungry and weak to cook for themselves I do not know. I find in another record they had just received a hundred and fifty bushels of raw unground wheat for their own winter supplies. Several of the immigrants died from starvation or from eating after too long fast. The Wallers used up all their winter stores of raw wheat, peas and potatoes. Anyway, the two caravans were at last down on the Columbia and rested four days before preparing to descend the rest of the way by boat and let the stock come on slowly by trail. What Mrs. Waller had left in her exhausted larder is not told. Fish were always in abundance here and root flours and berry pan-

cakes could be bartered from the Indians for an
awl, a jack knife, a handful of beads, bullets, or
little packet of needles. The Indians fished chiefly
from the north shore. The north shore also offered safer channel down than the south shore.
The stock might follow the narrow game trail of
the south shore. Indian dug-out and Indian canoe
and settlers' raft and wagon-box must follow the
north shore.

What a mongrel, motley, mosaic of life it must
have appeared for those first Overlanders. The
missionaries were so cramped for space to house
families and stores, they used to preach from
Pulpit Rock, where an inscription commemorates
their courage if not discretion to this day. It was
a pillar about twenty feet high, with a natural seat
in stone and desk in front. Below the stone pulpit
in a rabble, lounged naked Indians of every tribe
known on the Columbia—some gambling with
bone dice, all gabbling in a dozen different dialects
with the mazed Overlanders moving among the
aborigines almost as naked of clothing as the Indians—all in rags, many barefoot, but all adult
armed, which was a good thing amid these most
insolent of all Columbia tribes. Indeed, the missionaries themselves by 1843 had come to realize
you can't convert Indians in a day, no, nor in many
days, nor bring them up to white status of living
in forty years. You will find in many of the discouraged old letters back East at this period the

frank acknowledgment that while the Indian was physically a man, he hadn't yet acquired a white man mind of even primitive order. There was not a missionary in Oregon at that period, except Whitman, who did not acknowledge discouragement; and even Whitman had come to the point where he frankly hoped to do more by educating the half-breed children and inducing white settlers to come to Oregon, than by concentrating on Indians, who right at the Waller Mission of the Des Chutes this very year had buried living slaves with dead chiefs to serve their masters in the next Happy Hunting Ground; and, what is more, neither by lash nor pleadings could the missionaries stop the hideous custom.

Meanwhile, what was happening back at Walla Walla, the Hudson's Bay Fort and thirty miles east of it at the Whitman Mission this fateful year? It seemed a triumph for the new policy of all the Missions, but was really a triumph ushering in a most terrible tragedy. It wasn't the triumph saved Oregon. It was the tragedy.

We have already come over South Pass and seen the Tetons where the Rev. Samuel Parker preached in 1835 to an audience all attention till some one shouted "buffalo." On the instant hunters and trappers and Indians squatting on their haunches scrambled before benediction to a wild buffalo stampede. Then a year later on a beautiful September morning of 1836, came Mrs.

Spalding and Mrs. Whitman with their husbands through the Blue Mountains to the ever friendly tribes round Walla Walla. When Joe Meek down in Idaho saw that four-wheeled wagon from which the two hind wheels had to be taken to go on down the Snake River Canyon, tradition has it that Joe exclaimed—"Thar goes the end of the fur trade. When wheels kin cross the Rockies, then the settlers"; and when the Whitman Mission was established about thirty miles east of Walla Walla at Waii-lat-pu—place of "the rye grass"— Joe acting on his conviction left his little half Indian daughter Helen Marr to be educated at the Whitman School. When the missionaries swept on down the Columbia by boat to the ever welcome gates of Ft. Vancouver on the north bank of the river opposite the Willamette of today, Dr. McLoughlin begged and advised both Whitman and Spalding to do as the Methodist Lees had done—open the mission nearer the protecting arm of a Hudson's Bay fort. But Whitman was not thinking of safety. He was thinking of his evangel to preach the faith to all nations of every race; and here at Walla Walla were races friendly to all white men from Lewis and Clark's day. When the Whitmans had passed through the Walla Walla Plains of the Nez Percés and Cayuse, hadn't every warrior turned out in regalia attire to welcome them? Hadn't they galloped their horses and marched and countermarched and

beaten drums, and blown whistles, and rattled cas-
tanets and uttered whoops of joy to split the welkin? Hadn't the coppery squaws, bedizened with
paint and porcupine quill buckskin suits white as
chalk, seized Narcissa Whitman and kissed her
impetuously? Hadn't even the treacherous Snakes
of the dangerous canyons put Mrs. Whitman on
stiff elk skins, then with cords in teeth, swam across
to land Narcissa safe on the other ide? Of course,
missions would be safe among such tribes.

"Aye, Doctor," warned the wise white-haired
chief factor, McLoughlin, "but not for ladies—
not for gentlewomen." An Indian was an Indian
and the best of chiefs could not control their un-
ruly young bucks, much less huge grown brutes
in the shape of man, which Mrs. Whitman learned
to her heartbreak and anguish that awful winter
when her husband went east on his famous ride to
rouse the country, especially the Mission Board
about to close all missions. Whitman had gone
east by the trail of the Indian raiders for ponies
from the Spanish Settlements, down by way of
Taos and then out across the plains eastward; but
he Indian raiders made their forays in summer,
not midwinter as Whitman did on his famous ride.

It is barely six miles out from modern Walla
Walla to the site of the old Whitman Mission.
The road is posted and easy to find. A sharp
ointed monument marks the crest of the hill from
which the Cayuse and Nez Percés used to spy

down on the Mission and the passing Pioneers were housed and helped there. Down behind that hill inside a little white picket fence lies a flat grave flag-stone, marking all the mortal remains of the Whitmans. This grave stone does *not* mark the site of the Mission. The remains trampled in the middle of the mission yard were brought here and buried high above the risk of overflow from rain and spring thaws in the river, which you can see about a quarter of a mile behind Monument Hill. It now becomes plain how little Clarissa Whitman's life was lost. There was a beautiful spring of water on the bank down here. The river flowing past—just below the modern red barn and timber bridge—is deep and swift enough to carry away a little child, though not deep enough to en- danger a half-grown boy or girl. The little girl evidently tumbled back and was swirled away, or essayed to venture in depths too great for her. A farmhouse and farm barns now occupy the site of the Whitman Mission, where Narcissa came with flaming faith and Marcus with his unflagging zeal. No true picture exists of the Mission as it was at the time; but we can picture husband and wife puzzled by the failure to make converts wounded to the quick by the Mission Board's de- cision to close down the Mission, wounded still deeper to see their aforetime friends among the Indians—young Dorion 3rd, Lewis, Garry, Dela- ware Tom, a dozen others, who had attended

JEFFERSON CANYON

FIRST MISSION BUILDINGS OF THE SACRED HEART MISSION, ONE OF FATHER DE SMET'S MISSIONS, LOCATED ON THE ST. JOSEPH RIVER

school more or less—now turn to whispering foes and go round carrying tales of more and more settlers coming in such numbers that the younger chiefs in a rage broke down "Doc" Whitman's fences and rode their stock right through his grain field. The settlers wouldn't get that anyway, they jeered.

The gloom of tragedy thickened all that winter of 1839-40.

I know of nothing sadder than Narcissa Whitman's letter to her father Judge Prentiss of New York State at this time. The Spaldings had established their Mission on up northeast near modern Lewiston. It didn't make it easier for Mrs. Whitman that Spalding had been a former lover of hers rejected for Whitman. He had been her pupil in the village school. He was older than his fair-haired blue-eyed teacher but they sang together in the church choir and Mrs. Whitman had become the master passion of his life. Temperamentally, the two families were poles apart, both equally loyal to the faith, but the Spaldings raw-boned tough New England fiber, the Whitmans gentle born, perhaps better educated, certainly with a background of culture and breeding that excluded all personal animosities from work. Narcissa writes of Spalding's "wicked jealousy and pique towards her. If this mission fails, it will be because peace and harmony do not dwell among its members."

"Doubtless before this you have heard through the Board of the melancholy death of our most precious and only child, Alice Clarissa. I would describe to you if I could her bright, lively appearance on Sabbath morning, the day of her death. She had always slept with me until just a week before then, and that night she proposed, of her own accord, to sleep on the mat on the floor. This gave me a very strange and singular feeling, for I never before could persuade her to lie away from me, not even in her father's arms . . . It being very warm, and because she preferred it, I let her sleep on the floor all night—but did not sleep much myself. Ever after this I made a bed for her by the side of mine, where I could lay my hand upon her."

Whitman came back from the East in 1843 with a great train of immigrants. It was not all of his organizing. He had been joined as he pushed westward; and then came more immigrants and more immigrants in flood tides right to 1847. The Indians had acted badly enough during Whitman's absence. A brute had broken into Narcissa's room at midnight from which she thrust him out by main strength and courage. McKinlay had carried her off to the Hudson's Bay Fort for safety, and then sent her down to the Dalles till Whitman's return; but now even with Whitman on the ground, the Indians' conduct became more outrageous. They broke down his fences. They trampled his grain. They stole his vegetables. They brought their sick for him to heal or bury, then threatened to kill him for not healing all. Unfortunately measles came this year, brought by colonists.

It wasn't the man Whitman they hated. It was those colonists he fed and housed and befriended. Some of his most trusted confidants and converts became his bitterest foes as McLoughlin had forewarned. Monday, November 29, Whitman had come in from attending some sick Indians and burying others. Joe Lewis, a half-breed who had acted as guide for some of the immigrants, had ridiculed the Whitman cures for disease. So had a descendant of old Dorion. So had Delaware Tom, an educated half-breed from the East. They suggested the Indians pick three of their worst cases—measles or influenza—and try Whitman's cures. Two patients recovered. One died. Of this Whitman knew nothing. He had ministered to the sick and helped bury the dying. Four and five Indians a day were dying. Therefore the edict went forth among the Indians that all the Americans at the Walla Walla Mission must be forthwith slain.

Dr. Whitman was sitting with his back to the door serene in his faith, wearily turning over the leaves of his Bible, when an Indian knocked and entered. No one lived to tell coherently what happened. Of the white survivors, one hid under a board lifted from the floor. Whitman was clubbed to death and fell weltering in his blood. Narcissa rushed in to be shot in the breast by Joe Lewis, and she, too, was clubbed to death. Little children like Helen Marr Meek and Mary Ann Bridger died of starvation. The young women of the mission were carried off to the warriors' camps and though they were not killed, they suffered a fate not to be told till rescued by Peter Skene Ogden of the Hudson's Bay Company a few weeks later; but those weeks blasted their lives and brought early deaths. All bodies were trampled, horribly mutilated in the mud. The Indian reverted in an hour to the man-killer of his primal instincts; reverted lower, to instincts which only the basest of the beasts possess, the wolf pack, which devours its own fallen and destroys its own mate; and three of the worst instigators of the tragedy had had white man blood in their veins for three generations.

It is the saddest tragedy in missionary annals.

If retribution be any consolation, Tom McKay —son of an Astorian martyr—coming up the river with Peter Skene Ogden, knocked the wrist off one of the worst miscreants by a well aimed shot; and of the other assassins, many fleeing to the lava hills and canyons south of the Columbia perished of smallpox and measles during the early winter. Of the other murderers, five were carried down to Oregon City and hanged, with Joe Meek as sher-

iff. In June, Mr. Spalding, up at Lewiston, over
one hundred miles distant, escaped. Coming back
from a conference with Whitman, he had met the
Roman Catholic priest, Brouilet, who told him
the terrible news and bade him escape for his life
and get the protection of the Idaho chiefs not so
hostile because they had had neither the epidemic
of the Walla Wallas, nor the bad influence of half-
breeds like Dorion the third, or Joe Lewis and
Delaware Tom, all educated renegade half-breeds
with hate in their hearts for both races because
they belonged to none. Spalding, himself, knew
there was danger in the air; for one night as he
slept, he was awakened by the old Indian women
chanting their hideous death song; but perhaps
that was for those dying of the epidemic. He was
just about to go back and warn Whitman there
was trouble in the air, when he met Brouilet, and
the priest had to speak in a whisper for fear of
being overheard by his Indian guide and bringing
like doom on himself and the nuns. Please remember here the Roman Catholic missions were
French, largely French Canadians, and the half-
breeds of French origin were not so hostile to the
French priests as to the Protestant Americans.
Spalding escaped back to his mission by abandon-
ing his horse and running by night; but the experience left him and his wife nervous wrecks for
the rest of their lives.

Every visitor to Walla Walla should go out reverently to view the site of these most heroic pioneers' work. A spiral monument marks the graves. It is one of the most sacred shrines in American history and always will be and always should be; for the Whitmans brought the blow by befriending the ragged starving barefoot immigrants, who had come in clouds like locusts from 1843. They could have saved themselves by refusing or by flight to a zone protected by Hudson's Bay fort walls and guns. They did neither. They stood on the firing line of duty and perished there.

There were 12,000 people in Oregon by 1848. Thousands had perished on the Trail; other thousands turned aside to California, to Salt Lake, Montana, or Northern Idaho.

While the immigrants were toiling over the Oregon Trail, what were the diplomats of two nations doing? Peel and Gordon out for the British Government in the middle forties were reporting "the country was not worth a ——, let it go." The Royal Navy martinets didn't like the beds of the forts, despised homely fare, found the hunting not to their taste of deer stalking in Scotland, and the fishing by nets and harpoons a bore when they had been used to line and hook. Wilkes, out for the United States Government, had advised the Oregon settlers to go slow on statehood; for statehood meant taxes and self-protection in an era when there were no United States troops and any weakening of Hudson's Bay Company's power would embolden Indians. The traders, themselves, regarded the Oregon country as pretty well trapped out and were preparing to move up to Victoria in modern British Columbia.

CHAPTER X

Spokane

NEXT on the Overland Trail comes Illum-Spokanee, Indian Chief or God of the Sun.

Summer heat or winter cold, sunny, Spokane always is. You see this in sunny faces on every soul you meet, in peppy pace of everyone encountered, whether going up hills that take breath, or hustling along city thoroughfares; perhaps too peppy for high-geared nerves at that altitude, but a mighty fine omen for teamwork progress.

Spokane does not lie on the Great Overland Trail. The Oregon Fever was a racial river torrent that came up by Walla Walla following the Snake River windings to join the Columbia, but if you left Spokane out of your itinerary along the highway (whether traveling by rail or motor) you would make a mistake. Spokane is unique both in its past and in its present. It is, indeed, a curious melting place where blend both past and present. You reach it from the Overland Trail by a few hours run up from Walla Walla. Spokane is well worth the run. You will skirt the wonderful wheat plains to the East where the Palouse comes in from the borders of Idaho. This

was desert half a century ago. Today if you
chance to pass through in the early harvest season
of the Inland Empire you may witness a sight
almost unbelievable to eastern eyes—forty-horse
teams, or tractor with two men drawing combined
reaper and thresher to do in a day what formerly
required forty teams and forty men. The dry
season renders outdoor storage quite unnecessary;
and if you pass shortly after harvest you may see
bags of grain piled high beside the shipping points
to go round the seas through Pacific ports via
Panama to European markets. This is a far cry
from the old days when all dry lands were tabbed
"Desert." In the Northwest Empire, Spokane is
such a rialto for travelers as Bal'beck for ancient
caravans hieing from India to Egypt.

"If I go West," asked a woman traveler, who
had traversed the whole ancient and modern world
except her own native land, "do you mean to tell
me I can have as good accommodation as I can, say
in New York, London, Paris, Rome?"

I laughed. What had she seen in theaters and
movies to ask that question? Rodeos, bucking
bronchos, bad men in ten-gallon hats with shooting
irons round their waists, or what? "You will be
housed," I assured her, "in the most beautiful hotel
in the world bar none." I left her looking after
me as though I belonged to an Ananias Club. Yet
it is the truth. Because that hotel embodies the
very spirit of Spokane, I am going to describe it.

It does not need a name. It is world famous. In winter cold, you enter the rotunda to find summer glow. In summer heat, you come in and the cool quiet restfulness is the repose of a Spanish patio. I do not know a big rotunda in the world that is not noisy, exhausting if you happen to be tired from a long journey. As you enter this rotunda something seems to touch you. I have seen it thronged by Rotarians, by bankers' conventions, tourist excursions, such noise making little rabbles as Camp Fire boys and girls, whom some philanthropist had given the treat from an inland city to a day in Spokane. The youngsters would come ramping in like a herd of stampeding bronchos—all clamoring together at the top of shrill voices, when—no one said "hush"—they hushed with eyes and mouths agape and shuffled packs off backs and stood at an "attention," which a military commander could not have evoked. Onlookers from the big leather lounges smiled. They had felt the same.

There was the fountain—a real ice-cool artesian fountain, not a water works spray—tossing up in the center of the patio. There round the pillared gallery hung ferns and flowers of every tint under the sun. Do such give off invisible waves quieting to jangled voices and nerves? I have always believed they do. There among the hanging banks of flowers and ferns—hanging gardens—were birds from every clime, trilling, singing with gladness

of life, caroling back and forward, finches, cana-
ries, larks, thrushes, parrots, fiddling cat bird, the
little blue warbler with the streak of rose down on
his breast, who sings both day and night to his shy
mate in June. When I was younger and rode the
prairies obstreperous as any youngster in the group,
I loathed the sight of caged birds—no matter how
large the cage. I thought they must long for the
free-as-air life I felt on a good horse. I no longer
have that feeling. I have seen too many chicka-
dees stabbed by a cruel starling, or the starling
pulled to pieces by a hawk, or the shy bluebird
torn by an owl, or the warblers coming north
caught by a relapse of winter, dead of pneumonia
on my own doorsteps, or—the meanest sight I ever
witnessed—a glorious golden oriole stabbed in the
throat as he slept on a branch and sucked to death
by a measly little weasel, who had tracked him
up the tree.

Children ramping into the rotunda of that hotel
somehow just stop ramping. The boys naturally
encircle the big basin, where the spray iridescent
in the lights falls on gold fish darting among the
stones. "Shut up," I have heard one boy nudge
another, "you'll scare that big goldie—see him—
he is just peeking out of the rocks"; and the noisy
voice clamps down. The girls as naturally come
to a stand under the birds; and in two minutes,
little pocket bird-guides are out; and no teacher
could command such attention as those birds.

Grouped heads are together and the youngsters forget there is a dining-room off one corner and a grill room off the other, where they are to be fed till their little belts swell. It is much the same with the grown-ups.

The same atmosphere pervades the three eating resorts—grill, dining-room, hastily served restaurant. No noise. There are days of society luncheons and nights of dancing; but I have never heard a blasting blare of noise called music. It may be the flowers and birds have insulated or consecrated or dedicated you to peace. It may be the waiters are not waiters at all but high school and university graduates garbed in the velvet tunics of Switzerland, or of Poland in pure white linen costumes, with the modulated voices of well-bred homes; but when such a voice says to you— "Do you know I have so enjoyed seeing you"; and you look into her eyes and see she means it, you realize it was her own good manners evoked yours; and, as she served, the smile that "doesn't cost a dime but is worth a million dollars."

And there is more to Spokane than the hotel. This is the rialto of the Inland Empire—an Empire by the way as big as a Germany and Switzerland combined. I can not say as big as an Italy; for though the Inland Empire has numberless lakes from green to jade bronze, it has no sea front.

Do you remember the first time you crossed the

Southwest Desert and came unexpectedly on Grand Canyon? It is much the same in sober tones on lesser scale with Spokane. When you come up from Walla Walla way, especially after passing the great wheat and orchard belts, you become aware in the hot winds of midday of something fine as flour called by courtesy dust—dust in billows of an ocean wind-waved, tossing and flopping up and down with a demon restlessness that pebble-dashes your motor glass or rail car windows and if you hang an arm out peppers and burns you to the marrow of nerves and bone. Quite otherwise if you approach by the river bed of the Spokane also hurrying west to join the Columbia. The most of trains arrive or depart at night or early morning. The distant snow peaks are opal clouds and send down a breath of ice and you must don a fur collar coat and are glad to hug it tight. You are magically in the lap of the Rim Rocks with rivers that are white torrents from the mountains dashing in spray beneath the bridges crossed. The business section of the city lines in parallel streets, as always, the water front; but the city lies in terraces up the hills like the seats of a great outdoor stadium. You get your first glimpse not only of the city's history, but of its character; for every city has as much of individual character as a person or a race.

There at the water front is the old camping place—a portage—of Illum-Spokanee and his

tribes to barter with the fur traders going up and
down the Columbia from the Saskatchewan on the
north to the Columbia on the west or the Missouri
on the east or Snake River to the south; or to act
as middlemen between Coast tribes west and Plains
tribes east and Mountain tribes north and south—
all as different as Hindoo from Arab, or Turk
from Egyptian. Why were these marvelously picturesque tribes as inevitably doomed to pass as the
buffalo? Because they were a race of man-killers
and man-raiders by vocation, choice and practice.
The man-killer has never yet lasted as a nation or
a race. By the nemesis of his own weapon, he
passes. Here was a region with fish and game,
fruits and roots to support a hundred—yes—a thousand times any Indian population ever known. Yet
its people—Cayuse, Spokanes, Nez Percés, Flatheads, Cœur d'Alenes, Kootenays, Snakes, never
had any vocation but man killing and enslaving
man. Even the Nez Percés—who never pierced
their noses, and the Flatheads, who didn't flatten
their heads—the best of all the mountain tribes,
had no other vocation; and however frightful the
crimes of rough-scuff frontiersmen, they were as
gentle zephyrs to the sandy desert's tornado gales
compared to the crimes of these peaceful tribes
against one another, of which I shall presently give
you some concrete cases.

Look up the terraced slopes from the white rushing rivers hurrying down from the melting moun-

tain snowy peaks to the Western Sea. You read
the history of the city as from a movie film. Here
closest to the city thoroughfares, paved as the best
of your own in the East, remain the early homes
of the first pioneers—staid, set in the center of
gardens that are groves of trees and flowers. Spokane is a city of homes, not apartment caves; and
dingy enough these old gray frames look today,
with their front pillars in imitation of the Old
South, or shuttered oblongs with a door in the
middle and an eye winking on each side, and such
cupolas and domes and turrets as were the decora-
tive vogue when women wore false bangs and men
starched collars high enough to cut their throats.
Business is rapidly crowding these old places up
the terraced hills. The white man is doing just
what the Indian portage tribes did before him.
He is becoming by bank and by wholesale and
factory mill the middleman between East and
West. Up another tier of the terraced hill encircled by the Rim Rocks and you come to the
Middle Period mansion houses of the middlemen
who didn't perish by business cut-throat competi-
tion but waxed prosperous; for Middleman City
of an Empire vast as Germany, Spokane is bound
to become. These mansion houses are in brick and
stone with rock gardens and paved walks and per-
golas covered with roses and little surprisingly
restful seats in the shade for one to sit and watch
and dream over the past and present of the city be-

low, if anyone in Spokane ever takes time to dream. But mansion houses, whether Gothic, Queen Anne, or New England, are again giving way to another type higher up the tree-shaded terraced streets. Caused by what? Business, commercialism again? No. Rather by a gradual sense of the eternal fitness of things—elusive of analysis, but terribly real in its enforcement. You cannot pick up cheap competent help as you could twenty-five years ago; and the Garden of Eden, itself, could be kept weed-free only by the sweat of the goodman's brow. These big houses and big gardens especially after young families scattered became a heavy care. You might deny it, but you felt it. Then there was climate. Here was a climate that was neither North nor South but had the character of both. You wanted a house that would be cool in summer and warm in winter; so Spokane began to develop a type in architecture of her own—as every city must. Plenty of windows for the beautiful view below and for the cool air from the peaks but plenty of shade, from piazza and patio combination against heat; but not such large houses. Here the people own the houses. The houses do not own the people. Every householder knows the difference.

Now up another terrace of hills and you are on the crest of the Rim Rocks and get that curious resemblance to Grand Canyon in soberer tones on lesser scale. There are tall pines free of under-

FATHER DE-SMET

WHITMAN MONUMENT, WALLA WALLA, WASH.

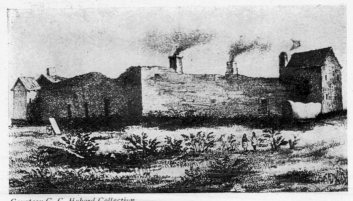

FORT HALL, NEAR POCATELLO

ALL THAT IS LEFT OF THE FIRST SPOKANE FORT

brush like the yellow pines in the Southwest smoking with an incense of resin from heat to that sun-god of Illum-Spokanee. There is the sage brush, lavender purple and pink in spring, tawny green and scented as frankincense in summer. There is cactus, a dwarf compared to Grand Canyon, but with the same blaze of red flowers. There are wild spiræas and other shrub flowers for which we scour catalogues down East—all like the waitress' smile—they do not cost a dime and are worth a million dollars—in beauty.

What sort of people dwell in these houses? That explains the Spirit of Spokane—peculiar fragrant beauty not of grace but rather of graciousness and sincerity, a rather rare combination. I remember as children in the West, we were schooled to an inviolate pioneer code which I wish someone would reintroduce. We were taught if we violated that code, we weren't well-bred. We were scum. It was partly frontier ranch code, and partly Indian code. If we broke bread and shared salt with a host, our lips were sealed to any utterance against that host. If we didn't like him, we could avoid him; but whether we liked our host or didn't, no kisses on the lips and poison pin stabs on the back. That is the very marrow in the nerve of Spokane charm.

Where did the people acquire that? From inheritance and necessity. Where did they come from? Indian era was followed by fur trade era.

Fur trade era had its scum tossed up by wild racial waves as by ocean tides; and too often the West has pictured as its heroes this scum, of a dialect never heard on land or sea and with bullet belts, dying in its boots. Whereas, these were only the underlings of the real western leaders. Who were the fur trade leaders—Dutch merchant bankers from New York, who came west by the Great Lakes; Baltimore traders who hied down the Ohio or across the Cumberlands and so on up west from St. Louis, in other words, cavaliers from the Stuart Period in England; French grandees of New Orleans south and Quebec City north; Scotch merchant princes from Montreal; English aristocracy from London. Of course, the great leaders, themselves, did not often come. They sent their sons and their personal representatives—the very best blood and brain stock in the world. Following the fur trade came the missionary movement and the Oregon Fever, and the gold rushes before and after the Civil War to California and Montana and Idaho and Washington—again plenty of scum; but scum doesn't stay. It boils over the edge of the pot to evaporate or skim off. It may leave a stench but it doesn't stay. Again the very best blood and brain stock in the country. It is the descendants of these people who dwell in the home cities of the West we know today.

I regret, I deeply regret, these halcyon days of Spokane cannot last. It is as inevitable Spokane should become the great hub of an Inland Empire wheel as that Pittsburgh became one of the greatest commercial centers in America. Mines, farms, fruit lands, railways that must radiate from that hub along lowest grade, factory, wholesale, retail, bank, all the activities of a great middleman city were created by Spokane's position, whether she welcomes or retards the transition. One of the best examples I know of that is what is happening right now in Spokane. Spokane is like the Eastern leg of a triangle going west to the Pacific. Down the Pacific from Seattle, Tacoma, Portland runs the other leg of that triangle to San Francisco, Los Angeles, San Diego. Now any schoolboy knows that to clip time and freight haul, it would be a short cut to San Francisco across the base of that triangle. Link by link through timber areas a line of rails has been creeping that way for a number of years till the unified links in one system now plan a straight line along that short cut to San Francisco. Nothing can stop Spokane becoming a great middleman center for lumber, mine, farm. You may regret the passing of a reposeful era but you cannot stop it. It is forced by geographic position.

The Rim Rocks with filtered haze hanging over them in a blue curtain and their hard lines of ocher brown softened by distance are not the whole of Spokane's scenic beauties. You can run up in great spiral highways to mountains high as the rims of

Grand Canyon and when the day is clear see the whole world of the Inland Empire in one circular sweep. Or you can follow out the river road of the Spokane where the Little Spokane joins the main stream in a willow thicket; and if the season be spring, there are iris gardens blue as the deepest velvet spotted with golden centers. There are pansy gardens and violet gardens and row on row of orchards in blossom. Or if the season be autumn with its junipers yellowing and the oaks shading to flaming reds and browns, the very air is fragrant with ripening fruit.

Little wonder retired fur traders, lumber men, miners, centered here to build them their mansions to enjoy repose. As you motor out you pass over the very ground where the first rival traders had their forts and fought their duels with more danger to dignity for the tailor to repair than bloodshed. Of the old fur warehouses, only one remnant remains; and it has been rebuilt and moved many times in the passing century. Nevertheless, this was the place where the famous redheaded and redder tempered Finan McDonald dominated the tribes, partly through marriage affiliations and partly through his own dauntless rash dash of courage with audacity. A hundred yarns, the most of them true, could be related of the big "red-headed white chief," how in a gambling game he slapped an Indian chief in the face, then challenged him to a pistol duel, from which

the Indian shrank saying white men were fools
to stand up in the open to be shot, better each hide
behind a tree, then whoever shot first "could pot
his man." Or you can see the caves where the
little Irishman Ross Cox left asleep at nooning
hour for rest lost himself from the main John
Clarke brigade and tried to take refuge from rattlesnakes and wolves, howling hungry, only to have a
wolf rush out almost under his legs, then when he
tried to sleep on the ground in the open with a log
for a pillow found a rattler under the pillow. You
can understand how when the brigade sent a rescue
party back to seek the lost man, the riders galloping
along the crest of the Rim Rocks missed seeing
poor Cox frantically waving his shirt torn by
brambles down in the hollow between the two
precipice walls.

What of the Indians in this wild lawless era?
Numbering thousands when the whites seldom exceeded a dozen, why didn't the red man wipe the
white man out? Because—say the modern senti-
mentalists—the Indian was friendly to the white
men till white ruffians changed that attitude to one
of deadly hate and bloody feud. Nay—nay!
Much as one would like to believe such explanation, that is not the truth. The Indians wanted
white man firearms to beat their Blackfoot neighbors to the east. Here comes in the blood-stained
truth as to the primitive Indian. In all white
man warfare you can find no trace of as bloody

and cruel tortures as these tribes inflicted on helpless captives. Girls were flung to the ash heap to be torn to pieces by young warriors or dogs; and of the two, the dogs were the less cruel and less beastly. Warrior captives—the braver the merrier—were tied to stakes, and while hags with streaming hair and eyes half blind from age screamed out their ferocious rage to inflame the torturers, the one man standing fearless of death, bound hand and foot, was burned by inches, with eyes gouged out or lips torn away, while he shouted back defiance to the end. And the Indians here were the finest specimens of their race—Flatheads and Nez Percés. You have to go back in white man history to the Nero era in Rome or the dark Middle Ages of brutal ignorant religious persecutions to find anything remotely resembling their savage rites of conqueror over conquered; but the story does not end in an eternal hopeless black for the human race, red or white. It ends in a glorious dawn of more and more light dispelling the black night like the dawn of sunlight coming over the opal peaks. The killers had to pass as they always pass. The peacemakers inherited the earth as they always do, whether they had to use the sword to enforce the peace, or absorbed the best of the worst and brought it up to the higher level.

Move round the rotunda of the hotel that is the rialto of the Inland Empire, and you can meet the descendants of these old fire-eating warriors. One

is Paul Wapato, a modern educated leader of his
race.   Others are young girls, beautiful of form
and feature, singers, teachers, in every vocation
which their white sisters enjoy.   But did not the
white man dispossess the red man of his lands?
Of course he did, though the red man never acknowledged any race could possess lands; but if
you think the red man serf to white conqueror go
out to, or pause as you come up to Spokane at
some of the Indian Reserves where the tribes were
assigned, especially just on the border line of Idaho
and Washington.   You will find white men renters
paying as their share of a half crop by dry farming
six thousand to three thousand dollars a year to
Indian landlords.   Are the Indians better or worse
off under such conditions?   What is the use of asking such a futile question in the face of obvious
facts?

CHAPTER XI

ON FROM WALLA WALLA TO THE DALLES

IT is almost impossible for the modern travelers running westward from Walla Walla and Spokane down the Columbia to The Dalles a hundred and fifty miles more or less—according to the rails or motor roads followed—to realize the perils and heroism of the first far wanderers over this section of the Oregon Trail. I have traversed it before there was any Columbia Highway and many times since the famous scenic route on the south shore was opened. I used to plan my trip to cross this dreary dust desert at night to escape heat and monotony. Then, having been brought up amid many descendants of old Hudson's Bay men, who pioneered here, I began taking this run by day. Perhaps I peopled the wind-tossed furrowed dust billows and hard black rock with ghosts of the romantic past. They assumed filmy shadows heroic as on that other famous world highway for the races of humanity up from Ur of the Persian Gulf to another Promised Land.

Here, where the Snake joins the Columbia, David Thompson in the hot July of 1811 had posted his famous notice on a little pole—*"Know hereby this country is claimed by Great Britain;*

and the North-West Company of Montreal . . . do intend to erect a factory"; but Thompson was just two months too late. The Astorians had taken possession of the Lower Columbia; and Thompson, the explorer, racing from Lake Superior up the Saskatchewan, crossing the Rockies, reduced to a diet of moccasin leather, hounded by Blackfeet and Piegan and Blood off his course farther south to get on the headwaters of the Columbia and beat Astor's men from New York had risked his life in vain. Here Lewis and Clark had seven years before come out on the broad blue waters of the Columbia, clear as the sky compared to the yellow floods of the Missouri, to record the sight as the object of "all our hopes and dreams." Here the Overlanders usually greeted the great blue river of the West almost a mile in width with an exultant shout. Little they realized that their race against autumn rains and starvation like many another race tested vim and staying power hardest on the last lap of the race. Muscles had hardened to iron. Death had taken toll of the weaklings, old and young. Children had been born on the Trail and died. Fathers and mothers had gone down to premature graves, leaving orphan families of whom the eldest might be twelve years to find their way to the Coast as they could. Little marvel, Oregon people regard their pioneers with almost the sacred reverence the Children of Israel held for their patriarchs. Of the two great racial trails westward, Oregon was from two hundred to three hundred miles longer than from the Persian Gulf to the Dead Sea; and while the Promised Land was an Eldorado of hope and faith to both people, each had to fight for every foot gained. If you question the ethics of one racial movement, then you must question the ethics of the other. I question neither. You cannot question progress. Races have to keep up with the procession or go down under it; and murdering races and raiding races and the stagnant races have never yet lasted in human history.

From Walla Walla to The Dalles, the Overland Trail forked. Families followed a stream bed across Walla Walla Plains to come out on the Columbia somewhat south from the junction of the Snake. More and more each year, cows, exhausted horses, oxen teams were driven by picked herders overland to reach the Columbia at Umatilla, John Day's River, the Des Chutes, The Dalles. This was really an old game and Indian trail. It was very dangerous and exhausting for farm stock.

To comprehend and realize the beauty of this region, you really have to telescope imagination back to the most epic era in all earth's history. As you go on down to the Coast, mountain climbers will tell you when they ascend Rainier and Baker, amid eternal ices and snows far above cloud line at the very cones of the peaks, they come on sulphurous holes, almost suffocating in poignancy and rimmed with solid sulphur edges. These are from the unknown past of vast crater sinks, when the Coast Ranges blew their heads off in a mighty volcanic explosion that must have rocked the Inland Empire for five hundred miles. The upheaval threw up the vast Cascades Mountains above a wallowing inland sea or lake and heaved the plains between far above water level. The plains were heaped with rocks the size of a house, with gravel from little pea-sized pebbles to "Olympic Pills" thirty feet in diameter. The gravels were then covered with the most productive terrain on earth —rocks ground to a soil fine as flour by the icy glaciers flowing downward eon after eon, and the tumultuous irresistible waters not to be confined by granite wall or basalt barriers. You see both granite and basalt here, where waters and ices have ripped a channel through solid rocks as if by a god's saw with diamond edge to the dark awesome canyons, which have quivered and yet quiver to old earth's cosmic processes of tearing down in order to build up. You see old earth's invincible destiny working the same changes still—the sea levels of gravel in layer on layer along river cuts; the giant and dwarf stones boiling and boiling round and round in "pot-holes"—the fur traders' "kettles"—till polished as a ball scored by diamond point.

How long ago? We do not know. Over this

scientists have broken heads. The discreet lay-
man will sidestep the controversy and let the wise
wigs fight it out. The yearly whorls of the branch-
ing evergreens overhanging the canyons do not
help you much in the quarrel. Tree growth came
ages after volcanic upheaval, perhaps helped by
birds dropping seeds. Did man live before or soon
after the cosmic upheaval? Neither do we know
that, though weird rock drawings have set archæ-
ologists guessing. The chances are he didn't
because he couldn't. There were too many vast
water monsters with as vast unpronounceable
names as their own bulk—ninety feet long, beaks
and necks from twenty to ten feet. Though these
big fellows were largely vegetarians with only saw-
notched bills for teeth to chew up a poor little
scrub-human, they had huge hoofs to trample and
claws to rip man to shreds. How do we know for
a certainty such marine leviathans did exist? Because their bones have been dug up from Alberta
to Texas and can be seen in any of our modern
museums. Perhaps the most astonishing of all
these revelations from the spade is the fact that
before this upheaval, the whole region was tropical
in climate both as to vegetable and animal life.
How do we know even that for a certainty?
Because horses, camels, saber-tooth tigers, water
buffalo of huge bulk, mammoths, mastodons, ele-
phantine in size, have been dug up. So have pet-

rified trees from Idaho to Arizona, of a size and variety purely tropical.

People with rudiments of astronomy know the earth took a great dip over on its axis toward the sun at this period, converting the Equator into the Poles, and the frigid zones into the tropics. Plato had told this long ago and was called a liar, though he put the date right or wrong twenty-five thousand years before his day, followed by terrible volcanic upheavals for eleven thousand years. Scientists are not quite so cocksure now the ancient traditions of the philosopher were romance. Both marine and astronomic sciences are proving he was correct; but dates are still in the realm of controversy. Again, if you are wise, dodge dates as you would brickbats. When one scientific society says one thing, and another says another thing, you'd better get out of the way of brickbats and stick to the facts visible to your own eyes; and those facts are visible all along the high cliffs of the Columbia in sea level sands, in glacial silts, in volcanic rocks that tear the waters to a white lace of foam and roaring rapids.

On these waters, the Overlanders had to descend the Columbia to their promised Land. How did they do it? Remember they were racing rains and starvation. Some reached the river barefoot. Some, who afterward became famous, with one moccasin only, which they shifted from foot to foot, as rock stab or cactus had put the naked foot out of commission. Clothes had been torn to shreds by cactus on the plains, devil's club in the mountains, wear and tear in spite of nightly patches darned on from canvas and flour bags. Broad brimmed hats strapped to chin for the man, sunbonnets for the women, were pretty nearly all that survived of head gear—lovely picture to the contrary of stalwart men amarch in buckskins and lovelier gentle women on side-saddles coming down trails with hats perched on their ears, which any passing branch would have brushed off and thrown under the teams to rear. I might think the narrative in old annals overdrawn and enlarged by the shadows of time as sunset stretches shadows of the day, had I not come in myself from luxurious camping trips of six weeks garbed in an attire which a ragged beggar would scorn—skirts in tatters, hat a sloppy brim, shirt waist shrunken, boots —well I knew the essential of keeping boots unimpaired so I usually came in sound-shod; but as to heaviest of golf socks, changed as they went into holes and rips, the least said about socks the better? I've had thrifty friends ask, "Why didn't you darn your socks each night?" Gently, such questions, friend! Because darns, heel or toe, each night on the same place produce blisters. Then you are out of commission. Better the frontiersman's trick of a soft moss or floss from mullen leaves and no socks at all than a blistered heel. A blistered heel in a hot boot may mean infection. As Lincoln

said, an army advances "on its belly and its feet."
Feet and stomach must be kept unimpaired; and
the most of the Overlanders now almost two thousand miles from home base were crippled both as
to feet and stomachs. Do you marvel they greeted
the Columbia's broad blue highway sweeping in a
mill race to the sea as we would greet a luxury
train after two thousand miles on a bumping ox
cart?

Stock had now to go on single file over trails
not wide enough for wagons; so the settlers prepared to shift wagons and all their families and
all their belongings from these wagons to the
North Shore of the Columbia. There had been
a terrible shedding of the superfluous as to baggage from the Platte to Walla Walla. You could
pretty nearly follow the Oregon Trail by old bed-
steads, chippendale tables, cradles, rocking chairs.
Much had been chopped to splinters for firewood.
Much had been thrown out on the rush westward
to weather and fall apart. Wagon-boxes were now
calked anew with tallow and rosin and tar.
Wagon tongues, whiffle trees, wheels, were taken
off and thrown on the boxes with feather-bed mat-
tresses on top and families helter-skelter perched
on the feather beds. Though swift, the Columbia
above the Dalles did not seem to threaten great
danger. There were sand bars. There were shifty
white-banked sand islands. There were rocks and
reefs; but broad channel ran between and to each

side. If an oarsman or polesman were alert to get
on the racing channel of water to carry his cargo
through the deep channels, he was safe and woe
betide him if he didn't. The most of the settlers—
I think you will find if you read the old records—
built large log rafts sometimes with a railing,
sometimes without. A raft is an extraordinarily
safe device for broad waters. It will not sink, especially if well balanced in its cargo. Water may
overwash the edge. If it hits to one side and tilts
and the cargo slithers to the low side, it may tip
freight and passengers in a channel where a swim-
mer's strength has about as good chance as in a
Niagara. Sometimes big iron nails were used as
spikes; sometimes ropes and chains bound the logs.
Rafts were made from driftwood logs. This took
from a week to two weeks. On these the settlers
launched down the Columbia. Lucky, the group
who could engage a polesman and steersman from
the Hudson's' Bay hangers-on of French water
ducks, who could feel the mood of the forward
current and sang at the top of lusty lungs the
chansons of Old France to keep up courage.
Waters racing to such a gallop they seemed to
arch and collect in midriver too swift to spread
out, ever forewarned of rapids and riffles ahead.
Waters beginning to froth and foam meant shal-
lows and lesser rapids. Waters with a roar were
ill omen of rocks ahead—safe enough if you succeeded in getting on the main deep channel to con-

FORT WALLA WALLA

OLD FORT BOISE

ALL THAT REMAINS OF THE FIRST FLOUR MILL USED BY
SPOKANE

AN INDIAN SWEATHOUSE

vey you past the danger where human strength
would be quite unavailing but disaster if you
didn't. Now remember, easily ninety per cent. of
all the Overlanders were inland people, land lubbers used to boy's swimming pools but utterly
ignorant of voyageur perils, on a river which had
often sucked down to death some of the very best
canoemen in the fur trade service—yes, even one
daughter of Sir George Simpson, Governor of the
Hudson's Bay Company, Mrs. Banks, out on a
holiday tour with her husband and London
friends. In spring and early summer thaw of the
mountain snow, when Columbia waters were high,
all but the worst "shoots" and falls could be passed
by good boatmen. Deep waters are safe. Shallow
are not.

There is confusion among the old and new
names of the Columbia here. There are cascades
above the falls and cascades below. Enough to
say the cascades are usually regarded today as
westward of the Dalles or "big shoots" of Lewis
and Clark. The "big shoots" are the falls proper.
The word Dalles is usually ascribed to the old
French steersman at this point standing up and
yelling to his boatmen—"d'allez, d'allez" "let her
go!—row for your life"!—"head her off the
rocks!" Here, comical to relate, Sir George
Simpson famous for his speed across the continent
from the St. Lawrence to the Columbia, used to
lean over the canoe gunn'ls and sticking his hand

in the water to guess the pace shout to his boat-men "faster—faster, men" and have his piper Colon Fraser strike up a Highland song on the bagpipes—"The Campbells Are Coming" or some similar tune—to spur them to greater effort and indifference to danger. The Columbia here has reechoed about "Marlborough Going to the War" and "The Campbells Are Coming" and "Old Hundred." It has heard the triumphant shout of the French boatmen plunging to the race of rapids rearing like galloping horses. It has heard the mouth organ and concertina and bagpipes—yes—and the war drum of the Indians beating time to the paddles thumping the gunn'ls. Get out of your head the idea that paddles were used in the final plunge. They were not. The French boat-man caught the swirl of the current away from rocks, plumped his paddles athwart, braced himself back like a hunter on horse and away shot the river craft to the whirl.

I could tell the story of many a pioneer down this section of the Columbia, but shall pick only a few not generally known. Hancock says the autumn his party came to the Dalles, the river was very shallow for a distance of four miles when it narrowed to a channel a hundred yards, descended fifty feet, then took "a shoot down," twenty-five feet. Franchère thirty years before describes the river as much wider and the fall not so great because in deep water the fall is not so apparent.

He tells how when they drew ashore for the portage past the Dalles, they always backed the canoes in stern foremost to avoid the backwash sidling the craft and swamping them, little boatmen tricks of natural-born water-craftsman of which land lubbers knew nothing. One of the most terrible experiences, which has almost gone into oblivion, occurred in the 1843 migration. There were nine hundred men, women and children in this band. They could not delay one day; for the rains were falling and thick heavy mists veiled the dangers of the river. Canoes, rafts, cedar boats, dugouts—all were used.

The Applegate families from Missouri had several boats.

Whatever errors tricks of memory may have played on young Applegate age nine when he witnessed the experience, we may as well accept his recollections in old age as the most reliable. To the little inlander, as the crude craft shoved out from the shore at Walla Walla, the motion of the boat seemed very great. At first the riffling current interested him, then as the hours and days passed, the reaction from great activity to idle hands with oars at rest to let her drift, produced an almost overwhelming heavy drowsiness. Of course, the descent from high ground to low level had a good deal to do with the lethargy. At first, out from Walla Walla, camp for noon and night was made

on either side of the river as convenient with driftwood for fire.

Aunt Cynthia, wife of Uncle Jesse—after whom
little Jesse was named—had a streak of superstition about birds in her make-up.　Watching a
raven winging over the camp in circles one day,
she remarked, "There is going to be a death in this
family"; but the youngster's eyes were attracted
by a darker nearer figure—a half-negro Indian,
son of Lewis and Clark's old colored cook, York.

This was just after the Potato Battle, and that
supposedly dependable Indian selected by McKinlay was leading the boats.　The boy remembered
the river curving and circling.　There was a sound
of rapids and his boat began to rock.　Some one
yelled "breakers ahead" and all squatted low to
throw the center of gravity as far down in the craft
as possible.　The Indian's red handkerchief round
forehead was seen ahead bobbling to the lift and
fall of great waves amid foam-crested billows;
but babies were asleep in mothers' arms, when just
twenty yards from the north shore a boat in which
rode Alex McClellan age seventy, two men and
two Applegate boys was seen to whirl on a rock
and split.　The boat wreckage disappeared in the
boiling waters.　A wail of anguish followed by a
shriek came from the boats behind.　Two of the
Applegate men were about to leap out to the
rescue when Aunt Cynthia's voice was heard above
the roaring turmoil, "Men, don't quit your oars!

To your oars, or we are lost." The boat shot past the wrecking reef so close a hand could have touched it. But what was happening to the settlers engulfed? It is here the little Jesse's recollections must be accepted.

McClellan, Warren and Edward were struggling in the water. Elisha was thrown on a rock with his foot through the pocket of a ragged coat. A feather bed went whirling past. McClellan, the old soldier, was seen putting one boy on an oar, then both were sucked down. It had all happened so suddenly there is great confusion in the various narratives as there always is in swift tragedies. It is said little Applegate's cousin or brother caught at the feather bed and went drifting down with it two miles. Two miles is a long distance to hang on in buffeting waters. It is said the feather bed caught on the rock when Applegate fainted, but came to consciousness to see the other lad whorling past. He caught at the older boy's clothing by his teeth. The reef running ashore was slippery as ice. Both boys were barefoot. The young Applegate boy, only a few years older than Jesse Junior, made the run first hanging on with his toes. The other boy followed; and the breathless spectators ashore grabbed both youngsters.

There is still one point here for savants to scrap about. The Applegate version distinctly gives the impression that the tragedy occurred east of or above the Dalles. A survey of the river gives the impression this was almost impossible and the confusion must arise from the name "cascades" formerly applied to all rapids but the Falls themselves. Says T. C. Elliott, of Walla Walla, who knows that section of the river as you do the fingers of your hand, "The river runs on edge for about three-quarters of a mile. After passing through an underground gorge it widens, then narrows to the Grand Dalles and the next mile and a half are narrower and more dangerous."

The gloom over that night camp cannot be described. The whole section was called the Devil's Gullet. Mamalose Burial Island came soon below; so you can survey the river for yourself; and your guess is as good as another's as to where the tragedy occurred. Jesse's next recollection is he awakened at Fort Vancouver on the north shore of the Columbia in the morning. Another question comes in here; and your answer to it is as good a guess as any other. Did the Indian pilot in revenge for the Potato Battle back at Walla Walla lure the first boat on the wrecking reef? He was never again seen; and his lighter skiff was not seen either in the wreckage below or along the banks. An Indian never forgets. It is part of his blood code unless wiped out by a gift.

In clear weather the Overlanders were simply dumb with wonder at the beauty and majesty of the Columbia. You can see it today from either of two rail lines, one on the north side, one on the

South, or from the Great Columbia River Highway for motors. Any ramparts they had previously encountered looked like toys compared to
these ramparts of the Columbia. On the crests,
the conifers tremulous to the rush of river below
overhanging the edge of the ledge, gray green in a
moss like lace. Ferns covered the southern rocks.
Waterfalls came over the precipice iridescent in
the sun to lose themselves in a spray fine as naiads'
hair. What if the pioneers did give some of those
falls names commonplace to the extreme, like
Horse Tail? It proved their love for the beauty
if they had not the culture for a more significant
name. The pointed isled rocks sticking up in the
river were dubbed "Cape Horns" and "Castles"
till they mix the passing traveler with the real
Horns and Castles and Coffin peaks farther down
the current.

Go back another generation to the fur traders
of 1812 to 1830. On no section of the Columbia
had these doughty sons of adventure more trouble.
The Indians at the Dalles were not properly a
tribe at all. They were a heterogeneous collection
of all tribes and mixed bloods, who assembled here
spring and summer for the salmon fishing. They
became known as Wishrams—people of "the warehouses"—board houses of hastily extemporized
planks—who came up from the Lower River in
dugouts and lighter cedar craft, or down from the
Upper River in canoe and overland by horseback.

They used baskets for pots, stones for tools, cedar "tea pot" hats, and as little clothing as possible till the traders came with blanket and bullet to barter for furs and food. At Wishram on the north side of the Columbia you will see a monument commemorating the white heroes of this period. Of red men heroes here, there were few. The Falls offered too great temptation to rascality. The white man had ordinarliy to make a long portage and the Indians, given bullets and guns to help carry the packs, often turned bullets and guns on the white travelers and then ripped and robbed the packs.

It was here John Reed, the Astorian, trying to go back overland with letters for Astor of New York in a tin box, proved too shining a target for Indian bullet and lost his box and almost his life. The Pirates, as the Wishram rabble of Indians became known, clubbed him with a skull cracker and got away with the box of despatches for Astor. It was close to this point Crooks and John Day coming westward with the Overland Astorians were met, stripped naked for the second time by the plunderers. It was here the despatch-bearers trying again to get through to the east were again beset by showers of arrows; but this time, there were forty-five men in the white party armed with carbines. When an arrow penetrated the lobe of a sleeper's ear and the whites let blaze a shower of bullets in the dark, the raiders scampered howling and yelling and hid in the woods where "they whooped all day." They didn't mean to stop the white travelers but were determined to charge toll for safe passage up the portage, or to loot every pack. Waters were high that spring and the French boatmen with lightened loads preferred to breast the current answering the whoops with songs sung at the top of their lusty lungs. The others ashore kept guard at each end of the portage while couriers ran over the slippery rocks with packs on shoulders, line across forehead and line noosed over shoulders to lighten the weight on the straining necks. One partner got an arrow just above his heart, stopped by his stone bowl pipe in a left pocket; and by shooting quick he dropped his assailant in the rascal's tracks. There was a free-for-all hand-to-hand fight—the Indians with war clubs trying to wrest the white men's guns, the white men wielding their guns, bullets or butts, whichever came first, and then on the river from the north side swarmed Indian dugouts with warriors chanting defiant answers to the French boatmen's songs. Many packs were lost to the Indians and these provided them with just what they wanted for the next raid—bullets. It is hard to realize in the profound sleepy quiet of Wishram today those old scenes, when hags with streaming hair came screaming from apparently nowhere to cheer the warriors on. They seemed to know these white men would not shoot a woman and their

boldness took courage from immunity. One especially—an old priestess, wife of the chief who demanded toll—used to stand lashing herself till her
lips frothed, cursing in every language of insult
under the sun. Too often, the whites paid the
pair of old rascals and went on; but once it was
deemed too dangerous to have the Pirates in
possession of fifty guns, though powder and bullets
had been rolled by the keg into the river, and the
whites paused to give the old rascals the licking
of their lives. They sent six men across the river
and told the Indians unless the loot was restored at
once, they would shell every village on both sides
of the river with the brass field pieces in one big
cedar canoe. Each village lied and protested it
was the village lower down held the loot. The
field piece began to crack out shots from one side
of the river to the other. The old chief Coalpo
advised the white men to seize one particular
chief. They did and tied him to a stake and got
out swords that glittered in the sun. Within
twenty-four hours wailing came from the women
hiding behind rocks. Guns, brass kettles, bullets,
came back to be pitched on the ground for ransom
of the captive chief. All guns were recovered and
a third of the goods. The prisoner was given a
flag and ordered to scamper. He did.

Not until both Protestant and Catholic immigrant came was Wishram so troublesome to the
whites; but in the interval from 1824 to 1840, Mc-

Loughlin—the great Tyee—ruled these rascals with rod of iron. He warned them if they as much as harmed the hair of a white man, he would hang the culprit and he did. If they raided a single brigade of traders' canoes, he would cut them off from traps and bullets to hunt; and they had learned "the great white haired eagle" kept his word. When we learn that later missionaries, robbed, knocked about, mauled in impudence, caught the culprit and counted him out fifty lashes on the naked back, we may say it was not very ethical but it was effective and saved many a life; but with the weakening of McLoughlin's power returned the old mood to the Wishram mongrel plunderers and with the return of the old mood came ferocious retaliation from frontier white ruffians, some of whom exhibited in pride the ears of Indians they had scalped. I have often wondered, "If Whitman? . . . " But why wonder? Whitman and his beautiful wife were martyrs to the Cross of the Prince of Peace as truly as any martyr ever canonized in Christian annals.

Descendants of the Wishram tribes you can see today on the Yakima Reserves. They are physically the most magnificent specimens of Indian life in America—tall of stature, thick of shoulders, muscular, faces of granite, chiseled by storm, wind and sun, long lived, almost a hundred, some of the older folks, and just as hard to handle as in the old days. Their physical type must result from

abundance of food—game, fish, roots, fruits—and
the fact that for centuries the weak and the small
must have perished in wars. Scrub slaves were
buried alive with masters or sold for horses to
other tribes. Only the strongest men and women
were absorbed in the Wishram people; and they
hold the most productive Indian Reserve in America today and draw royalties from fruit and root
and wheat lands rented by white farmers that run
from twelve hundred to six thousand dollars a year.
Whether this will lead to deterioration from idle
lives remains to be seen. Down to the present—
as you can see if you run up to Yakima North—
these people have not degenerated physically.
They are still a mighty stalwart looking lot of
men and women, whether the men are careening
about in limousine motors or the women decked
in the silk stockings, patent slippers, bought dresses
and most chic hats of their white sisters.

The run up to Yakima—the great orchard garden of the West—is worth the trip if you have the
time. So is the cross country traverse to Wenatchee, farther north. Many travelers keep to the
main Oregon Trail straight through west to Portland and Seattle, then detour going east to Yakima
and Wenatchee. See that your brakes are in good
order if you take the High Road, in midsummer,
when snows do not block the steep passes. Otherwise, keep to what is known as the Low Road.
Both roads are now broad beautiful highways with

bridges across the Columbia fine as any in America; but I promise you on both roads as many thrills as the pioneers'. I have had them and I am not a particularly easy person to thrill on mountain roads. I have traversed too many when they were not roads at all, only blazed game trails.

CHAPTER XII

"A PINCH OF SNUFF"

FROM THE DALLES PAST THE CASCADES ON TO FORT VANCOUVER

A S you go careening over the Oregon Trail westward, how would it be to figure what a pinch of snuff is worth?

While the fat-heads of the Hudson's Bay Company and the wise wigs of befuddled brains among the diplomats were denouncing Sir George Simpson and Dr. McLoughlin for advocating the purchase of California from the Spanish, and Alaska from the Russians, a Senator in Washington with a smug self-satisfaction over his own phrase was declaring sententiously he "would not give one pinch of snuff for all Oregon"—meaning, of course, all the Pacific Northwest Coast.

Whether speeding westward by train or motor, north shore or south shore, you have passed through wheat, barley, oat fields heavy headed with grain high as your car wheels. Do you realize what they are worth in actual dollars? They are worth each year over eight hundred million dollars in farm crops. You have passed through fruit orchards, which in blossom time drugged the air with the elusive perfume of Persian gardens, in the ripening season with the odor of luscious berries, golden peaches, apples so large and heavy the crop bent branches in pendent arches, pears where bees and wasps set up a humming above the spin of your speeding wheels, plums and prunes so large you could not dispose of one in two bites. Do you know what they are worth in actual dollars? They are worth in shipments forty million dollars a year at lowest price. Then as you came out of the dry irrigated zone to the humid forested slopes, you passed from the tall stately pines on down the Columbia along highways shaded and scented, literally smoking in a blue-yellow haze from the gigantic Douglas firs, broad of girth as a dining table, plated with the armored bark of a thousand years. Do you know what they are worth in dollars? There are trees here which yield lumber enough from a single tree to build five small bungalows from the shingle roof to the front door step. Do you know what they are worth in actual dollars? I cannot put the figures down. The price of lumber has as wide swings up and down as a crazy stock exchange in a city; but where the cut for 1917 was seven million feet, it was about two billion in 1928. You can look up what you paid for lumber in your own houses and get the total yourself. From one area alone near Spokane, over thirty million dollars in gold and silver were taken. Or perhaps you are passing the old Oregon

Trail on one of the electrified rails operated with the water-power from these countless cascades and falls. No jars, no smoke, no water tanks except far and wide apart to supply boilers for heating the passenger cars. Do you hold the faintest conception of what that water-power means in savings to rail men, investors, travelers, freight shippers? On one line alone, it has saved twelve million dollars in the few years of its use.

The lure of Oregon was bigger, vaster, more poignant and compelling than any of its own fevered Pioneers ever dreamed of a Promised Land.

Sometimes one wonders—has the heady wine of the West's ozone atmosphere given an exaggerated mirage of the true facts? Does the West keep its feet on the ground? Such facts are the answer to such doubts.

Above the Dalles are many Cascades. Below the Dalles are the Cascades as we today know them. It does not matter which side of the Columbia you follow. You are on a majestic path. The river is three or four miles wide in places and seldom less than half a mile. You cannot get a comprehensive view of both sides at once. They are too far apart. As I have said before—Go west by one shore, come back east by the other. From each you will see the same mad mill-race of waters blue as midheaven, glistening glass in sunlight, lifting in midchannel because crushed and crowded to narrows by rocky shores, through which it has torn its torrential course, roaring white-foamed over reefs sharp as whipsaws, sand bars in the billows of a tempest sea. Whether the name Oregon is from Wauregon —Indian for "beautiful waters"—historians dispute; but that the famed Oregon River is "beautiful waters" fortunately common sense cannot dispute. Where the rim-rocks break to clefts in the hills, you glimpse the far opal domes, which at first you mistake for clouds, of Mt. Adams, St. Helen's, Rainier to the North, Hood and Jefferson to the South. It may be the high dry tense air. It may be the race-horse speed of the galloping river, but the very atmosphere seems to quiver with the universal whisper—"hurry - hurry - hurry." As Commodore Wilkes reported away back in the 1840's, the very keynote of life seems to be, "Go ahead—go ahead—go ahead!" If there is a rock in the way, cut through it, jump it, swirl round it. "If there is a sand bar or any other kind of bar, do not stick on it and whirl round it without going ahead—go ahead—go ahead—go ahead! Get on the back of the race-horse—Progress—and let it carry you through—over—in a hurdle jump— round in a detour—pause to portage if you must— but go ahead—go ahead—go ahead the way I do."

That is the spirit of the Wauregon—beautiful waters. You get it from the water nymphs tossing their foam locks in spray. You get it in the wood dryads quivering from the ferns overhanging rocky ledges. You get it from the waterfalls so beautiful on the South Shore of the Columbia Highway, drifting and swaying and blowing rainbow colors in the sun. You get it in little boiling pots and kettles and caves of rock, worn below each waterfall by the age-old spray. You get it in the trumpet triumphant shout of the great and little falls—white-maned water-horses they may be; but not riderless. There is the very Spirit of the West invisibly riding those water-horses to a Destiny not one of us has dreamed.

The first thing that strikes you is that the character of the country has completely changed. You might be on another continent in another world. Interspersed with the ever-present grave cathedral spired pines are the broad-branched flat-leafed cedars, gnarled oaks with leaves a darker green than in the East and branches tied in tough twisted bow-knots, branches in the ash red-berried with jewels, in the maples so silver you mistake them for poplars, in the honeysuckles growing wild whereever rock or tree gives their tendrils hand hold, in the laurels of waxy white bloom in spring and waxier leaf of deep green in autumn, in the madrone or arbutus trees with boles and branches of peeling cinnamon brown, which never sheds its dark leaves at all till blown and crisped off by wind. Left far behind is the French voyageur's *"triste"* country of sand and lava rocks. Mallards and teals and hell-divers and inland gulls you will see in thousands, as well as the eagles and hawks soaring high overhead ready to swoop down on any salmon come to grief in the shallow pools. Indeed if you take time to watch at some nooning hour, you will see some very comical battles between these magnificent birds of prey from the upper air and the water fowls below. The ducks can dive. The gulls cannot. The duck spears a fish too bulky for a quick swallow, which sticks half swallowed till the gulls come to snatch him away. The gulls kick—kick with their webbed feet. The ducks dive but cannot stay down. In the noisy clamorous fight, the half-dead fish may be dropped when with a swoop down curves eagle or hawk. If the fish is too big for one swallow or requisitioned for a family of open-mouthed nestlings, the hawks and eagles have too much sense to risk dropping him where the gulls and ducks can come in flocks and snitch him away. They fly back over land, soar high above and let the poor fish come smashing down to break his head or back on the rocks. Then they swoop down after him and carry the prey back to their screaming open-mawed nestlings.

There is another sort of wild lift here, too, not so cruel but most exquisite. To the credit of the thousands of tourists motoring over the Columbia Highway, I never have seen a single car molest this gentle friendly type of wild life. It is the squirrels —so tame they will almost feed on nuts out of your hand. The gray squirrels are, of course, the beauties with their bushy tails, but the glossy Douglas squirrels are the saucy chittering little warriors, who will "sass" you in every squirrel dialect, chattering and scolding in every keynote, take all the nuts you toss their way and then scrabble up the armored bark of the great fir trees defying you to catch them.

Years ago—I don't know who did it first—some one imported Chinese pheasants to these great forests. They multiplied amazingly in the mild climate and almost impenetrable thickets of protection from all foes—two families of twenty to twenty-four a year—till now they are known as Oregon pheasants; and you can see the gay red-and-green winged fellows with their immense families scudding boldly across the roads, peeping shyly from branched coverts, rising with a whirl where you come suddenly on them.

Do not miss all this beautiful wild life in your hurry over the Oregon Trail. There are two points at which you should stop on your race to the Pacific Coast. One is at the Pioneer Monument east of Portland and Fort Vancouver. The other is at Lookout Point between Longview and the Sea. There is almost any type of accommodation you may want near each point. You can park your car in any of a dozen shanty camps and buy or cook your own meals and have the man in charge of the gasoline stations look over your machine for loose nuts, wabbly axles, worn tires. A defective ma-

chine is more than dangerous, here. It is death;
and the only explanation of there resulting few
accidents is the breadth of the highway with its
guard railing on the precipice edge, the frequent
service stations for aid and repairs, and the fact
that so many travelers here own their own cars and
do not take the risks of high-speed maniacs on safer
roads. Or you can leave your car at one of the stations and get accommodation for the night at any
of the little bungalow or Gothic stone inns, with a
bathroom and food as good as at the finest city
hotels at half the cost.

Pause at these points if you possibly can; or you
will miss half the delight of the Oregon Trail.
Particularly, pause near the Pioneer Monument.
It resembles the Grant Monument on Riverside
Drive, New York. It has the peculiar atmosphere
of reverential awe that sets the most thoughtless
thinking and lowers the most clamorous voices and
lifts the veil on dreams. As you wander round the
rest inn in early morning or at nightfall, you will
see such a blaze of blood-dyed glory from sunrise
or sunset across the Columbia as will send racial
memories harking back to the age-old question—
must all races pass out from their darkest Egypt
of slavery under sacrificial baptism of blood to
their Promised Land?

Here, too, you should ask where to look out for
Mamalose Island, the last of the Indian Tomb
Rocks, and Coffin Rock and Castle Point farther

down the river near the narrows. Coffin Rock is rightly named. Here the Indians did deposit their dead swathed like mummies trussed up in cedar weavings and buckskin; but you cannot find coffins on Coffin Rock today. On Mamalose Island, you will. Outside Blackfoot Land, it is the only place you will find the Indian burial ground in its primitive condition. The bodies were placed in little wicket-protected boxes with slope slab roofs to shield from rain. Totem- or clan-carved poles marked each family grave. Skulls and bones lie all about; but you can see the last of the ancient Indian graveyards on the American Pacific slope.

But far other thoughts had Lewis and Clark, the first Overland Astorians, the first Overland fur traders, the first Oregon Pioneers as they came speeding West. Lewis and Clark, like the Pioneers, were racing autumn rains and hunger to reach the Coast. The French voyageurs, who could sleep wrapped in oilcloths under the rains happily as under the clear summer stars—chanted their Quebec chansons of Marlborough and his eternal wars — "Malbrouck has gone-a-fighting, Malbrouck has gone-a-fighting— But when will he return? My Lady climbs her watch-tower, As high as she can go; She sees her page approaching—All clad in sable hue—" and when the more than seventeen verses of the warrior brought him home dead—and when the whole was ended, each one went off to bed—"I say no more, my Lady, as nought more can be said." Of course, the Marlborough was not "brought home dead"; but many of his warriors were; and it is their death the plaintive ditty has celebrated for centuries.

The Scotch and American fur traders tuned up bagpipes and concertinas and mouth-organs to cheer courage flagging. What did the Pioneers, also racing rains and starvation, do? Ezra Meeker describes one of the scenes. After the awful trials of the desert plains and Snake River Canyons and the Falls at the Dalles, a heavy drowsy lassitude settled on the exhausted men and women gliding down an open water highway on raft and in cedar boat and in canoe. It was the snap back of elastic spirits stretched to the breaking point suddenly relaxed. True—the Promised Land seemed to fulfil all hopes; but the travelers were terribly tired— how tired they did not realize till they could relax. The silence was so tense in the gliding boats, so depressing, that someone struck up "Home, Sweet Home." The most plaintive refrain on earth was caught up by more than five hundred voices gliding down on the river craft; but the second verse was never finished. Nerves snapped. Tears and sobbing came unrestrained. "Be it ever so humble"—aye—but it was home, a home now two thousand miles away never to be seen again; home in safety and security, with those cradles rocking which had been flung aside in the desert because the little occupant lay in an unmarked grave; home with the Sunday organ pealing out its hymn in New England and the Middle West; home with its spinning wheel whirring to wool and flax garments, when now the wanderers had few garments of any sort; home with its cobbler coming back each spring and fall to outfit little feet with stout boots and copper toes, when at the Dalles men had whittled out wooden soles and bound them with rags and buckskin for footwear down to the Coast; home with great Dutch bake ovens, turning out every Monday or Saturday huge loaves of bread and pies in tiers of pumpkins and apples and plums and berries, when now was no bread, only hunger— the constant gnawings of poor meals or no meals or stomachs deranged by the alkali waters.

"Old Hundred" was a safer tune to cheer up the flagging hopes of the Pioneers. Of course, the weeping over "Home, Sweet Home" lasted only a moment. Other voices struck up "My Old Kentucky Home," "Swanee River," "The Campbells Are Coming," and tears were wiped away to look clearer ahead to the Shining Peaks. When you have "burned your bridges behind you," you have not only to look ahead but go ahead and fight ahead and win the fight—or die; and that kind of desperation kills weaklings or forces them to become strong.

Ordinarily on high water and clear weather the trips down stream from the Dalles to Fort Vancouver could be made in a single day; but start-

ing on the Platte in spring, few of the Pioneers
reached the Dalles before the autumn rains. High
water was not in the rains. It came in the spring
thaw on the mountain snows, and the fogs that lay
on the river made dangerous slow-going and zig-
zags from north to south shore as the channel
seemed best. Wilkes in the 1840's describes this
section as the very billingsgate of the world as to
beggarly thieving tribes. Every portage was beset
by the begging braggarts and petty pilferers. Old
Slyboots was one of the chiefs at this time and
whether he was frankly friendly or hostile depended on the presents given him; but the Pioneers
had no gifts for bribes of safe passage. He describes
all the missions as on the North Shore, where the
Indians fished—the Dalles missions as seven miles
from one falls and four from another, but always
within hearing of the roar from the falls. Waller
was here as missionary part of the time, Perkins
and Daniel Lee at other seasons, but the missionaries had almost decided to abandon the Dalles
when the Whitman Massacre occurred and Dr.
McLoughlin sent word to hold the Dalles at all
costs. This was the strategic point to catch and
defeat the triumphant Walla Walla tribes emboldened to rush down the Columbia and massacre
all the settlers; and sure enough it was below the
Dalles that Tom McKay caught the war-painted
Cayuses and shattered the arm of Five Crows, who,
before he died of the epidemic back in the hills,

had pestered the missionaries and settlers for a white wife and dragged one poor girl from the Whitman Mission off to his tent. The Dalles became that year a rough stockaded military fort. The Dalles were known as Fort Lee; the Cascades as Fort Gilliam.

Cox of the later Astorians describes the Dalles Indians as the filthiest and most malicious of all the tribes. He describes Mamalose Island as near the fourth Cascade, below the Dalles. No fur brigade ever portaged here from 1813 to 1843 without three sentinels on watch by turn all night with back to a good stout tree and hand on a loaded pistol. The path on the south shore was horribly narrow. On the north shore, every rock might conceal a human rattlesnake. Cape Horn at the Narrows was named because of its resemblance to the South American cape which so many of the old vessels had rounded in the early days. Hair seals from the sea used to come up far as the narrows and bask and bark from the black rocky islets. How many portages were made? Sometimes four to six coming up stream. Sometimes more going down. The treacherous current was safer than Indian raid.

At the first Cascade below the Dalles, a little waif, age fifteen, who had lost both father and mother and gone astray from one band of Pioneers was picked up by another party and lived to become another of the Pioneers whose name is lost to history.

How far was it from the Dalles to Fort Vancouver? It depended on how often you had to zigzag across the river. Certainly not less than one hundred miles. I recall my asking a pilot of mine that question on Saskatchewan River. "How far have we made today as the crow flies?" "We aren't travelin' as the crow flies," he laughed back. "We're travelin' as we haf' to! I reckon we've made about ninety miles but aren't got down stream more than forty. There is an awful lot o' difference 'tween travelin' on a map and travelin' on a river."

To return to the Pioneers from 1839 to 1840, bears grunted in and out among the camps at night, seeking fish offal. Wolves howled their dismal crescendo back on the hills. Indians who were friendly, diced and danced all night to their war drum's dull thud-thud-thud; and the wise Overlanders smothered out camp fires to avoid chance shots at ember sparks during the nights. Hancock says in 1845, three days were considered fast time down the Columbia from the Dalles to Fort Vancouver. Had it been spring, a sixty-pound salmon would have removed all fear of hunger; but it wasn't spring. The Columbia was a choppy sea from wind and rain.

Look out from the Pioneer Monument and recall all these filmy memories of a heroic past. Imagine if you can where your car is parked, trying to camp below the high rocks with Indian raiders taking pot shots at the embers of your fire. You are

shivering with chill; you are hungry; and then try
to realize a canoe with French voyagers galloping
up the river singing cheerily, emerging like ghosts
from the night gloom to your scant tent or bed on
a boat moored to a tree, and laughingly tossing
across to you a burlap bag filled with what? Fresh
fruit, bread, pemmican, dried fish, dried beef,
cannisters of tea and syrup and salt and oatmeal
and barley for broth.

"Man, where's this from?" asked the Pioneers,
thinking it must be a dream.

"From de Fort! From Dr. McLoughlin. He
send eet."

What!—Dr. John McLoughlin—the old Hudson's Bay Company ogre, who was going to drive
out all American settlers? The rough Missouri
frontiersmen who had come with hate in their
hearts and threats "to burn Vancouver about the
old aristocrat's ears," could hardly credit their
senses.

"How much was it? what cost?"

"Nodden' Nodden' at all! No cost! The Doctor
—he send eet as a geeft fur weemen and little children! He t'ink de maybee hungree and tired!
Eh? Non! Oh, oui, Messeurs, he say no man mus'
go hungree when big House have food to
spare——"

Hungry? Some swore loud profane oaths to
keep from weeping. Men and women fell to their
knees and thanked God; but too many when they

reached Fort Vancouver forgot to thank Dr. Mc-
Loughlin, forgot to repay the debts incurred in his
name on the Company books to save their lives;
and rather than force the collections of those debts
against needy settlers, he resigned his position and
salary of twelve thousand dollars a year in 1846.

CHAPTER XIII

On to Fort Vancouver

FROM the Cascades westward over the Oregon Trail, you are not following a river. You are skirting the shores of a lake called a river. In any other land, these rocky points jutting out in the Columbia would be called capes. These islets in Europe would be independent principalities. It was because of the vast width of the river, that canoes, rafts, cedar boats, fir dugouts clung close to the shore line. It was unsafe to thwart across these wide waters in wind or whip of tides. You recall Lewis and Clark hugged the north shore going west and the south shore coming back east. The Astorians ten years later did the same. The Pioneers did both except that "the cow column"—a name for all stock, oxen, horses, mules —kept to the narrow game trail below the modern Columbia Highway on the south shore, because Indian villages dotted the north shore in an almost continuous line.

Few lives were lost from Indian raid or rough waters west of the Cascades.

Keep track of the rivers pouring into the Columbia as you go West—the Hood first, then the Willamette from the south; the Yakima, then the

Cowlitz from the north. Keep track of them, because they open to back country where lie some of the most fertile areas in the world. They are really hidden vales of a paradise. From the rim rocks of the river, you may see only a cleft barely wide enough for a horse and its rider; but the cleft leads to an open vale, and in that vale may grow the Skookum or Hood River or Wenatchee or Yakima or Wolf River apples you eat for breakfast in New York and Chicago, or the chilled fruit you eat as strawberry shortcake for dessert. Or the river may come out to the Columbia amid swampy islands as the Williamette or the Cowlitz; but up that river, you will find fertile plains, which were the first settlements of the Pioneers; and in the midst of such fertile plains sprang up such modern cities as Portland, Longview, Seattle, Tacoma.

It is amusing to go back to 1844 and find many of these Pioneers were even then counting on "getting in on the ground floor" of future cities and acquiring homesteads—640 acres for men, 320 for wives, 160 for children—which would in some far hazy future be cut up in city lots. Those who guessed right and stuck it out and did not lose their heads and dash off in the gold strikes from 1848 to the 1880's became the richest families of the Pacific Coast. Those who guessed wrong didn't; but that is another hard luck story. You realize, of course, that down to 1852, rails were almost unknown west of Chicago and scarcely dreamed west of the

Mississippi; so the guess was a long shot in the future; but for the most part, those who reasoned or guessed that all roads must lead to tide-water terminals were the lucky ones; and as you read some of their stories later, you will find the guesses reenforced by such sensible proceedings as sounding the depths of water where they took up squatters' rights, or reckoning carefully that waterfalls stopping steamers going inland and creating factories and mills would determine the sites of future cities. Portland and Seattle and Tacoma are examples of this—the Pioneers' hard practical common horse-sense.

But of another type was the Indian's view of all this movement of whites like clouds of locusts or ants over the land. I have not the remotest idea on earth where the Indian prophets—call them "medicine men," "mystics," "witches," what you like—acquired their clairvoyant visions of the future. Said the old Seattle chief when Seattle was only a hog-wallow between high hills and tide backwash: *"These shores swarm with the invisible dead . . . at night when the streets of your cities and villages are silent and you think them deserted, they will throng with invisible hosts that once filled and still love this beautiful land. The white man will never be alone. Let him be just and deal kindly with my people; for the dead are not powerless. Dead, did I say? There is no death, only a change of worlds."*

OLD BLOCK HOUSE USED IN PIG WAR, SAN JUAN ISLAND

Photo. Arthur M. Prentiss

FORT VANCOUVER, FROM A DRAWING BY CAPTAIN WARRE OF
THE ENGLISH ARMY, IN 1845

Courtesy Great Northern Ry.

SACAJAWEA MONUMENT, AT PORTLAND,
OREGON

Courtesy Great Northern Ry.

AN UMATILLA CHIEF, 106 YEARS OLD, WHOSE
FATHER MET LEWIS AND CLARK

Seattle, the chief, was born six years before Captain Vancouver came to the Pacific Coast in 1792. He was regarded by his own nation as a prophet. This prophecy was uttered about the time of the Stevens' Indian Treaties in the 1850's.

Or read the weird utterances of aged, gray-haired, almost blind, ragged, starving Indian "wise women" in the terrible years of Indian Wars from 1847 to 1857. I cannot account for them. You may, but I am not foolish enough to deny they foretold the future. Mt. Hood was acting badly. So were the sulphur holes on Rainier and Baker. Mt. Hood erupted. The air was darkened so that lamps had to be lighted at midday. No damage was done; but the cinders, the dust darkening clouds above and atmosphere below, created an apprehensive depression among the whites and terrible gloom among all the tribes. The Indians always believed these crater-holes on mountain peaks were ruled by the dark demons—unchained to work mighty transformations at set times, but for the most part kept in subjection by the good spirits.

It was in 1843, the year of the first great Overland migration following Whitman. Mrs. Dye gives it best in her beautiful narrative of McLoughlin:

"Old Waskema returning with berries from Mt. Hood, had seen the immigrants in bateaux going down to Fort Vancouver. Waskema set out for Fort Vancouver.

"It was a dark and heavy day. Not even when the great

forest fire came down and threatened the fort had it been so oppressive. Dr. McLoughlin went out to observe the lurid sky. Candles were lit in the hall, and the cattle came lowing up from the marshes at midday. The air was full of fine, light ashes that fell over a radius of fifty miles. For the first time in the memory of man the white robes of St. Helen's were blackened with dust.

"Down by the boathouse Dr. McLoughlin saw old Waskema landing from her canoe. With the kindness of heart that would not slight even a withered old squaw, he advanced and took her hand. 'Well, what's the good word, grandmother?'

"The decrepit old figure tried to straighten itself. In spite of her taciturnity, the white-headed Eagle had won the heart of old Waskema. A smile that was a pathetic contraction of leathern muscles long unused to laughter, danced over her face and was gone. In a sepulchral tone, shaking her bony finger, pointing to the erupting mountain, the old squaw spoke words which were prophetic of the evil days that befell from 1847 to 1856 in raid and massacre.

"The attitude, the tone, the darkness, all corresponded with the gloom of the doctor's spirit. Only too well he knew that with this influx of Americans the Hudson's Bay régime was over. A wind loaded with frost blew down from Mt. Hood."

Mrs. Fuller Victor in her life of Joe Meek refers to the same creepy prophecies among the old witches of all the tribes. We know how Spalding was awakened by death chants round his camp in 1847. I could tell of similar predictions among the fourteen Olympic tribes in this era—yes, down to the 1870's; and these tribes isolated from all white contact by forests impenetrable on the land side and quite as unapproachable on the ocean side

owing to pinnacled rocks, knew so little of white
man values that when a great vessel was wrecked
sixty years ago, they tossed the seaman's chestful
of gold coins among the children for baubles in
play, and ripped the bags of flour to strew the flour
as useless on the sand but saved the cotton sacks
for clothing. They, too, had their strange clairvoyant prophets of white races, of terrible wars
among the nations of the whites, of a Messiah
Saviour to lead the red man to higher things by a
golden paved Path of Peace upward to the Great
Spirit behind the visible sun.

But of this, more anon when we come to the
Olympic Highway.

You speeding westward will see a new Vancouver in Washington, where sign boards will tell
you where to look for the two sites of the old fort
on the north shore. You will cross bridges over
the labyrinth of swampy islands, some of which
will always be swampy from tide and summer
thaw, others now islet gems of emerald green almost hidden in fruit ranches, or girth deep in
pasture for the best sheep runs and cattle feed on
the Coast, others again famed for what are called
"salt air" peas. If you once taste these peas and
this mutton, you will never be quite satisfied with
the flavor of any other. Unluckily for the East,
the demand is greater than the possible supply.
Though canneries are running for the peas, few

reach farther east than the Rockies. It is the same
of the chilled mutton. You do not need to label it
"lamb." Its area is restricted pretty much from
the San Juan Islands on the north to the Columbia
on the south. The delicate almost melting flavor
seems to result from some peculiar chemical combination of sun, light, soil, salt air. It has never
been advertised so far as I know; for all output is
absorbed without advertising; but when you eat
chilled "lamb" elsewhere, you have a suspicion that
lamb may have been an ancient and somewhat
tough woolly old ram; and when you eat peas elsewhere, though the amount of pure nourishment
may be the same, you may feel as if you had been
shot full of a small boy's spring marbles.

While we are on the subject of Pacific Coast
foods, you will find equally curious differences in
different areas only a few miles apart. There are
raspberry and loganberry and blackberry and
strawberry areas round Everett—berries of a de-
licious flavor unknown elsewhere. The same of the
fisheries. At Astoria, or up on the San Juans,
you will taste a clam delicate as no other sea food
but the rare "cod tongues" of Labrador and Newfoundland. In other localities not a hundred miles
away, a clam is just a clam—good, poor, indifferent. The same is true of silver salmon and deep-sea
trout. Right in the San Juans with their one hundred and seventy-two islands and as many harbors
between crab-shaped coastlines, you will find one

harbor famed for its trout, another for its silver salmon. Whether the flavor, flaky and melting, results from the temperature of the deeper seas, the fish food, the sunlight—I do not know. I only know it is a fact and every wise fisherman hies him to the harbor, not where he will make the biggest catch, but the best. I mention these things for two reasons. I have seen Eastern tourists go to hotels in all these areas and order—not "the feast for the gods" they might have if they knew, but the same type of New England or Middle Western dinner to which they have been accustomed; and I have gone to Western hotels where I could not get a blessed morsel of the local delicacy because, as the waiter told me, "tourists don't know enough to order it and it is left on our hands." In such hotels, engage your room separate from the dining-room. Then go out for your meals to the little water-front restaurants, where the floor may be sawdust, the table covers cheap oilcloth; and you will get what you want at a third—yes—a tenth the price. It is the fault of the tourist demand, not of the local hostelry.

Old Fort Vancouver had two sites. Both were on the north shore for reasons obvious as you cross the bridge. The south shore was too swampy. When McLoughlin moved headquarters up from Astoria on the Pacific ninety miles to Fort Vancouver to be farther away from free-lance tramp-ship traders' rum and near the point from which he could send his fur brigades south to the Snake tribes, north to the Kootenays and Flatheads, east to the Nez Percés, the Cayuses, the Cœur d'Alenes, the Spokanes, he found he had built the first fort on a prairie where it was too difficult to get pure water. Some of it was torn down and a new site picked on better ground three miles distant, giving ample space inside the log palisades, and a fine plain behind for farm and gardens to render the fort independent in food supply of Indian trade or the long wait for canoe brigades across the continent and the longer delay for provisions shipped round the world from England. Fort Vancouver had to be independent of all chance supplies for its great brigades of two and three hundred men in each of its large departments. It was a vast empire in itself, covering a territory a third the size of all Europe. Over this empire, John McLoughlin was virtually king with the autocrat's power of life or death in his very word, but obedience to that word depended on the justice blended with mercy of the king; and never in either justice or mercy did the great Tyee fall short. In stature, he was kingly— over six feet tall, straight as a lance to his old age, deeply religious, with hair whitened before he was thirty so that the Indians called him "the White Eagle," majestic in deportment from the inner majesty of his soul, a stickler for etiquette in dress and manners because he knew Indians despised familiarity and slovenliness and vulgarity, however low they might themselves fall. He always carried a gold-headed cane. In dress, he was meticulous as a courtier. The white choker collar was fresh each day. The black flowing silk tie always unwrinkled, the long black or blue coat with the gold buttons of the period impressive as the vesture of a knight commandant seeking his first honor at a king's morning audience. When the weather was inclement, he wore as overcoat a long cape lined with silk. He was always fond of dancing and tripped the stately steps of the period with grace and agility till he died. When in doubt about some vital decision, or in fear for the safety of some of his brigades, he would be found on his knees in his library praying to God Almighty for help or wisdom. In brief, he was a true gentleman of his century.

When others like Douglas and Simpson of the Hudson's Bay Company took titles from their king as insignia of service, John McLoughlin, as one of the Oregon settlers who had gone West most hostile to him, afterwards acknowledged, "John McLoughlin held his patent of nobility direct from God Almighty." He had married in early life the widow of that McKay massacred on Astor's ship the *Tonquin*—a fine Indian woman of the Soo, daughter of a chief on Lake Superior; and Tom McKay, his step-son, carried into his career on the Pacific Coast the finest traditions of both races; whereas, McLoughlin's son—David—educated in

Paris, seemed a throw-back to some unaccountable blood strain; for he died a drunkard's death.

How many bastions had Fort Vancouver? Wilkes says that in the 1840's, when he was there, it had none. Other annals of guests give the impression of the usual two, one at each diagonal corner; and it is possible both are right. As the great Tyee's influence for power and justice spread from the Coast to the Rockies among all tribes, the bastions may have been converted to storerooms for powder and ball and guns. As Wilkes was there just when the great migration began in a tidal sweep westward, the fort seen by him was possibly the fort which received the most of the homeless Pioneers. The stumps, broad as a dining-table along the river road, were already overgrown with red honeysuckle in full bloom. Behind the fort was a village of fifty comfortable log houses. Here the Hudson's Bay Company's servants, Indian wives and children "swarmed" like bees. The log pickets were upright, twenty-five feet high. Inside were houses, shops, warehouses, bachelors' quarters, reading-rooms, a library. The palisades enclosed about four acres, every foot in gardens. Just outside were huge granaries. At one end of the inner square was Dr. McLoughlin's house—one story log but weather-boarded, painted a spotless white, with a piazza and grape vines and flower beds in front. Before the steps stood two old cannon on "sea-carriages" with piles of

balls "to speak to the natives" if they needed it.
The Catholic chapel with flag-staff stood near the
center with the lettering H. B. C. in white on blue
flag. Warehouses lined all walls of the fort. A
little square cabin known as "the butter tub" did
duty as prison. It was seldom occupied and did
duty oftener as cold storage for milk and cream
and butter than for some renegade man, who had
imbibed too much rum for his head.

Vessels of fourteen feet draft—deep for that
era—rocked at the docks. Wilkes notes the two
islands in the Columbia here and the Willamette
coming in on the south shore. The centers of the
islands were prairies, but the shores lined with
oaks. Several tables were in the long dining-room,
one for the great Tyee, and his head officers; another for the missionaries; another for the ladies
—who never dined in public for the simple reason
the Hudson's Bay Company would not expose its
women to the gaze of Indian chiefs, who were
often guests. Here, a regal hospitality was main-
tained with all the formalities of a feudal barony,
and five hundred guests could be seated. The
lights were tall candles. To be sure, the stores
sold goods at an advance of eighty per cent. over
London prices, but Wilkes doubted if that more
than paid the expense of freighting the goods
across Canada or round the world in ships. It was
on furs—not goods—the Company made its huge
profits. A big bell summoned to meals. At the

end of the supper-time meal, pipes and tobacco
were passed to be puffed leisurely over sips of rare
old wines.

At dawn, the big bell sounded. In half an hour,
anvils, carts, little bells on horse brigades, ham-
mers, a chatter in French habitant patois, made the
air hum. Breakfast rang at 8 A.M., dinner at 1
P.M., supper between 6 and 7. "Everybody," said
Wilkes, "seems to be in a hurry." Each had his
duty. On Saturdays work stopped at 5 to give all
hands a chance to buy goods at the stores. Year in
and year out Fort Vancouver ran on clockwork
system. Except for the use of light wine for the
last meal, or rum for the brigades caught in a
chill or spill on some of the rapids, liquor was absolutely taboo. Its use was too dangerous among
the Indians. In the bachelor quarters, arranged
much like a ship's bunks, pine boards made the
beds, four point—meaning pound—blankets of
pure wool in red or green with black stripes to
mark the weight for Indian buyers, feather mat-
tresses mountain high to defy cold. There were
six Protestant missionaries dining at McLoughlin's table when Wilkes was there. Though the
great Tyee was a Catholic, on Sunday the big
dining-hall was loaned to the Protestants for service and Chief Factor Douglas read the Episcopal
ritual if no other Protestant were present.

The gardener was Billy Bruce, a famous old
Scotchman who had been trained on the Duke of

Devonshire's estate and found when his term had expired with the Hudson's Bay Company and he had returned to England, he could no longer be happy in a congested old land so came back to the Columbia. In all, thirty-eight children from the fort and village were being educated under a teacher paid by the Hudson's Bay Company. The boys were expected to pay for their education by working in the potato patch and yearly raised six hundred bushels of potatoes. Orchards were everywhere, inside the fort walls, and outside the pickets. Peach stones were said to have come from Robinson Crusoe's Island in the South Seas, apples from seeds tucked in London apprentices' vests by loving damsels, who never saw their lovers again, and heard vaguely that many had married women of Indian blood.

Wilkes notes plainly what so many writers have ignored—that by 1840 the fur trade had fallen off so greatly south of the Columbia that the Company were preparing to move north to what is now British Columbia.

Behind the fort was a farm nine miles square. Here roamed the finest of three thousand milk cows produced by crossing the long-horned rangers of California with imported guernseys and jerseys from England. There were also twenty-five hundred sheep and three hundred brood mares. At night or during inclement weather, when the stock was not driven in lean-to sheds, it was herded. No chances were taken of loss from weather or raid. And south of the farm, rose Mt. Hood in all its blaze of glory. Grist and saw mills lay six miles above Vancouver on the Columbia. Boards were shipped to Hawaii as ballast and brought returns of eighty dollars a thousand feet— our War prices in this century. The blacksmith shop not only repaired all metal implements from horseshoes to guns but made axes and hatchets, twenty-five to fifty a day. The destruction of axes in this big-tree region necessitated a home factory. Yet Wilkes remarks when the thaws came, the Columbia rose eighteen inches in ten hours and the floods swept the great trees past "like chips."

From 1832 to 1840, when the first missionaries came to Fort Vancouver, the fort undoubtedly presented a more warlike aspect. There was at least one tower doing duty as bastion loopholed for musketry fire. McLoughlin's house is described as in the center. Front and back gates were kept locked at night and wicket window slides to the side gave glimpse of all comers. Here had come the Lees and the Whitmans, and the Spaldings in the 1830's to '40's. Men-of-war, sailing vessels, Indian dugouts rocked at the docks. Up the Willamette at Champoeg or French Prairie lay the only settlement—chiefly old Hudson's Bay Company servants with their Indian wives and half-breed families; but it was as Wilkes had seen the fort that the most of the immigrants now rushing madly to Oregon must have had their first view of Fort Vancouver.

All day and all night, the broad river gates stood open to receive the wanderers. Often in the wildest weather, Dr. McLoughlin, himself, stood on the docks, his long cape blowing to the wind, his cane in one hand, a lantern in the other, directing where to house the women and children, where to put up tents for the men, who could not be housed, shouting to his Hawaiian cook to hasten with hot tea to the immigrants soaked and chilled by the rains. Day dawn saw him or Douglas at the cashier's desk behind the main office-counter dealing out provisions and food to people who had been denouncing "that old aristocrat" all the way from the Missouri. The fire eaters did not know what to make of it. Some had bank drafts, but here were no banks to cash them. McLoughlin offered either to take their bank drafts against purchases, or deposit them in the strong box to be held against future needs and gave them a receipt. Some had not a dime in cash or drafts. To them he sold beds, food, blankets, rough flannel clothing, boots, implements on credit with no security for pay but their own word. Flour was becoming scarce. Well, then, here were so many bushels of wheat or oats, which they could get ground at the great mill and pay by working at the lumber mill or delivering shingles at three dollars a thousand, or pay next year in wheat at seventy-five cents a

bushel, a better price than many had received back
on the Mississippi and the Missouri; but to all,
McLoughlin's last words were "go to work—go to
work"; for there was work for every man and the
Fort, acting as a clearing house for all comers, had
to hasten laggards away or be eaten down bare as
a bone in its own supplies.

No need to starve now. No heed for cold.
Bark in great slabs would smolder all night like
a coal hearth. There were fish for the taking.
There was game for every shot—grouse, duck, elk,
deer. Little Applegate tells how the apples tossed
by sailors from the ships rocking at anchor seemed
the best apples ever tasted in his life. The press-
ing need for these people was to get busy, pick
their squatter areas, build their cabins for the
winter and lay in supplies for the early spring—
January—when they could plow up the prairies
and and get a crop in for the next year. The
habitant chatter in French, the broad Scotch
brogue, the haste, the clockwork routine, left the
newcomers in a sort of daze for a short time, when
groups began to disperse to various areas, seeking
sites for future homes. Those who were ill remained at the Fort under care of the Company
physician; and it was natural that groups from
different States went out together and sought their
homesteads as near neighborhoods. It is an actual fact that some families of two or three made
their first house for a winter in big cedar stumps

hewn out, one stump at each end then boarded before and behind with slabs in a sort of three room contraption, with fireplace in the central room and sleeping quarters at each end. Floors were mud or puncheons; roofs, slabs; beds, board berths; table, a board; seats, a rough bench; doors, on leather or wooden pegs; windows, buckskin or a sliding board; but that was palatial compared to the six months of roofless life all had known. In fact, out on the Olympic Highway to this day, you can see a big cedar stump post-office with slabs for a roof.

How the bagpipes, the concertinas, the mouth organs, the fiddles sounded to ears starved of joy for six months—one can guess. Hopes came up with a rebound. Especially hopes came up as December rains gave place to warm genial weather with roses in bloom and later all the orchards heavy with blossoms of fruits the colonists had known in their old home land. Their Promised Land was then no phantom mirage. By the fourth of July, people who had been starving on the Platte or the Snake but a year ago, were feasting on a barbecued ox and dancing on the turf to celebrate weddings of troth plighted on the long trek westward. Then, of course, all through each winter, the slow "cow column" of stock came drifting in. What these settlers thought when they saw their own cattle coming gaunt as skeletons— cattle they could have sold back East for twenty to thirty dollars—when they could have bought Hudson's Bay cattle at ten dollars a head, and ponies at five dollars and heavy horses at fifty to seventy-five dollars, is not on record. It recalls the follies of mining stampedes in our own day, when people shipped from England bales of hay for the Klondike and lamp chimneys from New York and Chicago. As for dishes, many settlers learned how to whittle out cedar plates like the Indians, and cook over a spit, bury clams on hot stones below a smoldering fire, and then for the rest cook in bake ovens of earth till they got permanent cabins up with cranes to swing copper and iron kettles in above the roaring blaze of fir and pine. A few needles or bullets bought mats from the Indians for the rough floors; and the second winter found the majority of the settlers as enthusiastic as when they had set out from far home lands.

And then four years after, the very winter that St. Helen's had sent her smoldering gloom over midday, and later when the Whitman Massacres sent shivers of horror down every spine, came the most astonishing news, news that transformed Oregon from a moneyless Arcadia into a commercial bee hive—gold—gold had been discovered in California. Almost overnight Champoeg or French Prairie was deserted by the French Canadians. The missionaries had no children left. Provisions jumped to such prices as the frontier

VIEW OF LONGVIEW, LOOKING ACROSS JEFFERSON SQUARE

LEWIS AND CLARK SALT CAIRN, AT SEA SIDE, NEAR ASTORIA

PIONEER MONUMENT, COLUMBIA HIGHWAY

had never before known—from twenty-five to fifty cents for an egg, from no price for fruit to ten and twenty-five and five hundred dollars a barrel for fresh apples, pears, any fresh fruit or vegetable, three and five dollars a bushel for grain and more for flour. Many a pioneer left his family in Oregon and hurried by ship or horseback south to the Sacramento to try his luck placer mining in the pay sands, or to sell what he had raised. Those who stuck to their squatter farms and worked like demons—men, women, girls, boys—made more selling what they raised than the argonauts, who flocked south to mine. For the first time in its half century of history, Oregon knew the sight of real money. There were three hundred thousand people in California clamoring for supplies. There were twelve thousand people in Oregon— half women and children—selling them supplies at reckless prices. Where had been farms, sprang up towns; where towns, cities; where muddy flats at tide water, or mills at waterfalls, like mushrooms up over night grew great cities. Oregon and California were now American territory.

If you can explain such coincidences by anything but Destiny, I cannot. The Pomised Land had become a fact. The weeping had turned to laughter and the harvesters "were bearing home the sheaves" of their own blind hopes and blinder faith.

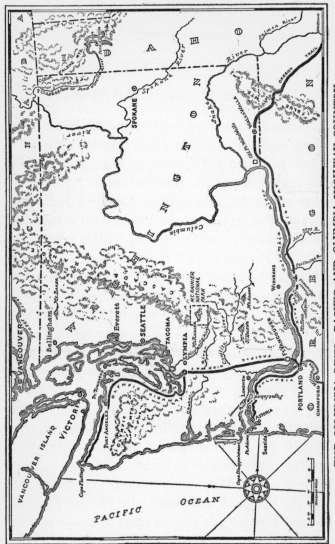

THE COLUMBIA RIVER, PACIFIC AND OLYMPIA HIGHWAY COUNTRY

CHAPTER XIV

ON DOWN THE HIGHWAY TO THE PACIFIC

IF you will take any map of the United States and measure roughly from Southern Oregon and Idaho to the Canadian Border, you will find a region about six hundred miles square, or roughly about the area of New England and New York and Pennsylvania, or all of Ohio and Indiana and Illinois and Kentucky. Or compare to Europe. The Oregon of the Pioneers' Promised Land would be about the size of France with parts of Switzerland and Italy included.

It is hard for Easterners to grasp such dimensions, especially to grasp them in terms of farm, mine, timber, fisheries. Neither is the comparison to the mountain areas of Europe enlightening. Some of the best wheat lands and fruit territory are in what is called the dry zone; the greatest wealth of mine and timber in the mountain wilderness; and the fisheries where swamp, waterfalls, pinnacled rocks seem to bar human efforts.

Though Fort Vancouver seemed to mark the end of the long trek westward, the Pioneers had to pick their homesteads like an oasis in a wilderness. As you go on to the Coast, over roads as fine as the Boulevard in Chicago or the Thames Embank-

269

ment in London, you are following the trails chopped out by their pick and ax as they sought those homesteads. Of course, they had to follow more or less the river beds; as you will. From Vancouver on the Columbia, you strike that great Pacific Highway, which runs in a continuous broad paved road from Vancouver, British Columbia, to San Diego, California—thirteen hundred miles. You can go down the Columbia Highway to Astoria on the sea; or on up north to Seattle and Tacoma which connect with one of the most uniquely beautiful regions in all America—the Olympic Highway from Puget Sound to Cape Flattery. You can do each from old Vancouver Fort in a few hours by train or motor in luxury comfort with pauses at hotels as fine as the best in New York or humble and inexpensive as the little inns of Brittany or Cornwall. The thing is to plan your trip ahead and do one going west, the other coming back east.

For ninety miles from Fort Vancouver to the Sea, the Columbia takes a great bend north almost as confusing as the canyons of Snake River. To the right of the great bend, you will see the reason. Mt. Adams, St. Helen's, Rainier, hang like opal domes dyed in rose on the northeastern sky. You will mistake them at first for clouds set on fire by the sun. Each mountain pouring its floods of snow-thaw in the Columbia throws out its long ramparts of rocky foot-hills, which divert its tor-

rents through canyons and narrow passes to the
Cowlitz at Longview; and the Chehalis, which
cuts across to the Pacific by Gray's Harbor, site of
Aberdeen and Hoquiam—two more tide-water
cities; and the Snokomish and the Skykomish and
the Snoqualami rivers and passes and swamps from
the main Cascades till I wish that old Chinook
jargon had passed with the Chinook tribes to oblivion. As a rule, the old Indian names should be
preserved. They tell so much of the past; but the
Chinook was a mongrel tongue for the benefit of
old traders, who could not pronounce Pacific Coast
phonetics; and it confused all early records from
Lewis and Clark to the Pioneers. Enough for you
to remember, whether traveling by train or motor,
the passes follow the streams; and these passes
were all hewn out with ax along Indian and game
trail by the Pioneers seeking their homesteads or
short cuts from the Columbia to the Willamette,
or across to Puget Sound.

Many made mistakes in their choice of homesteads. As many of the mistakes are being repeated today, I want to emphasize them with
offense to no particular area and, still less, favor to
any. They are mistakes tragic to people over fifty
years of age seeking repose in a genial climate for
the rest of their lives. Mistakes can be retrieved
before fifty. Few can after fifty, especially if all
savings have been sunk in one mistake; and the

choice is so varied in areas almost certain of success, such loss is unnecessary.

If you take a map, you will see how the Cascades form a great moisture zone running north and south. Almost at right angles to this ridge are the Olympics, east and west. Now there are areas in all these zones—I do not name them, use your eyes and your head—where the soil is of a deep black humus with exhaustless fertility for a thousand years. It has been formed by glacial silt and prehistoric forests. Comes a break no wider than a lead pencil; and the soil is pure gravel. I do not know the cause. It may have been the sweep of glacier or volcanic upheaval; but I do not need to tell any sane human being one type of land is not worth ten cents an acre, the other type pretty nearly valuable in proportion to the brawn and brain invested. There is a still subtler difference in these values. Many of these areas are logged-off lands. The usual history is lumber, first; then shingle mill or paper mill; then the lands for sale at five dollars an acre up or down. Now the Pacific Coast with three hundred days of sunshine out of three hundred and sixty-five, has uttered such howls about rains, we are apt to forget that the normal rainfall of the Pacific is much less annually—less by almost half—than in New England. What creates the moisture is the clouds breaking against the snowy heights in a wall, when down fall the rains; but there are places in the

Olympics, in the spurs of the Cascades, where the clouds from the ocean do not float across to the high ridges; and in behind these blind spots, the soil is dry as a bone. It may be too elevated to pump for irrigation. Much is so gravelly that if it were irrigated, it could grow nothing but such short sheep pasture as an inch of top soil can raise. It is absolutely valueless for farm, fruit, truck. It is not worth five cents an acre for spring pasture. It cannot regrow in a thousand years the dank forests that come up on better soils in humid airs in less than fifty years. Fortunately, such spots are rare and I would not draw attention to them but that passing through them you must sometimes ask yourself, Why this little city full of banks, warehouses shipping? Why this little city, its next door neighbor, with abandoned hotels, bank buildings empty, long streets of vacant blocks where the windows have been shot out or removed? Because behind every city must be background of forest, farm, mine for shipment. You must use your head as well as your eyes; or five dollars an acre will prove dear land and twenty to a hundred dollars cheap.

There is another equally subtle point about irrigated lands. There are places where irrigation charges are high a year—as high as twenty dollars an acre and worth it for productive lands; but why pay that if you have a slender purse and can buy equally good lands right on the water front of some mountain torrent coming down so steeply from the snowy peaks? You can build your own intake, put in your own flumes and have your irrigation for nothing; or stick in a gas engine and pump water for your own farm.

Even in the choice of a future city site—and many a suburb will grow into a city and many a village into a shipping center—there is a similar gamble with the goddess luck. I have known all the Pacific Coast for years and in nine cases out of ten, have seen growth go southwest; but I think of a dozen places where for no reason I could fathom, the blessed town took a jump northeast, or sprawled so swiftly in every direction, you could not guess ahead one year where the next jump would go. Doubtless in time the little bungalows lying between wholesale and retail blocks, or between declining business areas and residential sections, will be absorbed by one type or the other; but in the meantime, your taxes go up and up and your values go down; and they may not retrieve in twenty years; and twenty years is a long time after midlife. I have friends in the West who guessed right, got hold of little lots at two hundred to a thousand dollars, and saw them go up like a rocket to twenty, forty, fifty thousand dollars and sold. In other words, they got the little egg, sat on it and hatched out year by year by sheer "stick-to-it-iveness" a fortune. I have others who paid four thousand, seven thousand dollars for their areas and did even better—saw them go to a million in value. I have others who paid three hundred thousand for the best areas on a main street, when away jumped that main street in a kangaroo leap two or three miles. Came in the Chinese laundry, the little foreign shop, and down went values and up and up and up went taxes till the investor was glad to let the property sell for taxes. I think of one particularly, who let a three hundred thousand dollar property go for taxes, held on to a little five-thousand-dollar backwater block and recouped all his losses by a jump of the city in that direction. Is it a gamble? Partly; but more it is eternal vigilance, watchfulness and that most uncommon of all things we crave—common sense. If one could zone cities and make them go as you zone them, it would be safe gambling; but like horses in a stampede, they do not go as you zone them. Few of the Pioneers trekking west ever dreamed such cities would grow up on the Pacific as exist today, just as few of us today realize that in our lifetime many Pacific Coast cities will equal in size and wealth some of the Atlantic's greatest ports; but all the Pioneers had vaguely in the back of their heads, that a wise choice as to homestead site was the key to their future success.

Having reached Vancouver on the Columbia, your next objective is, of course, Portland, less than ten miles away. What created Portland, you do not need to be told. Every factor was there to

make it what it is: the head of navigation from the
sea, easy grade in haul for the rails to and from
the Inland Empire, background of farm and fruit
land and mine, waterpower from the Willamette
and—most important of all—the spirit of its people descended from these old Pioneers, who prepared for what they foresaw in splendid civic
docks, deepened water, libraries, museums, stadi-
ums, music halls that should be called temples, and
such conceptions of beauty as are yearly celebrated
in their rose festivals instead of in the rough raw
stuff we too often foolishly ascribe to the West in
our Eastern movies and theaters and fiction. There
is a lot to see round Portland, both sacred from the
past and augury of a greater future. See the residences both bungalow and marble type if you want
to know the character of the people. No vulgarity
here of boomster or newly rich. No sign of poverty.
Hardly an unhappy disgruntled face from failure
and blasted hopes. Go to the Historical Museum
and leisurely let the Secretary, himself the son of a
Pioneer, show you the relics of the first comers,
from Captain Gray's sea voyage of discovery in
1792 to the Pioneers of 1839-56. When you survey
gold hair mixed with Indian raiders' scalp locks
you get an idea of what Oregon cost in heroism.
But go also to the Market of a Saturday morning
and price the fruit and vegetables and the fish.
Silver salmon, deep sea trout; figs and oranges and
lemons and grape fruit from the South; plums,

apples, berries, vegetables of every variety fresh
from the fields. Pineapples from Hawaii, avoca-
does and nuts from Panama, candied fruits from
the Orient. It is like a Fair in the Far East, or one
of London's great food markets after the ships have
come up the Thames from the Channel Islands.
Taxes and clothing may be high; but these prices
are to us from the East a joke. Also realize that in
a genial clime you do not pay out in fuel enough
for a winter trip to the Pacific. A bit narrow are
the streets down town; but who could foresee Portland, Oregon, would one day outstrip its patro-
nymic parent, Portland, Maine as seven is to one?
It is almost comical to recall when Portland was a
village of a thousand or less and coins were tossed
whether to name it Boston or Maine, the flip of a
silver piece decided the name. It is almost equally
ironical to reflect that when Joe Meek, the guide
down at a famous meeting of settlers in Champoeg
called for "a divide" whether to leave Oregon as it
was, a no-man's land, or set up American Government, the votes of two Canadians brought Oregon
under the ægis of the Stars and Stripes; but these
two Canadians were French; and the French were
not particularly partial to British rule. Again, I
ask—was Oregon's fate Destiny or what? Vancouver, the great British explorer, was just a few
days too late behind Gray, the American, on the
Columbia. Thompson, the best explorer the fur
trade of Montreal ever sent out, was just a few

weeks too late after Astor of New York had sent his blundering and traitorous if not cowardly underlings to Astoria; and neither Simpson nor McLoughlin could prevail on the fat heads of London to back their venture to buy on the Pacific Coast what they had lost by ignorant diplomacy. Where Wilkes, the American, foresaw a great new empire, Peel and Gordon, the British navy men, reported the country as worthless, and American senators thought Oregon "not worth a pinch of snuff." If John McLoughlin "held his patent of nobility from God Almighty," Oregon held the patent of her future from a Hand greater than any human factor.

I am not going to describe Portland as it is, because I have never known a city with a background on the Pacific Coast which did not surpass its own highest hopes in ten years, and double its wildest guesses of future population in twenty years; not one from Vancouver, British Columbia, to San Diego, California.

But you must not miss Champoeg, south of Portland. You can go out and back in a few hours' run. Champoeg is now a State park rightly dedicated to the Pioneers of the past to keep their heroism, though it was a heroism in buckskin, fragrant in our memories and perhaps encourage in us some of their dauntless spirit. Gone are French Prairie and Champoeg as the first happy French Canadians and discouraged missionaries knew them

from 1834 to 1850. Even the split-rail fences on
the lowlands have been swept away by floods; but
you can camp on the turf where they danced away
care to bagpipes and fiddles with moccasins for
dancing slippers and drink from the same old pure
spring which the famous Jacque Cardinal called
his "barrel of rum which never ran dry," and eat
your picnic supper under the same old oaks and firs
where the Methodist Lee brothers standing six
feet in their moccasins thundered against the sins
of the flesh and invoked to the love of God, or
the priests, Blanchet and Brouilet, held up their
lurid painted pictures of a fiery hell and a tender
Christ to recall these wild children of French
Canada to the faith of their Quebec fathers. All
the old memories are there, shaming our softer
civilization and flabbier faith and half cynical
smile at all ideals. There was the faith in these
simple children of wilderness Wilds. Here in
modern Oregon is the realization of that faith. Besides, on your run out to Champoeg you can pause
and see the last home of McLoughlin. When Mc-
Loughlin realized that the fur trade had passed
forever and resigned his position in the Hudson's
Bay Company, he built a house beside the falls at
Oregon City almost a replica in type of the old
house in Vancouver Fort, but on smaller scale; and
when great water-power companies began to
cramp space close to the falls, the old house was
carefully torn down and rebuilt higher up, board

for board, log for log, floor for floor, just as McLoughlin had lived in it. There, you can see the heavy puncheons and board floors worn thin by the moccasin tread of copper-skinned visitors who came for his wise advice to the day he died; and when he was dying and was asked was all well with him, he whispered "A-dieu," not "Farewell" as we thoughtlessly utter our good-by, but "to God."

It was natural that many of the Overlanders after their few days of rest at Fort Vancouver should first take a look round Portland and up the Willamette far as the bounds of California. Ezra Meeker tells how in the 1850's on a bright moonlight night of October he carried his exhausted young wife up in his arms to where the only lodging house in the village of Portland was, a colored man's cabin. They had come down from the Cascades in a little grunting steamer and warped in as close to the steep banks as they could; but the steep bank was slippery and the most of the town was under tent roofs. These huge trees and huge stumps in mid-road seemed to demand more strength than their exhausted vitality possessed before a homestead could be cleared. They had not yet found that higher up the Willamette were park openings amid the trees where a few hours of work would erect a cabin and the plowshare could be driven through the sod for the next year's crop.

When Commander Wilkes came to Champoeg

in the 1840's, wages were a dollar a day for unskilled labor, three dollars a day for husky choppers and men scarce at that. Salmon fisheries
afforded food, though they were not very good so
late in the season and far from the sea. When
Frémont went south of Champoeg in the same
decade, this was mighty dangerous country from
weather and Indian raid. Snow loaded the pine
forests and was so deep in the mountains, where
Oregon merged to California, that horses plunged
to saddle girths and Chinook guides refused to go
on. They could see the warm green plains far
south between headwaters of the Des Chutes-Wil-
lamette height of land and the Sacramento; but
where they stood "storms raged fiercely." Snow-
shoes and sledges had to be whittled out before
Indian guides would go on. Kit Carson was head
guide. The provision column of pack-horses and
mules fell in behind the trail blazers and on Feb-
ruary 13 to cheer advance scouts, the poor little
pet camp dog had to be sacrificed with one worn-
out mule to add nourishment to thin pea soup of
snow water. Flocks of geese kept winging north
in their wedge-shaped lines and their weird
screams cried, "Spring—spring," but the men
round the camp fires had to tighten belts from
hunger. The height of the pass was nine thousand
feet, two thousand higher than South Pass up the
Platte; but even Frémont in all these perils could
not resist the influence of the majestic mountains

—"purple ranges bordered with bright yellow
gold, the peaks a narrow line in crimson cloud,"
the atmosphere a singular "greenish orange"
against cerulean skies. The game trails "were
steep and slippery with ice," and the naked storm-
stripped branches tore clothing and human skins
and exhausted the most toughened guides to a
breathless stall. Some crawled down the ice backward rather than risk a slide into snow waters,
of which Frémont often had more than one in a
single day. Guns were lost. Men delirious from
weakness strayed off and had to be found; but
at last all were down in California's butterfly
meadows.

This trail was followed by many an immigrant,
who tore off from Oregon to California in the
gold rush, but it was not a territory to attract the
Pioneer settlers.

When Hancock came in 1845, he was tremen-
dously pleased with the Willamette and set out
to see what lay south farther up the river. He
went on foot with one companion, each having a
rifle over shoulder and a blanket with five pounds
of flour inside strapped to shoulders. Each night
and each morning, they shot grouse or rabbit for
food; but horse hoofs marked Indians in ambush
following abreast and one night when they had
killed a bear for steak and could not sleep for the
howling of the wolves tearing at the carcass, they
were aware those Indians were too near for com-

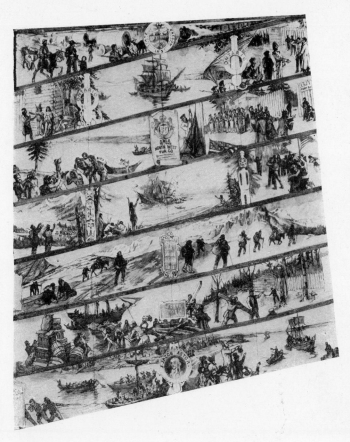

ASTOR MONUMENT, ASTORIA, TELLING WHOLE HISTORY OF
THE NORTHWEST PACIFIC COAST

(Upper portion. See over for lower portion.)

ASTOR MONUMENT, ASTORIA, TELLING WHOLE HISTORY OF
NORTHWEST PACIFIC COAST

(*Lower portion. See over for upper portion*)

fort. Friendly Indians didn't hide from two lone whites. Sometimes a naked coppery skin flitted away among the shadowy cedars. The campers put out fires and with backs to trees smoked all night to keep awake. The parked prairies right on the water front promised ideal homesteads. But these Umpqua and Rouge River Indians, notorious for treachery! What would they do to settlers? They didn't go far without finding out. The hidden warriors charged with a whoop one night when both men rose and met them with leveled guns and stood their ground within "eight steps" of the advancing zigzag line. The Indians snatched off an elk hunch hanging to a tree and dived for the woods. By this time Hancock was "getting pretty mad." It was unsafe to light a camp fire and almost unsafe to fire a shot at game, and food was down to less than a pound of flour. The next time they killed a deer, they kindled a fire to cook it, then went off some distance in the woods to eat. Hancock had had enough of the Upper Willamette. They decided to make a raft of "sticks" and "get off down stream" back to Portland. It would be altogether safer to settle nearer Portland, then a clump of "12 or 15" log houses. Three years later, in the mad stampede to California, Hancock found these Indians just as hostile; but as the gold seekers were going south this time in convoys of twenty-five men with wagons and horses, they kept sentinels on watch each night and fired at every snaky gleam of a naked copper skin sneaking through the brushwood. Even with a stronger party, half the wagons turned back for Oregon City and Portland. Those who went on left many a raider "kicking on the ground." "Dat," said an old Dutchman, "ish de vay de Dootch fights." Those who went back to Oregon made much more money than those who went on. Hancock says pork sold at a dollar-thirty-five a pound, flour at thirty-five cents, sugar at a dollar—and a barrel of apples as high as five hundred dollars. It was placer mining in California—easy money—easy-come and easy-go; and the most of it went recklessly. Before final choice wise heads wanted a look at the lower Columbia and up round Puget Sound.

Thither let us go!

CHAPTER XV

ON DOWN THROUGH LONGVIEW AND ASTORIA TO THE SEA

PORTLAND really marks the western end of the Oregon Trail; but it does not mark the end of the Overland Trail. Lewis and Clark and the Astorians went on down the Columbia to the Pacific, and the Columbia River Highway follows their river trail. So do the railroads lining the broad waters of the river now slowing in its progress; for it is no longer descending the rock steps of stairways from the Cascade Mountains and resembles more the majestic entrance of channels from tide water than an inland river. You see the big ocean liners plowing up the channel, as they beat up the Thames to London, or the Hudson to New York, from every port under the sun; but all the scenery is on a more majestic scale. The deep draughts of the waters between rock walls are almost unbelievable—forty feet in places from the terrific sweeping momentum, a sort of annual natural dredging. In other places where the sand and silt islands cut the river breadth up in narrow straits, the same impact of restless flood tides behind keeps the narrower mid-channel dredged out for deepest ocean liners. The width of these mid-channels seems to mark the only limit to these inland ocean ports. Up to the present, delays or accidents from this narrowing of certain stretches in the river bed have been almost non-existent; but when the Pacific numbers its population in the twenty and forty millions as it undoubtedly will, the question comes up in one's mind whether Collis Huntington of the Central and Southern Pacific was not right when he said that sooner or later these river highways would compel commerce to follow the lower grade haul of river bed, and rails would have to meet that lower grade by tunnels through mountains, shorter cuts across bends in the streams, swifter speed to cut costs as against water carrier; for Huntington not only foresaw that the great growing Inland Empire traffic would tax rails but would ultimately crowd space on the river channel for steamer room, just as it has sent New York traffic sprawling across East River to Long Island City and Brooklyn and Hudson River and on the west to Hoboken and all the New Jersey docks till Greater New York waters resemble a perpetual shuttle of ferries and barges and tugs and tows.

The changes impending on the Columbia are not in the far future. They are very near and on them hangs the future of Longview and Astoria as great cities. The rivalries among these Coast cities over this very point are so acute that a prophet becomes very canny about becoming too cocksure. As a holiday, I once summered at Quebec City. The docks were a pathetic reminder of a glory that had passed—passed on up the St. Lawrence to Montreal. No longer did masts countless rock to the tide. Except for pleasure tourist steamers, the most of the great ocean liners went churning past leaving deserted Quebec Harbor rubbing its eyes. You could have bought some of the most beautiful old residences for ten thousand dollars—residences with dining rooms that were banquet halls; and business blocks for less. You could not buy them today for a hundred thousand. With the increase of commerce for the whole country multiplied two and three hundred fold, Quebec revived—revived in a way you can describe only as the dead coming to life. The same thing is now impending on the Columbia and you will see two of the most marked examples of this at Longview, thirty miles from the Pacific, and at Astoria, right on the Pacific, or rather on the arm of a deep bay that is the Pacific.

Longview is not an old city. It is at this time of writing barely six years old from the plowed ground of farms amid a park of oaks, lying on the Washington or north shore; but Longview was deliberately laid out, created and established as a city site thirty miles from the Pacific to catch and hold in its web that increase of river and ocean traffic as time goes on. As background it has the finest areas of fir and pine forests which will reforest themselves in fifty years and if protected from fire cannot be exhausted. That means lumber mills and paper mills of which three of the biggest companies in the United States have already established scientifically equipped plants that are marvels in their curious combination of educated brains handling electric machinery, which is the nearest to human I have ever seen. When you have gone through some of these mills, you have literally followed a narrow railed board walk amid whizzing saws and automatic carriers and cranes for miles; and all are driven at electric speed with three shifts of men a day and non-stop in speed from the engine room with its belching-flame smoke-stacks to great hoists loading lumber on the ocean liners lying at the docks.

But Longview has more than a background of lumber. It has a background of finest farm land both along the Columbia and along the Cowlitz coming in from the north, as well as the hinterland of fruit and wheat and stock from the Inland Empire. It has one of the finest climates on the Pacific—never hot, never cold. You can count five snowy peaks hanging in rose domes on the sky line. These send down cool breezes at midday and the Pacific sends in warm breezes at night. Look from any window, on any street you like, there passing in the kaleidoscope of cloud and sunlight is beauty. Summer or winter, there are flower-bordered walks and broader streets of one-way traffic so wide that a half dozen cars can run abreast and not be impeded, or make your ears hum hooting at one another to get out of the way. It gives a delightful sense of restful repose—an oasis of peace in a whirligig of trade. It is really a dream city—a utopia if you like to call it that— but a dream come true and not likely to awaken with "the headache of the morning after" because it is not a boom city. It was laid out a zoned city from the first; shipping on the river front; mills along the river front; trade and shop streets next; small bungalows for workers next; residences back from the terminal last, with community libraries, athletic-club houses, union churches, centralized for all.

The time will come and very soon when growth of all the Pacific Coast will provide more trade than the present cities can handle and the rivalry will fade as it has faded between Quebec and Montreal. It is on other ground that Longview is worth while for you to stop and see. It is to study out a modern utopia city. Can the utopia be realized? Will the turmoil of success as a big center defeat its avowed aims as an ideal city for every class of worker, humblest to highest? It is bound to be one of the most interesting experiments in the United States. Other utopian cities exist, some in the Southeast as tourist centers, others in the Middle West as manufacturing centers, but Longview aims to maintain her utopia for all classes. It began in the dream of Mr. Long, one of the foremost lumber producers of the Southwest, where a dozen mill centers used almost all their supply of raw lumber and the company was looking for a new supply of longer duration where mill hands trained for a lifetime and executives from boyhood, from shirt sleeves up, could be transferred and beginning on a new basis plan for almost an exhaustless life to the city.

Two or three years were spent seeking the site. There must be water front first. There must be nearness to tide water. There must be healthy all-the-year-round working climate. There must be background to create and maintain a future city. There must be deep draught not requiring expensive dredging. All these requirements the site of Longview answered; so Mr. Long, the head of the big lumber company, began his utopian dream with the best architects and city-planning engineers money could command. One of the first things was a new move in all Western cities. To avoid a boom and the sprawling of the city in all directions as real estate promoters got hold of this and that site—with consequent loss to holders of stagnant areas—the first act was to lay out the site in zones at absolutely equal and stable prices for each zone; and to put these prices where buyers paying 25% cash down and a low rate of interest on future payments in instalments could begin humbly and profit from growth by each developing his own business or his own residence. The primary figures were fixed by a visit to and comparison with every growing city in America. The first values were put very low, indeed. All anyone needed to do was get his foothold, improve it, be industrious and keep it. As the seller was the town site company "the hideosity"—if I may coin the word—of a foreign shanty town with all its slovenliness and unsanitary surroundings was forever prevented. Though the town-site architects and engineers did not try to dictate the type of building, the zoning really compelled it and the ugly type of new raw incongruous building eliminated itself by comparison to its neighbor. I do not know of a single ugly building—big or little—in Longview. Then the laying out of the streets gave a vision of beauty certain to react on all owners of property. Down the center of the broadest thoroughfares runs a concrete or cement walk with gardens of flowers lining each side. Along the borders of the one-way traffic concourse to each side of these central walks run more flower and shrub lines. It would be hard for a newcomer with less idea of beauty than a Zulu to live amid such surroundings and not catch their contagion of something finer than his own crude ideas.

Will its own success force a change of this utopia city? I do not know. I do not see how it can. As one of its younger executives said to me—"We don't aim so much at Big as Fine"; and that is a mighty high ideal. All I can add is—do not miss Longview. Go and see it. It isn't a creation of Babbitt. It is a wonderful experiment and one worth while. As you enter and leave the city, passing the Cowlitz River, you will see both Coffin Point and Castle Rock of Captain Vancouver's first charts. You will pass over the very island where Lewis and Clark camped on the way eastbound and the Astorians did likewise after them and so did many an Overlander because there were always deer in the thickets and shelter from rains. You will see why many of the homesteaders tried to hew out a short cut from the Cowlitz up to Puget Sound instead of down the Columbia and round by sea; and instead of the beautiful Pacific Highway you traverse today, from the Cowlitz to Puget Sound, the early ax brigades found themselves bogged in the worst mires encountered from Kansas City westward.

When Wilkes tried to explore this trail up the Cowlitz for report to the American Government, he found the current so strong he could make only twelve miles a day. Walking along the bank "mud was ankle deep." Between the Cowlitz and Chehalis, way was cut open with axes or jump over the trees. Ten years later, a stage-coach over terrible roads was plunging through the mud up the Cowlitz to what is now Olympia and many farmers had cultivated clearings with the fine

stock and beautiful orchards for which the region
is now noted.

There is another point on your way on down to
the Pacific, where you should pause for a day or
a night. It is Lookout Point above Puget Island.
The river far below sapphire blue, the islands
countless as the Thousand Islands in the St.
Lawrence, the ocean steamers passing up and
down where long ago Indians acted as pilots
through the narrow channels, the rolling blue
hazy veiled foot-hills with their evergreens giving glimpses of rosy domes which you now recognize as distant mountain peaks belted by cloud
wreaths fine as gauzy silk, the vistas at every twist
and turn of the road revealing vales, dalles, lesser
waterfalls, the atmosphere changing in color to
every slant of the sun,—are a panorama up to the
present defying artist's brush or photo film. It is
like the changing expression of a beautiful human
face, the sort of face that compelled Gainsborough
to paint an idealized type, or landscape that forced
Turner first to get his color in true to atmosphere,
then create his human or boat or mountain center-
piece to focus the spectrum lights. Some day, a
great artist will discover this region. He will
have his own fight with himself to portray it.
Then the world will see it. Many do see it today.
You never pass Lookout Point but you see half
a dozen cars parked and it has amused me to observe that it is little children with minds still an

unpainted mirror and noses barely above the white railing lining the high declivity, who first explode with sheer glad joy at the glorious view.

A few hours' run and you are down at Astoria famed in story and I wish I could add in song; but the songs are yet to come. Here was Gray's windfall in 1792; and Vancouver's belated explorations a few weeks later; and Lewis and Clark's wintering haven; and the rendezvous of every fur trader from Astor's ill-fated crew to the struggle between Montrealers and New Yorkers for possession till the Treaty of Joint Occupancy settled matters for almost fifty years. This Treaty of Joint Occupancy recognized the American claim resulting from Gray's discoveries and Lewis and Clark's Expedition; but Vancouver was the first to discover and explore in detail Puget Sound; so the Treaty of Joint Occupancy really left open the claims from Puget Sound south to the Columbia, where American settlers poured in from 1839 to 1859. There is not a year in this half century when an exciting novel could not be written on the episodes of twelve months. Why such novel or poem has not caught its inspiration from Astoria, I do not know except that the true seems to surpass any fiction that could possibly be fancied.

You can hear the roar of the ocean breakers nine miles away, which from Drake's day in the 1500's barred discovery of the Great River of the West for two hundred years. Only the Spanish

ships up from old Mexico suspected that a river
lay behind the boiling breakers, but they could
not find the safe channel between reefs. Gray
found it with his little *Columbia* and drifted safely
in and anchored and won immortal fame. Vancouver followed with his large ship, chagrined
beyond measure that he had failed where Gray
had succeeded. Here wintered Lewis and Clark
in a fort where you can see their fresh water
spring, their dining table off a huge stump, the
rotting debris of the great trees felled by their
axes now overgrown by trees just as large.

Astor's poor *Tonquin* sailed away from the
rough-hewn log fort to be destroyed with all its
crew up at Nootka off British Columbia. Here
came the riotous old Governor McTavish with his
barmaid Jane and his drunken jealousy on a hair
trigger till he and all his carousing crew trying
to cross the Bay were engulfed in a watery grave.
Here came Thompson with galloping canoes
round Tongue Point, which you see sticking out
in the harbor as you enter Astoria. Thompson
had been half way down to Montreal, when orders
from Ft. William sent him back to beat the Astorians to the Columbia. Here came ships from
Salem, from Bedford, from Boston, from New
York; from Hong Kong and Bombay; from London and Hull—some whalers, some sea otter
hunters, some general traders, some plainly rum
carriers to bedevil the Indians till McLoughlin

moved the controlling fort up to Vancouver on the Columbia and Willamette. Here rocked Coast Indians' big fir-tree dugouts, Wishram Pirates' cedar boats, fur brigades' long canoes, New England clippers swift of flight over the seas as gulls, four-masted windjammers creaking and groaning to the great sweep of sail, and finally little steamers up from San Francisco or down from Sitka to exchange hides and tallow and grain for furs and later fruits and provisions. You will find monuments and signs marking the site of each era and the hero of each episode; but the monument telling the history of all Astoria is the Astor Monolith crowning the hill from which you can see two hundred miles to the Pacific or one hundred miles from the Pacific. As the War Memorial Monument at Kansas City stands on the site of the beginning of the Overland Trail, so the Astor Monument marks the terminus of the great adventure. Between the two beautiful obelisks lies a century's heroism. Spiral drawings engraved in stone round and round the aerial column tell the long romantic story in picture. It is today one of the most artistic and beautiful monuments in the world and worth the time to go up the hill by motor or bus. On the way up you can stop to see the City Park of flowers unsurpassed in size and glory of coloring by any flowers except in the tropics. Or you can view the sights and go out to play at Seaside Beach below Cape Adams on the South Shore, or Long Beach beyond Cape Disappointment on the North Shore.

In growth and development commercially, Astoria embodies one of the puzzling things in all Pacific Coast cities. It has farm and timber background. It has fishing and shipping foreground. It has splendid docks and deep-draft waters. It is hilly, really terraces up the hills; but it is no more hilly than Seattle, Tacoma, Portland. Why have these cities farther inland gone ahead and Astoria sat still? The same type of splendid American citizenship is in both. Is it that trade seeks the farthest inland tide-water port? Or is it in the frank avowal from one of the most prosperous citizens to me: "Why have we sat still? I'll tell you brutally why though it won't make me popular. We have been so blessedly prosperous—lumber, shipping, fisheries, general trade, cranberry marshes—that we didn't think we needed to stir our stumps—I mean our human stumps—till those other cities gave us a jolt by shooting past us."

I did not dare say that. He did and I let it stand.

CHAPTER XVI

Up the Pacific Highway to Olympia and Tacoma and Seattle

I
T is hard to think of the Puget Sound cities with either restraint or sense of proportion. It is harder to grasp the portent as to their future from the present. From Vancouver, who first chartered these waters for the British Government, and Wilkes, who did likewise for the American Government half a century later, all navigators were impressed, enthusiastic, prophetic in their descriptions of Puget Sound as a harbor for world commerce. Here, the danger was not shallow water at tide line. It was deep water—so deep that in places the difficulty was to find dockage against the hills jutting out in the Sound. Similar amazement instantly obsesses the casual visitor today.

If all the cities and towns on Puget Sound were gathered in one fold as the more restricted areas like New York compel, the population would easily number three-quarters of a million; and the most of that population has grown up and gathered there in your lifetime and mine. Yessler, who ran a "one man saw mill" at Alki Point when Meeker reached the Sound in the early 1850's, and who

left his name to one of Seattle's cross-town centers
—thought to arrest development north by the aerial
gothic-towered building now poking its turret
among the morning clouds. Yet Yessler Building
today marks the southern line of great thoroughfares paralleling the water front. When the
World's Fair was held in Seattle on the hill where
now cluster the beautiful halls, library, chapel,
museum, residences of Washington University,
numbering on its student roll almost half as many
scholars as Columbia or New York University,
this site was wild land. I recall crossing mud
puddles on planks and floundering among the
stumps and on a midnight ride out to see someone
leaving the city next day, having doubts in my
mind whether our motor car could get back whole
or in sections. When Colonel Chittenden began
to lay out Lake Union and Lake Washington as
fresh-water harbors and to connect them by canals
with salt water for ocean liners to come in to re-
pair-docks, I remember glancing at the invalid by
my side and wondering if he were dreaming
dreams. Yet in his life foreshortened by illness,
the famous army engineer saw his dreams come
true. Is there another city in the world with two
large lakes and three lesser ones within its circum-
scribed limits? I do not know of it. Yet look
across the lakes. Beyond each, the city is reaching out to vaster areas; and the sections where
denser housing has already cramped front gardens

to a width of thirty or forty feet are not interspersed with vacant tumbledown houses or unbuilt
lots or long lines of paved streets with nary a house
to line them, laid out and paved from city taxes
by ambitious speculators. Indeed, taxes are high
in Seattle because the city can hardly lay out its
streets, pave them and extend sewer, lights, walks,
fast enough to keep pace with population.

"You are discounting the future too fast," groan
the older conservative taxpayers. "We can never
keep step with the rate new bungalows, blocks
for business, apartment houses are going up."

"Well, show us the houses, blocks, hotels, apartment houses that are vacant"—responds the defense.

The same features of growth so rapid as to be
almost incredible are to be found on a lesser scale
in the other centers on the Sound. Of course, like
New York and Brooklyn and Jersey and Hoboken
in the 1850's to 1880's, more or less sectional jealousy and rivalry exist just now; but as that jealousy
and rivalry have had to merge in the common aim
of a Greater New York in the East, so the day is
not far distant when Tacoma and Olympia to the
south, and Everett and yes—out to Bellingham on
the north—all will have unified aims. Nothing
can stop it—not all the sectional scraps now so
vociferous. As Huntington said of the Central
and Southern Pacific rails long ago, "We may for
a time fight and run counter to geographic posi-

tion, but ultimately geography beats us to our senses and we have to obey and adjust our plans to it."

Where rocked the Coastal tribes' big dugouts for seventy warriors bent on piracy in the 1850's, rock to the lift and fall of tide waters the liners of every port under the sun. Where hogs gone wild from the Hudson's Bay Company's farm on Nisqually Plains to the south rooted along sow paths, now shuttle the trains of four transcontinental railroads carrying cargo down to or up from the Sea. Some of the cargo is from the South Seas. More is from Alaska. Much is from Siam, India, Japan, China, North Russia, Hawaii. Vastly more is destined for Panama way to the Gulf of Mexico, to the Mississippi, to South America, to Atlantic ports, to Europe, or round the world and back again for any port of call where a tramp vessel can pick up or discharge a cargo at whatever rate she cares to offer a shipper on the spot unhampered by American or European agreements as to rates and freights.

You will receive other surprises in the lesser cities. Do you want to see lumber rafts afloat where each log resembles a Grecian or Luxor column being hauled up, barked, slabbed, timbered, changed to shingles, shooks, boards while you watch? You will find it at Tacoma. Do you wish to make a study of beautiful architectural designs? Pause on the way up the Pacific Highway from the Columbia Overland Route and see the Capital buildings at Olympia. They are finer than many capitols in the States of the Atlantic Seaboard. Or you may care to see the great canneries whence come the fruits and fish you enjoy in the Middle West and East. You will see at Everett salmon being tossed from motor launches to factory and from the first grip of the machine claws untouched by human contamination, till cooked and sealed in cans. The same scenes can be viewed at Bellingham. How is it possible these outer towns and cities can become feeders to the great central zone round Seattle and Tacoma? How has it been possible a hundred small cities and towns from sixty to eighty miles distant have been feeders to London and New York? The motor highway and swift rail are explanation. Rails and motors may focus traffic and trade centers vaster than humanity has dreamed; but they also make it possible to scatter homes farther afield in healthier surroundings. You will find this as you follow any of these highways. From Seattle to Tacoma is one continuous roadway of little garden homes, whose owners can come to the big cities in less time than it takes to go from the Bronx, New York, to Wall Street, or Hyde Park, Chicago, to Lake zones of rail and traffic. If you come in or go out some night from Seattle northward, you will find the same—workers living in the country whose work is in the city. And wherever you go on a clear day—and three hundred out of three hundred and sixty-five are clear—you can see the translucent opal peaks in a luminous light of rose and fire.

As I have said before, it is hard to view the Puget Sound cities with a sense of proportion and restraint. You seem to glimpse a future vision where all present-day dreams may look drab compared to reality. There is almost every way to see Puget Sound that a capricious visitor could demand. You can bobble round in the sight-seeing harbor motor boats. You can ascend and look down from a sea aeroplane. You can turn tramp and go a vagabond in and out among the islands of the Sound at a dollar a day for the cruise. You can board a sight-seeing bus, or hire a taxi, or use your own car. Personally, I like the vagabond way where you bump against all sorts and conditions of people—the rich, the poor, the well-to-do, the industrious, the slack, the idle from whom you get a reflex that is really a composite of all sentiments.

Let us telescope back now to first comers from 1792-3 to the 1880 great migrations.

Said Captain Vancouver, the British Navy man —quoted again by Governor Stevens, when he came West to make treaties with the Coast Indians in the 1850's—"Had this insular production of nature been designed by the most able engineers, it could not have been placed more happily for the protection of the port." Said Wilkes, the American Navy man in the 1840's: "Nothing can exceed the beauty and safety of these waters for navigation. Not a shoal exists; not a hidden rock; no sudden overfalls of the water, no strong flow of the wind as in other narrow waters. There are in this region so many excellent and secure ports that the commercial marine of the Pacific Ocean may be easily accommodated." Yet at this very period all Oregon was "not worth a pinch of snuff" to an American Senator and "not worth a ———" to a British diplomat sent out to report; and Greeley, one of the ablest journalists in New York, was describing the whole Oregon migration westward as "sheer insanity."

Can't you see the picture of Wilkes, who was "the noblest Roman of them all," coming ashore to celebrate on Nisqually Plains? Because its charter gave it no explicit rights to farm, but yet on the Pacific Coast it had to farm for its own food supplies, the Hudson's Bay Company had formed a subsidiary company on the Plains of Nisqually for which the American Government paid in 1869 a quit claim of six hundred and fifty thousand dollars. Here from 1836 roamed its herds of horses, cattle, sheep, hogs—almost wild as deer—so wild that deer and cattle often fed over the same prairie and on alarm would spring alike timid into the hiding thickets of ferns and forests. Here, McLoughlin and his Nisqually manager, Dr. Tolmie,

proved wheat and barley and oats would grow.
Here peach stones from Robinson Crusoe's Island,
apple seeds from London, prunes and plums from
New England and Europe had been planted and
growing for almost ten years before Wilkes came.
Here McLoughlin had urged the Methodist missions to locate and Daniel Lee did labor for one
season to be succeeded by Dr. Richmond, followed
by Blanchet, the Catholic speaking the patois of
the French Canadian settlers. The Hudson's Bay
Company fort at Nisqually covered two hundred
feet square with high log pickets and not two, but
four bastions, which is the best gage of the Indian
character roundabout. Flowers were a mosaic
carpet on the plains. The first time he landed
here, Wilkes was enchanted as by a fairy land of
beauty. There were the peaks of snowy mountains
on the sky line, the flowers knee deep on the plains,
the herds of plenty roaming pastures, the crops of
grain waist high waving to the wind—this in a
no-man's-land of which the world hardly knew
the name. Beside Wilkes' squadron rocked the
little *Beaver,* Hudson's Bay Company's ship, 120
tons, a steamer but fueled by wood to carry supplies to posts as far north as Sitka and trade as
far south as California. She had pretty nearly a
belt at water line of small cannon, barricades,
board and netting—another gage of the tribes with
whom she traded of whose pirate tricks you shall
hear. The second time Wilkes came in to Nis-

qually Plains on Puget Sound, he wanted to give his crews a Fourth of July celebration, but as it happened to be Sunday the grand feast was postponed to Monday.

Even in those days the names of the Coast tribes were so unutterable to the white tongue with their "clicks" and "clacks" and "grunts" and throaty phonetics, Wilkes was already calling this, that and the other chief "King George" or Prince Something Else. He had experienced some ugly clashes with these rascals long before the Whitman Massacre lashed Indian bloodthirst to frenzy. Guns were missed wherever they were set aside for a minute and might be "found" in a chief's baggage or under some old fat squaw sitting innocent as a stone. They would just happen to be there. A sailor out in a small boat would be as suddenly encircled by pirate canoes as a floating loaf of bread by gulls and hell divers. On the sailor pulling out a pistol, the war canoes like gulls and hell divers would float away—all innocent enough but ominous. Wilkes thought it would perhaps be good for the health of those Indians to witness what a Navy Squadron could do. With this the Hudson's Bay men were in perfect accord. The Indians came flocking round in thousands— not so defiant on land as on water. The sailor cook had an ox barbecued whole on a spit above the big driftwood fire. On the morning of the 5th all men were mustered in spotless white frocks and trousers, and landing marched to martial band at quick step about a mile inland. All were armed. The sun shone without a cloud. Two bright brass howitzers had been trundled to the prairie. When Fort Nisqually was sighted, paused the marchers to cheer. The voices in return from the Fort were but faint, partly because the majority of the people were out among the onlookers, partly because the French Canadian settlers were not quite sure what this American invasion meant to their own holdings. Horse racing with many a head-over-heels spill by the middies, unused to bucking Indian ponies, three-legged races, fun and frolic, filled the day to sunset when "supper was ready soon as the tide went out," which meant soon as the clams could be dug and a clam-bake end a holiday. That night Wilkes says he could pick out on the horizon not only Mt. Ranier and Baker but far south and east—St. Helen's and Mt. Hood, "very distinctly." Some of his crews later in the season did ascend these nearer peaks if not to their summits at least near enough to see those sulphur pots of extinct volcanoes. The Indians simply refused to go up to the mountain crest. These crater holes were the doors to the Indian's demon dens. The Wilkes crew observed the wonderful belt of flowers round these peaks between tree and snow line. Today every tourist can see them from a motor car.

Whether the display of power had much effect, you must judge for yourself. I give it only because many maintain it was the failure of Stevens in the 1850 treaties to assign lands to the Indians, which enraged to massacre. Stevens could not assign the lands. They had not been surveyed and could not be surveyed till roads were constructed through the impenetrable thickets; and it is a good thing they were not assigned. Had they been assigned in the 1850's, settlers would have bought them up for a song, for old awls, bullets, beads, needles, muskets, pistols. The Indians did not value land as land. They valued it as hunting ground; and of hunting ground, they had more than they could occupy or ever had occupied. Whereas, when roads came in the early 1900's, these timbered areas west of the Cascades sold at public auction for the timber alone—leaving the Indian the logged-off fertile land and water front —for the prices of from twenty-seven thousand to ten thousand dollars even to a little papoose's share.

How about the settlers all these ten years from 1843 to 1853 when they came chopping their way along a game trail up from the Columbia, or bobbling out on boiling seas up the Pacific Coast in dugouts with tents for sail?

It reminds one of what must have been the experience of the Tribe of Dan in olden days, when Chaldean Invasion sent them from Palestine and Egyptian ports across the Mediterranean up the west Coast of Europe to Erin Isle or the city of

King Lud—the Briton, who ruled what is London.
We can only guess the wild deep sea adventurers
with pirate raider and tide rip and storm. Of the
Oregon Pioneers, I have met only two—one aged
ninety-eight and one aged ninety-two—who could
recall their experiences. I doubt if any more survive. One or two have left brief narratives in
writing. One might think with a two thousand
mile trek behind them, they would have been content to sit down rather than go farther afield. Not
so. They wanted before picking homesteads to
see those Hudson's Bay Company's farms up Puget
Sound way. Here were tide-water shipments,
fresh-water springs and streams, pasture girth
deep, orchards so heavily weighted with fruit that
branches broke, timber for houses and barns and
the price of stock five to ten dollars a head. Then
there was that shrewd guess, somehow, sometime,
rails would come. Rails were unknown west of
the Mississippi in this era. When rails met tide
water, there must grow a great city. Where would
it be? With squatter farmsteads free to each
member of the family, a right guess as to location
of that city meant a future fortune. There were
wild guesses and wild misses in the guesses, of
course.

Of the Pioneers who chose the dangerous trail
of a trackless sea up by Shoal Water Bay, round
Cape Flattery past the pinnacle rocks of Clallam
and Angeles and Townsend on to Puget Sound,

Hancock had knocked round the Pacific Coast for two full years before deciding Puget Sound offered him the best chances. The perils of this sea route were terrible. Out from the Coast Puget Sound affords as safe approach as New York or Boston; but scouting close ashore, in-driving tides from the ocean on one side and from the land side winds from the Olympics in hurricane blasts, roil of mountain stream boiling down torrentially from snow peaks, were rash risks for canoe and cedar dugout; and the dangers from the sea were as nothing compared to those from the Indian pirates. It was November when Hancock took one of his scouting trips. In coming down to Shoal Water Bay "our clothes were torn from our backs" by the overhanging thicket. He describes himself as "brushed and bruised" from head to heel. He had to hire Indians to push and carry their boat out over low tide to deep water. It rained on him in torrents and an ague of chills sent him back ashore to camp under a tent of blankets, which must have been about as much protection as to wrap one's self in a soaked blanket. Compelled to seek shelter in an Indian slab house, Hancock simply stretched himself exhausted on a mat over the mud floor; but when the master of the house came back, rain or no rain, Hancock was ordered out and found himself encircled by five warriors armed with knives. He crawled out weak and shaking with chill but when the surf of incoming tide began creeping up on him he crept back under the unwelcoming Indian roof and offered half his provisions for the privilege of passing the night. Rain was still battering the roof in the morning and he had to give a quarter of the provisions left to stay for the day. The war canoe of another Coast tribe passed his refuge that day. He had to bribe these greedy Indians with all he owned to take him back to Astoria on the Columbia. There he recovered under the care of the Hudson's Bay Company's physician and again set out for Puget Sound up the land trail by the Cowlitz to Nisqually Plains. He immediately secured employment making shingles for Dr. Tolmie. Five Pioneers were already on the ground here —prosperous and content.

In 1848 the American settlers built their first mill on the Tum-Tum Waters of Commencement Bay—Tacoma. This was the year after the Whitman Massacres roused the Indians to frenzied boldness and the settlers to terror. It was also the year when the discovery of gold in California drew so many settlers away from Oregon. Hancock joined the stampede to the gold diggings; but he was back on Puget Sound by 1849 prospecting for the coal lands inland from Pu-yall-up. He mentions passing Alki Point, as "an excellent harbor"; but the Indian pirates out for loot everywhere gave him many a bad half hour. The Snokomish, Snoqualimes, and Nisquallys were always at one another's throats, if not over a stolen wife then over some former killing and a raid in revenge; but the rest of his story comes in the Olympic Highway. Olympia consisted at that time of exactly one frame house, part store, part dwelling for an American trader. Ezra Meeker under a very thin disguise of fiction tells almost a similar story of experiences on Puget Sound in the 1850's. The Dennys came to the Sound in 1851 and staked out a claim at Alki Point, which was, as far as I can gather, the first settlement of Seattle. Young Mrs. Denny had a baby exactly five weeks old. It was this family used an old horseshoe or piece of iron or whatever it was to sound depth before picking a homestead for the future great city. It is a truism that from an acorn the oak grew. It is equally true that from a great faith grows a great realization; and you will grasp that more and more as you study Seattle.

CHAPTER XVII

On to The Ends of the Earth

HAVING reached the "Ultima Thule" of the long trek to their Promised Land, up the Willamette beyond Portland round Puget Sound, one might infer the Oregon Pioneers would seize their squatters' claims of six hundred and forty acres a man, or over a thousand acres a family, settle down and begin to drive the furrow that would create a new home foot-free of debt. That is where many narratives of the Overland Trail terminate. It was not where it really terminated. What urge, spiritual or material, drove them on and on to the very ends of the earth at its broadest belt? Fools—cynics may say—when they had attained all they had sought and left a trail of bleaching bones from the dead for two thousand miles? Fools, perhaps, but with something divine in their folly—that "divine frenzy" which Josephus describes in the wanderings and wars of the early Hebrews for more than two thousand years.

You recall the Oregon Fever was at its height from 1843 to 1849. Did any Pioneer really go beyond Puget Sound in this era? They did; and you will find something of the same folly in yourself when you follow the trail. You will find you

have viewed enough sublime scenery to keep a
phantasmagoria of moving pictures gliding across
your mind for the rest of your life. You will have
picked up unconsciously as you traveled scraps of
past adventure, romance, heroism to pale any the-
atrical or fanciful portrayal ever read or seen; and
yet you will go on, or want to go on to the end.
What matter if the trail out to Cape Flattery
"seems to hang on a hook" against precipice wall
above a torrential canyon—as one of our motor
drivers described it? You will want to follow to
the end of the Olympic Highway from the Pacific
Highway at Puget Sound right out to the Ocean;
and you will find as you go on whether you take
a week for it or a day, the urge, or whatever the
driving force, was a true intuition. The reward
will prove greater than hope. Call it "the faith
of little children," the folly of a blind faith, faith
it is, faith the key that has unlocked every great
invention and discovery since time began, the faith
ready to die to prove itself true—from Abraham's
trek up from the Persian Gulf for Palestine to
Lindbergh's trek across the Atlantic in aeroflight
and the great German "Zep's" more spectacular
first conquest of the Pacific by air route; from
Kepler's belief that the earth was round, not flat,
to Columbus' voyage to test out that belief. The
same fluttering flame of a faith that will neither
quench nor perish is in yourself. Out the Olympic

Photos by Arthur M. Prentiss, Portland, Ore.

INDIAN REMAINS AND TREVITT MONUMENT ON MEMALOOS
ISLAND IN THE COLUMBIA RIVER

Photos by Arthur M. Prentiss, Portland, Ore.

MEMALOOS ISLAND, COLUMBIA RIVER

ASTORIA, AS IT WAS IN 1813

ASTORIA. FROM AN OLD PRINT PUBLISHED IN 1861

Highway to Cape Flattery you will long to go. It is worth it.

You can go in almost any way that commends itself to your purse and time. There is a light-house boat service to all this coast. It would probably give you all the thrills if you covet thrills; but it takes time. Sometimes wind and weather permit this service once a week, sometimes only once a month; and what with tide-rip in and wind from the Olympic Range out, it is a rough trip. Few lighthouse keepers along this coast care to serve longer than ten years. The isolation, the desolate thundering seas, the lonely waste of wild-est waters, react on the most stoical natures and like the fur traders of the Far North, though safe themselves and utterly free from financial worries, they "have to come out" or gradually succumb to a whelming depression that ends in permanent melancholy.

Then there is train service far as the very west-ern limits of the Sound, where you can go on by private car, your own or hired. Charges for a hired car are not high—I forget what we paid—but no more than in a car of your own if you charge yourself for oil, and possible wear on your tires through taking a rough road where you might as well have followed a perfect paved highway. Or you can board a ferry boat to such points as Town-send and Angeles from which you go forward by car. The Olympic Highway from these points westward is one of the most beautiful in all the world.

As you swerve round the south end of the Sound through Tacoma, you will see Mt. Rainier far to the southeast—home of twenty glaciers, headspring of seven rivers to the sea; and as you proceed back up north to the west of the Sound, you will see Mt. Baker on the sky line far to the northeast, both examples of that amazing faith which materializes in realization out-reaching wildest faith. These two highways up to Mt. Baker by Bellingham or up to Rainier from the Tacoma road cost sixty-five thousand dollars a mile—more than many a mountain section for the rails. They are twenty-four feet wide—wide enough for three cars at sharp turns in the corkscrew trail-climb to the stars, with rip-rock foundations where sliding earth did not give grip for road by blasting out and heavy log railing on outer edges as protection. When the roads were begun, tourist travel hardly equaled eight thousand people a year. Today it exceeds two hundred thousand people a year. Drawn by what? Sheer beauty. There is no other answer. The lure from slime to stars, "The Great Silent Watchers of the Sky"—as the Indians called the peaks—have beckoned you and you had to go. Wiseacres said these roads wouldn't pay, couldn't pay—were madness for county and state to undertake. Yet they have paid even if you estimate that each tourist leaves only ten dollars a year behind

him. You can find almost any type of accommodation you want—free camp site if you have your
own tent and provisions; cheap "shanty tents" at
a dollar a day with a general commissariat if you
prefer that; luxury lodge with a bath to each bedroom and any charge you care to pay for luxuries
from six and seven dollars a day up. Just a word
of precautionary advice, though advice may be
superfluous. Unless your own driver has a mighty
steady hand on the wheel and equally steady head
combined with agility, hire a driver who knows
this road, or go up on buses handled by drivers
who have been tested. At the general office of
both mountain resorts on the Sound, you will get
the scale of all charges and sound advice. Also
dress warmly. You are going up to the snows.

Books could be written and have been written
on each peak—books about the vast silent forests;
the flower zone a mile wide above the timber line;
the ice caves changing each year above the flower
belt; the turquoise and jade and sapphire blue
tarns countless as the stars in the upper Alpine
meadows where Psyche from time beyond human
memory, has seen her own loveliness reflected from
a mirror that fades to silver under the moon and
tinges to rose under the dawn, and flames with fire
at sunset; the peculiar volcanic formation of almost a giant's causeway of rocks blocked like colos-
sal upright bricks; then the sulphur crater holes
at top of peaks, where the great mountains blew

their heads off in a fearful fire catastrophe eons ago and created the Inland Empire from sea swamps. If the earth is solid, what created these fire-holes—these gas and lava explosions? You will find as many theories as there are geologists.

A word as to the ice caves on which there are not so many disputes. You can see a variety of caves on Mt. Baker, Rainier and the Olympics. I know of nothing lovelier in mountain scenery. They shift and change each year; for though the push of the century's snows above seems to press the ice block in an advancing crystal flood to dissolve in mountain falls and torrents, the glacier is not gaining ground as it advances. It is losing ground. Each year, according to the zone in which it lies, it melts back a little faster than it pushes forward—by actual measurement, from one to sixteen inches. As it melts, it drops the pebbles impacted in its ice river. These may vary from a bullet to "an Olympic Pill" high as a house—polished as a billiard ball by the waters, scarred as by diamond point from the scouring of the ice; and when these are dropped in river bars, they are called moraines and create the little upper mountain tarns. Now snow on mountain peaks may blow and fall every month of the year, from hurricane blizzard to gauzy silk mist soft as veil; but it falls heaviest in winter and leaves each year's layer so you can count back the years from the blocked crystal layers in the laminated ice caves, each wall of which with its crystal prisms splits the white light ray of the sun into the spectrum colors of the rainbow. It is a sort of fairy world; but don't tarry there too long, or like another fairy world it may dissolve in a crash on your crown. The Indians have some beautiful legends about ice caves and they are much alike from those of Aleuts in Alaska to the Rocky Mountain and Cascade Range tribes. The ice caves were the dwelling place of Loki—the old Norwegian Demon of Evil, the Indian devil of wintry blasts. In these ice caves with his hair of hoary icicles and beard of curling snowdrifts and breath of blizzard winds sat Old Winter Demon sending blasts of cold out over the hunters' land till there came dancing north the Youth called Spring; and wherever the Youth's feet touched earth, the flowers sprang up, and the streams began to flow, and the land turned to green with pasture for the buffalo. The Youth carried a quiverful of arrows. Each arrow was a warm sunbeam. He peeped into Winter's Cave. Winter let out a blast of his icy breath with an awful roar of threats. Youth shot an arrow at the old ogre's head. The Old Man's beard and his hair came off like a wig and his head cracked and his cave crashed down; and Spring went dancing and singing away to the north. There is as much fact as fiction in the old Indian myth; so do not tarry long in any ice cave, or you might suffer the

fate of the old fellow's crown from a block of ice
loosened by your warm breath.

On your way out to the Olympic Highway, you
will pass some interesting human touches, too. For
instance, at some of the motor filling stations as
you pass through Tacoma, you will be served by
Spanish pirates clad in ten-gallon hats, with bloody
handkerchiefs round their necks, and mustaches
thick enough for a bird's nest, and boots thigh-
high. It may be good advertising but it is also
good history—a reminder that in the long ago
Spanish frigates poked their prows in nearly all
the North Pacific waters many years prior to American or British discovery but failed to make good
any claims by landing and setting up sovereignty.
Down late as the 1850's, sailor boys escaped from
the British Navy used to scoot in any sailing sloop
or rowboat they could handle across the British
side of Juan de Fuca Straits to Angeles or Townsend or Clallam on the American side, marry the
proverbial Indian maiden, act as interpreter,
trader, or what not and far as I can find, fare
pretty well even if they didn't live happy ever
afterward. The raiding tribes from Fraser River
might leave a hundred of their own heads sticking
up on poles along the shore front of what are now
Everett and Bellingham; for these tribes did not
scalp. They beheaded. Long as the white boys
remained good Indians, they did not suffer death.
It was only when the Pioneers came in hosts as

settlers and traders, the Indian resentment kindled to massacre and outrage.

If the day is not clear enough for you to see the great white peaks as you hum westward, you will not be disappointed. Your car will be going through boiling mists. You will glimpse tarn and canyon and white waterfall and get living and real pictures of Landseer's deer paintings of the Scotch Highlands on a giant scale. You will pass cedar stumps that did duty as a free-for-all post office box in the early days. If you do not go too fast—and do not, you will miss too much—you will pick up scraps of Indian lore and early settlement days, which in a very few years will exist no more for anyone to pick up. It is the only region south of Athabasca north of the Tropics where you can meet Indians in almost their primitive condition; and the change from poverty to great wealth through sale of timber lands is coming over them so swiftly even this charm will have passed in another ten years. Out at Jamestown, two hours from Port Angeles you can see one such transition.

Jamestown is not a reserve but has a primary Indian school under the Indian Bureau's supervision. It is not named after any Virginian or English origin. Lord Jim Balch was a Clallam chief. Hence the name. The Clallams grew weary waiting for the government to fulfil the old Governor Stevens' Treaty and to assign them lands. This Indian Treaty was to assign the Indians definite reserves; but the reserves could not be made definite till lines were run through the impenetrable thickets of forests; and the Treaties could not be fulfilled till years later. The Clallams knew they could make a good living clam digging, crab fishing, whaling and salmon fishing along the Coast; but to avert being ousted from the Coast into the sea by pushful white settlers, they wanted to hold their lands in fee simple and not by treaty, so seventeen or eighteen families clubbed together and bought two hundred and twenty acres along the very best section of the clam and crab areas on the Straits. Crab fishermen can clear eight hundred dollars a year. Farms ran back in strips from the water front. Congressmen and senators have come from Jamestown with Clallam blood. Before the Eighteenth Amendment was a Federal measure, this precinct voted dry. Washington as a State had beaten the Federal workers to the winning post on both temperance and suffrage; and the women voted, every soul of them, for dry. Only one old dugout lies beached on the sands. These Indians use motor gas launches for their fishing. Yet a century ago, they were the most ruthless fighters on the Pacific Coast. When a flotilla of Fraser River Indians came down to raid them some three-quarters of a century ago, the Frasers were massacred to a man. What transformed these Indians practically into whites in three generations? I asked the teacher, Mr. Taylor, that. He said: "I would prefer the Indians should answer you.   I want them to tell you the story."

He led us across to the little Indian church built by their own hands.   Was it Protestant or Catholic?   Neither—he said.   The Congregationalists had been here first, just as the Methodists, Presbyterians and Episcopalians had been first on the Columbia, and the Catholics first up in the mountains; but the differences of sects and creeds confused the Indians, particularly after their own Messiah craze came to such disastrous end in the late '70's and early '80's.   Though one reserve right now calls itself Methodist and another Catholic, basically if you won their confidence you would find the most of these Coast Indians were mystics. At Christmas, at Easter, on Thanksgiving, they might assemble for a rally to the mission church; but for the rest of the year, they attended only their own mystic Shaker or Quaker church.

We entered the church—just one text on a little blackboard above the expounder's head.   There was no pulpit, only a chair and a table and an open Bible, with plain benches back against the wall. The text was in part—"Christ makes all nations one brotherhood."   Bells on the plain deal table constituted the only music to lead the chant of men on one side, women on the other.   "I will take you out to hear about their curious religion from one of the chiefs," the teacher added.

Picture the scene—the bleaching skeletons of the

great firs washed in by the tide, the blue launches plowing through the surf and coming ashore to the sandy beach, the village with its rose gardens lining the shores and the shores, themselves, rose red as the gardens in the sun setting over the in-rolling tide. The present leader of the Clallams was sawing a plank from a tree trunk. His wife in a carmine shawl sat near; and here is the story of Billy Newton, great leader of the Clallams, preceding this man.

Billy Newton had not been a good Indian. His life had been stained by almost every vice on the calendar. Was Billy Newton asleep or awake? I do not know. Did he see a vision, or only dream he saw it? I do not know. I only know it produced marvelous results in transforming a scamp into the most powerful and compelling influence for reform among the Coast tribes. I could not gather in the broken English spoken very fast whether Billy had been getting over a drinking bout (for rum runners can get access to this section of the Coast), or a fight, or a gorging Indian feast. He was in bed irritable, ugly tempered, ready to whirl in an explosion on any intrusion. Appeared a vision clothed in "samite" as Tennyson would say, in fire as the Apostle would put it; and came a voice to the Indian's ears or consciousness.

"Billy Newton—keep your garden clean."

Why should Billy Newton "keep his garden clean"? That sounded too much like the whites with their mealy-mouthed treaties and broken pledges. Billy was as turbulently bellicose as an angry bull.

"What do you mean by that?" he exploded. "Why should I keep my garden clean?"

Said the voice of the vision, "If weeds grow, they will choke out flowers."

What did Billy care whether flowers or weeds grew? He flopped over—and there was the vision and there was the voice—"Billy Newton—keep your house clean."

Billy went mad clean through. "What do you mean by that?" It had pierced his muddy, turgid, angry brain that this voice, this vision, was trying to convey a message in symbols.

"If you keep your house clean—good people will want to come in and stay."

House! Was the vision talking about his carcass, or his shanty? Good people! Bah! Hypocrites!

Billy would have shut the vision out but he couldn't. It was here—there—everywhere—he couldn't get away from it. It was like some force lifting him out of himself. He could neither blind his eyes nor plug his ears.

"Billy Newton—keep your heart clean." This time Billy Newton neither shouted defiance nor beat the empty air. The voice was in him, through him, round about him. "If you keep bad thoughts out, good thoughts will enter and stay and lift **up** your life"; and Billy Newton heeded that voice because he could not help it. He arose and confessed his sins before all his people; and they were a black list. He became the great preacher to fourteen different tribes of as many different dialects. He was not the first of the mystics nor the last. He was one of a whole succession of them. I asked the preacher—did they still have such visions? They did; else how could they have kept unity amid such diversity of creeds? "You can have your pocket full of Bibles," he said; "but the truths of the Bible must be written on the tablets of your heart by the Spirit." "Then what do you make of all this clash of creeds and jangle just now?" I asked. "All religions will be one within fifty years," he said. "If you still have visions, what do you make of the prediction of another Great War?" I asked the Clallam leader. The man read no newspapers. All he got was such scraps of news from the outside world as children might bring from school, or fish buyers let drop.

He lifted his arms and pointed. The tide was moaning in, blood red and fiery as flame in the sunset to break in white wave fret on the sands—

"Lady," he said, "de nex' War will be to de las' War as de flame tide is to de little white waves."

"When?"

"Only God knows but not far off, not far off— too soon, too soon—but dis country will suffer leas' of all and de followers of de light of the Spirit not at all—after dat, a New Heaven and a New Earth —de Kingdom Heaven not far away—beginning in each man's heart."

I asked him much concerning the two sides to the next War, which I cannot give here; but in brief it consisted more of an Armageddon between anarchy—confusion—corruption—evil *and* law— order — government — integrity — righteousness, than a fight of nation against nation; but it was to be a war in which blood would flow as water; and when I asked him details he almost shaded his eyes from the dark horrors he seemed to see.

He spoke very fast and his broken English was hard to follow.

He had been reticent at first. When he spied a little Aleut cross hanging from the chain of my lorgnette, he asked was I a Catholic? No. Was I a Protestant? No. What was I? Just a Christian trying to follow the Light; and I showed him a mystic Swastika Cross from the Aztecs and a little seal from Ur of Abraham with the seven stars before the throne and the Serpent below the heel of the woman. Then he opened his heart and talked freely and asked us to attend church service next day. Our schedule did not permit.

"What do you make of it?" I asked the teacher as we got back in our motor.

"Make of it? That's it! I don't know. I have been here for years; and the more I see of it, the less I know. That's why I wanted you to get the

story from their own lips. Our civilization coming so suddenly blinded these primitive people.
We didn't understand them. They didn't understand us; and, of course, in a generation or two—"
he paused.

"There will be no primitives left. They'll be
us?" I asked.

"That's it," he said.

And away out on the Pacific among the Quil-e-
eutes, I found the same mystic beliefs, even less
tinged by white man creeds and customs. When
the Indian youth, who acted as our interpreter,
heard I was sympathetic with the Indians, he told
me he, too, was a mystic, though he was a high
school graduate.

If we had had time, he said he could easily take
us out in safety among the pinnacled rocks to a
whale hunt; but you cannot order up a whale on
notice; and I regret again we could not wait; for
the great whale hunts have passed forever among
the Olympic tribes except as a sport. Why should
a clan take six months to make a fir-tree dugout for
a whale hunt yielding four thousand dollars to be
divided among twenty hunters, when each hunter
is selling his timber limit by auction for from
twenty-seven to ten thousand cash and building for
himself a modern bungalow with 'phone and radio
set inside, and two or three motor cars in the front
yard, and a daily bus to carry the older children
to the nearest school?

Get the primitive key to his knowledge now; or it is lost forever. It isn't all as clean as the mystic's faith. On the other side is the Devil worship of the old priests, some of it sheer superstition, some of it rascality preying on ignorance, but some of it, a residuum, which our science cannot explain. It isn't a white page. It's a black one—a very black one; it's one we cannot explain in terms of our science, but it holds the oldest Indians in as absolute slavery to a sort of devil worship as the devil worship of certain tribes in Asiatic Turkey. In fact, there is so much similar in the two systems it sends the mind harking back through countless centuries to find explanation in a common origin for the human race. Our astronomy descended from Chaldean has the Great Bear with its five pointed stars. The Indian star lore has its Wolf of the Skies. We have our myths of the Sun-Rise an Aurora to drive a team of fiery horses across the Zodiac. They have their myths of a War-God prancing up from the East on a Rocking Horse (galloping) of stone. We have our metaphors of the beautiful Sunset of Life and flaming clouds and rising stars. They have their metaphors of Going to the Sun across the Track of the Milky Way with stars for guides to a Happy Hunting Ground. We have our written records of humanity falling from immortality to mortality through eating forbidden fruit. They have their oral traditions of humanity falling from Paradise to earth through grasping at forbidden grapes. So one could trace countless parallels.

But on westward along the Olympic Highway, aisled by trees two hundred and fifty to three hundred feet high, you go from Angeles. You can go by car, bus, boat from Seattle, Tacoma, Vancouver; but you really only hit the Olympic pace west of Port Angeles. We set out by boat from Seattle and it was near Port Angeles that we picked up the Olympic Highway. As always, the road followed a river's course.

Fine motors of every price and make met us with a wave. The amazing thing was that most of the finest cars had Indians at the pilot wheel, young bucks and squaws if you care to call them that. And there was no inferiority complex, nor sullen face among them. They waved hail-and-well-met to you gaily as you did to them. The back seats often looked like a collection of frisky brown kittens and puppies; only the kittens and puppies were papooses. Soon we were gliding through an aisle of the most magnificent Douglas firs that stand in the world. We paused at one, a landmark—three hundred feet high, thirty-seven round. We backed off to measure another—two hundred and fifty feet high, thirty feet round; and in serried ranks they stood for seven miles in one stretch and four in another, sentinels of the centuries. Green moss draped the branches overhead in a wild dryad hair. Ferns high as the motor car hid the undergrowth.

No wonder these Indians have prospered. Protected from hostile neighboring tribes by the wild coast to the north, the Olympic Mountains to the south, and the forests too deep to be penetrated east and west, with fish in the sea and fish in the mountain streams, and clams and crabs on the shore, and elk and moose and deer and rabibts and grouse in the woods, and planks for their long houses, and the soft inner bark of the cedar and the soft wool of the mountain goat for woven clothing, wind-proof and rain-proof—they lived from time immemorial, isolated from other tribes as from Europe or Asia, and safe from molestation as in an embattled fort.

Mr. Woodman, a highly educated white trader of Port Townsend, now aged ninety, with eyesight and hearing unimpaired, who married a Clallam girl in his youth, told us that, to his knowledge, there were between Juan de Fuca and the Columbia at least six different tribes, who not only did not understand one another's language, but were incapable of uttering one another's phonetics. In his youth four thousand Clallams used to camp at what is now Port Angeles, two thousand at what is now Townsend; so they were not a weak clan. The word Clallam means *strong men*.

What, then, I asked him, had reduced the tribe from ten thousand or more to perhaps not a third that number today, scattered on several reserves? Was it vice, smallpox, rum, starvation, war? Rum, there was none. Starvation, was then and is yet unknown. Vice, never gained the foothold known elsewhere among Indians; for these people were cut off from contacts. It was tuberculosis. When the white men came, offering firearms and blankets in exchange for pelts, the Indian began to change his mode of living. Though the Clallams lived in plank long houses always, they used to change their residence every six months. Now, though they hunted, they began to be more stationary; and the crowded indoor living made them easy victims to what we would call influenza, pneumonia, tuberculosis.

But through the columned aisle of the Olympic Highway came a whiff from the soft air of the sea, a tang of washed salty wind-puffs mingled with the resin of the great forests. As the car slid noiselessly over the padded mold of the forest road, there came the chant of those eternal tides amid granite and black basaltic dikes, which guarded and concealed this coast for three hundred years after it was first sighted.

We were at La Push. You will find it on the map forty miles south of Cape Flattery. Draw a rectangular boundary up round the cape and back to Seattle, and you have touched the high spots of the Quen-i-ults, the Quil-e-utes, the Makas, the Clallams and others now intermingled on the Puget Sound Reserves—Pu-yall-ups, Lummis, Sno-homish.

La Push is the village of the Quil-e-utes, with the Makas and Clallams, the most famous whale hunters of the Pacific. No more than two or three hundred people are today in the village; but each man, woman and child owns eighty acres of big timber back along the road. This is a tidy fortune in such an area, say for a family of five or six. As far as I could see the village perched on the black rocks differed little from the fishing hamlets of Newfoundland and Labrador, except that this one was more prosperous. Always these Coast tribes dwelt in oblong plank houses; and here were plank houses giving way to neatly painted five and six-room bungalows with radio wireless above and two or three motors in the front yards.

Timber is not the only source of income to these people. There are not a dozen dugouts left on the Coast for whale hunting—their great sport. But these folks are still the harvesters of the silver crop of the sea. The big fish companies are out to pay a dollar for the steelhead salmon, twenty-five cents for the silversides; and where the white man is forbidden to seal-hunt, the Indian by treaty can hunt "long as the sun shines, the rivers run, the mountains stand." They sell today of such seal pelts, twenty-one hundred skins worth ten dollars on the average; seven thousand dollars' worth of baskets and mats, chiefly the work of old people;

and the storekeeper told me that the timber claim would average easily ten thousand dollars to each individual—papoose, old and young, male and female. This timber is sold by public auction to the highest bidder. The sale price is handled by the Indian Department.

An old woman—almost a hundred, the storekeeper told us—padded barefoot across the sands with her crab or clam basket on her back; and another ancient crone sat in a door weaving the fine inner bark of the cedar into rugs soft as wool; but their somewhat impoverished appearance was not so much evidence of poverty as of disinclination to change their mode of living.

An old medicine man behind his smoked glasses called "How"! to us from his porch step; but he did not look as opulent as medicine men in the days when they got all a sick Indian's possessions before curing.

"These fellows were devil worshipers?"

"Yes, always. They no longer rule the Indians through superstition; but the Indians—even educated Indians—always hold them in deadly fear."

"Do you think these old chaps had any secret knowledge—occult, psychic, hypnotic—apart from vegetable remedies for physical ills—which the white man does not possess?" I asked that question of every authority on the reserves; some, storekeepers; some, Indian agents; two, judges in the courts; one, an Eastern university woman, married to a judge, who had made Indian life their joint hobby. In every single case the answer was: "Yes —absolutely; we have seen the proofs. Whether it was sleight-of-hand, hypnotism, what not, we don't know; but we have seen things done for which the white man has no explanation and can get none, for the medicine man only reveals his secrets to an oath-bound confederate."

Yet a century ago these Quil-e-utes were head-hunters. Sixty years ago, as already told, so little did they know of white man's life that when a great vessel was wrecked in this Graveyard of the Pacific, the Quil-e-utes tore up the flour bags for cloth and strewed the flour as worthless on the sand. When the seaman's chest was found filled with coin, the money was tossed out for children's play and the chest used as a trunk.

Now the little children go to the public schools; the older by bus to high schools.

What is their religion? No longer devil worship with the idea that the good spirit will not hurt you anyway; so, much better to make your offering to the evil demons. All at La Push are Shakers, Quakers, mystics; for they attained the revelations independent of white man help, eschewing creeds and sectarian differences almost as much as the old devil worship.

On the upper slopes where you crossed the Divide between the Cascade Mountain Range and the Olympics, you saw moss in sage green at cloud line. Here as you glide down on soft-padded black humus road, you see no sage-green moss but armor-plated trees straight as sentinels on parade in front of a vast silent army of trees. Here the mosses are a little world in themselves, ranging from the deepest green in tint to the intense light shades; and if you use a magnifying glass, each moss is a little forest in itself—a microcosm of the great macrocosm above it, as the ancients believed our little world is in all things just a microcosm—a child world of the vaster invisible world above it. Flowers in the crannied wall—Tennyson sang—if I could know you *all in all,* I would know all. It is the refrain of every seer from the prophets to the modern poets.

Fish pools are passed, amber and jade under the green shade. The rivers are no longer boisterous torrents but dimpled brooks "wimpling to the sea." A dozen lakes that might be in the Highlands of Scotland you will pass and at each are camps and elaborate lodges where you can have such accommodation as you care to choose, and pause to dream such dreams as the world of beauty suggests to each. That is why I reiterate—do not hurry on such trips. You have all eternity. Who is chasing you? You may say this, that or the other business engagement; but in many cases, it is your own restless nerves prodding you to the end of a trail foreshortened by your own folly.

Hancock was one of many Pioneers who worked

round to Cape Flattery by the sea. It struck him
as it struck many an old navigator, who could not
come past the reefs with a larger ship, that here
would be a great place for trade with the Indians,
who had never been touched by white man influence and had to barter with the fur traders through
middlemen tribes, so he erected a slab house. Because the experiences of Hancock are similar to
other white men's, who first tried to penetrate this
region, they may be given as typical of all. Meeker
had like experiences on Puget Sound. Vancouver
and Wilkes and the old Spaniards and sea rovers
such as Meares, who tried to establish connections
with the tribes of the Olympics and San Juan
Islands, all record details of these Indian pirates,
wild as wolves, unconscious of ethics as tigers, and
yet shy and furtive as forest deer. And do not be
too hard on Indian ethics as the code of the man-
hunter and man-hunted. In recent years, I was
on the roughest coast of Newfoundland, where for
three hundred years Devon fisher folk have dwelt
isolated from world contacts. "Well, how are
things coming along with you? Will you pull
through the hard winter?" a bishop asked of a
good holy father. "Aye—aye," said the priest of
a flock haunted by sea perils as were the Indians
of the Pacific Northwest, "with the help of God
and a few wrecks, we'll be all right." Says Hancock:

"Having my few goods in this house where I lived, it was necessary to stay there pretty closely, and I was visited by large numbers of the most primitive looking creatures imaginable; some with furs covering parts of their bodies, others entirely without and some with blankets manufactured by themselves from the hair of dogs. Of these animals they raised a great many which they regularly shear and weave the hair into blankets in a way very peculiar to themselves, quite heavy and very coarse. These people flocked round my house, manifesting a great deal of curiosity, and in such numbers that I began to feel somewhat apprehensive of mischief, as on all their visits they were armed with knives and bows and arrows, and seemed dissatisfied with my presence there. Pretty soon they informed me that they wished me to leave at once; to this I objected, telling them I intended remaining peaceably on my part, and that I wanted them to pursue a similar course toward me. I told them a great many things by way of reconciling them to my remaining, in regard to myself, but they availed nothing as they continued to visit my house with the demand that I should leave, this I always refused to do; in fact I did not know how I could, provided I had the inclination. True, I had purchased a canoe from them, which was at my disposal, but for me to have attempted to go anywhere would have been the height of folly, as they would have pursued and probably killed me; besides I could not manage the canoe alone in these waters.

"Finally, one day a large deputation, perhaps two hundred in number, approached, well armed, and ordered me to go immediately. On my refusing they told me that they would give me three days to leave, and if at the expiration of that time I still remained I might expect the most serious consequences. During the three days they did not visit me as usual, but occasionally a straggling fellow would come about, no doubt to see how I was progressing in my preparation to leave. On the third day they manifested a good deal of uneasiness and in

the evening came and took away one of their people whom I
had employed to wait on me. I was determined to defend
myself against any attack they might make, which I was fearful
they contemplated doing that night, so I put in order and loaded
all the guns I had, between fifteen and twenty, and calling a
little boy who was passing about dark, promised him a present
if he would stay with me all night. I supposed that by having
this boy with me, they would not fire in the house, or at all
events he could not get out without my knowledge, if I
chanced to fall asleep, as I had the house well barricaded inside.
About midnight I heard a noise and could soon distinctly hear
the Indians whispering outside. I then cocked a gun, lying
beside me, of which the boy was conscious, as also of the
fact that a number of his friends were outside, intent on mischief, and being alarmed lest I might shoot some of them, he
called to them and told them that I was well armed and on
the lookout for them, advising them to leave as I was going
to shoot; whereupon I could hear them running off in the
direction of their village.

"In the morning I found that my canoe had been consider-
ably broken the night before, and at the same time perceived a
number of the Indians coming toward my house. I determined
to try a ruse on them and see how it would work so I sat
down at a table and taking a pen, ink and paper, appeared to
be very busy writing; the Indians all the while were standing
around the door wondering what I was about, and seeming
to be very suspicious of my writing; of this they had some
knowledge, having seen one person communicate by writing
with another some distance off at the Hudson's Bay Company's
trading establishment on Vancouver Island, Canada, and I
knew what they thought of these suspicious articles, as they
had told me of their strange discovery. I continued writing,
notwithstanding I was frequently asked what I was doing,
and by this time about two hundred were congregated, all eager
to know what I was writing about. I finally told confidentially

to a lesser Tyee, that I was writing to the Boston Tyee, the President of the United States, of course, expecting that he would tell this startling news to the whole of them as soon as he would get out of my presence.

"Soon they came in groups and asked me in the most supplicating manner to desist from writing, but I paid no sort of attention to them; finally the chief came and begged that I would quit writing, and that I would burn what I had already written; I ceased for a moment and requested him to ask his people how they would like to have their canoes broken without having been guilty of anything to justify such conduct, and whether in fact I had ever done anything to them that they should so badly act towards me. This seemed to have a most salutary effect, for they at once proposed fixing my canoe up again in first rate order, and as a pledge of their good feeling offered to give me twenty baskets of potatoes provided I would burn this paper. I finally agreed to it provided that they would afterwards deport themselves civilly towards me, and said I would take nine baskets of potatoes; so I burned the paper, while they hurried off for the potatoes; and to repair my canoe."

Bribing some of the Macaws of Cape Flattery and then some Clallams, Hancock succeeded in engaging boatmen to go back to Townsend.

He had had enough of Cape Flattery Indians for some time. No trader could escape from these Indians by land and unless they helped him, neither could he escape by sea. It explains the isolation of these tribes until modern days. Big ships could not come in. Little ships could not safely go out.

It was when prospecting for coal up the Sno-

qualmie, that Hancock came on the famous Snoqualmie Falls. He says:

"About dark we encamped for the night about a mile and
a half from the great falls of this river, which the Indians
said were as high as two trees they pointed out, which I suppose
were one hundred feet each in length; and such was the noise
occasioned by the falling water that it was impossible to sleep
soundly. Next morning I took all my crew, except one left
in the camp to prepare breakfast, and set out to visit these
falls. We went right alongside the cataract in our canoe and
beheld a most beautiful and imposing spectacle, though the
roar was almost deafening. The river has a perpendicular
fall of about one hundred and seventy feet, with a surface at
the present stage of the water not more than thirty feet broad.
"The banks upon either side of the basin, where the cataract
deposits itself are perhaps two hundred feet high, and so steep
that it is impossible to climb them. After remaining some
time in admiration of this beautiful wonder of nature, I was
preparing to leave, when my attention was attracted by the
Indians to a beautiful rainbow, that had just made its appearance about midway the cataract, formed by the rays of the
rising sun upon the water—one of the most beautiful sights
I ever beheld."

In prospecting for coal, Hancock discovered
each of the passes now traversed by the great transcontinental railroads, the St. Paul, the Great
Northern, the Northern Pacific. He explored in
two years from the Sound up the Skykomish, the
Snoqualmie, the Snohomish, Cedar River; but the
possibilities of great profit in trade with the Cape
Flattery tribes drew Hancock back to the perils

of Neah Bay. He took passage in 1851 in November on a tramp vessel from San Francisco and accompanied by two Hudson's Bay men, Mr. Gosnell and Mr. Ellis, a passenger, Mr. Sargeant, and a sailor, Jim, with an arsenal of firearms, tried to pull ashore in a small boat. One begins to understand why this point was named Flattery —it lured, but it lured to wreck:

"At one o'clock P. M., we found the distance greater than supposed, the waves beating in the shore perhaps forty feet high, rendering it impossible for us to land, so we went around to a small bay or indenture in the island where the breakers were not more than ten feet high, landing with some difficulty. We saw that natives had been here some time previous but none were to be seen, so we determined to return as it was growing late, and rounding the island found a dense fog completely obscuring everything seaward. We went a short distance out to sea and fired our guns, hardly knowing in what direction we were steering and being apprehensive that we might be lost at sea, made our way to the land by the noise of the waves dashing on the rocky coast, for the fog was by this time so dense that we could not see beyond the bow of our little boat.

"Without stopping to take advantage of the fire they made, though both cold and wet, I took my gun and started off to find Indians from whom we might learn our locality or obtain shelter until we could join the vessel, being in our shirt sleeves. I traveled through brush and over rocks until night compelled me to return, and eating a biscuit with my companions three of us went to the end of the island and built a large fire of the beachwood as a beacon when the fog would clear off and enable it to be seen from the vessel. Four of our party lay down around the fire, leaving one to watch, and one of them remarked he would willingly dispose of all the present or future in this particular locality for a blanket thick enough to enable him to obtain an hour's sleep.

"In the morning one man went around to the outside of the island to look for our vessel, the rest of us remaining to look after our boat, and at noon we ate the last of the biscuits taken from the vessel, dividing the broken fragments in our pockets into five equal parts. Just then Mr. Gosnell called my attention to an approaching canoe with three Indians in it, and I hailed them several times, but such was the noise of the surf that they did not hear me, and I ran across the island to the other side where I called until they heard me and stopped, gazing at me with evident astonishment. I beckoned and waved my hat, but they would not approach the shore, and paddled off as fast as they could. I watched them until they reached a small island four or five miles distant, behind which they ran their canoe, and would frequently come out from their place of concealment to see whether I was still there, when I would renew the beckoning and waving of my hat. After continuing this about an hour, we saw they were coming towards us. We were delighted at this, as the brig was nowhere to be seen on the broad expanse of the water, and we were very hungry, as well as almost discouraged.

"They came within a quarter of a mile and ceased paddling, when I spoke to them in five different languages, none of which they seemed to understand. I then spoke to them in the Chinook or jargon that is used quite generally by the Hudson's Bay Company with all the different tribes; yet they could not comprehend a word I said. I was then pretty well satisfied they had not been accustomed to seeing white people, as all the Indians I had seen on the coast, who had ever had any intercourse with the whites, could give some evidence of the knowledge of the jargon so generally spoken. I then made signs inviting them to come on shore and show me where to find something to eat, offering to give them a handkerchief; but No! they made me understand they were afraid; I then thought it best for them to see our whole company, as they were probably suspicious of a considerable force. I assured them that we five constituted the whole company, and would not hurt them, when they ventured a little nearer and halted; I insisted that they should come on but in vain.

"I then recollected a number of brass rings I had put in my pocket as peace offerings before leaving the vessel, and offered them each one of them, and the head man a handkerchief, when they cocked an old flint-lock musket and ventured to advance to obtain them; I presented them kindly but they seemed frightened and pushed off a little distance in their canoe. One of my companions offered them a handkerchief, trying to convince them we were friends and wanted them to come ashore, as we were very hungry; after a great deal of persuasion one of them came and received the handkerchief and very hurriedly knocked off with his paddle a substance, resembling a gristle, from a rock and biting a piece threw the other to me, and jumped in the canoe, leaving us abruptly. They had not gone far, however, before we heard them calling in a friendly tone, and they soon came up, bringing some large mussels that are found adhering to the rocks on the beach; we asked them to carry them to the fire for us, hoping to cultivate a familiarity with them, and, giving them some brass rings, induced them to go there; they saw all our guns and sword, which again aroused their suspicions, and they hastened away.

"We were now pretty well supplied with food, such as it was, having provided a supply of the gristles (I know no other name for them) that were abundant along the beach. By the time we cooked them it was dark and the snow falling fast; leaving one man as guard, four of us endeavored to sleep. The weather cleared up and the moon shone brightly enabling the man on guard to see a large canoe a short distance off, full of Indians. He awoke me, and from the little knowledge I had of the natives thus far north, I concluded our better plan would be to open communications with them before morning, as they might attack us during the night. None of our party had a knowledge of the Indian character, never having been in this part of the world before, so, they were willing to take my advice, and secreted themselves behind a log, with their arms in readiness, while I went to the water's edge and hailed the Indians in a friendly voice several times. The Indians answered in an indifferent way, when I asked them to come to shore, as I wished to talk with them.

"After some hesitation and considerable talk among themselves they came, and wanted to land, but I objected, and requested them to remain in the canoe, at the same time shoving it gently off. I asked them their errand here at this hour, and they replied they had come to trade their furs and bring us something to eat, doubtless only an excuse for their presence, and a covering for their designs on us. I told them I had nothing to buy their furs with, when they showed me some bear and elk meat, which I proposed buying with brass rings, the only things I had to give in payment, but they refused. I then took off one of my shirts and offered it for a small piece, which they declined also. One fellow jumped on shore and others attempted to follow, but I laid hold of the end of the canoe and held it from the shore, requesting the one who had landed to return; he asked me to get in and go with them, but I refused, and taking him by the hand obliged him to get in, giving him several rings and charging him particularly to present a couple of them to his Chief. I then asked them to go home and come back if they wished in the day, as it did not look well to be coming in the middle of the night.

"They left, but went only a short distance to a little bay where they lay quietly holding to the weeds until morning, when they went slowly to another small bay, which I had before examined; a short way across the land there was another indenture so near as to almost cut the island in two, and concealing myself near them I heard them call several times, being answered by others on the opposite bay. I remained long enough to ascertain their design on my party and cautiously hastened back to my friends, persuading them to launch our boat immediately so we would have to fight but one party.

"We left rapidly but were detected by the Indians who were soon after us in quick pursuit having about fifty of them paddling and gaining on us every moment; finding they would soon overtake us we ceased our exertions, reserving our strength for greater need. Our sailor Jim, at this juncture was much alarmed, and wished to get away, but I laid down my oar and ordered him to be quiet and not manifest any fear, as we must be calm as possible, and by no means allow our enemies to obtain our guns; these we elevated to let the Indians see we were prepared for them, and I beckoned them to come and bring us some meat. They said they would furnish us all we wanted provided we would go on shore to receive it, but understanding their desires we declined doing it. I told them we were looking for our vessel, and they had better go ashore to our fire and remain there till we returned; they followed us, however, four or five miles to sea yet not venturing nearer than thirty yards, and still offering their meat and furs if we would go on shore to receive them as presents.

"I told them again to return to the fire and await our coming, when they stopped and we continued on our way to sea with our little craft—with nothing to eat. I suppose we must have proceeded twelve miles right out to sea, when it became so very foggy that it was only occasionally we could discern the land in the distance; we now felt satisfied that the Indians could not see us, and determined to return near enough to see land all the time, when we steered our course by the shore, watching for a place where we might land in safety, and fearing at times that both ourselves and our boat would become a prey to the angry waters of the ocean which rolled very high accompanied by a strong wind."

Photo by Asahel Curtis, Seattle, Wash., the great authority on Washington
SEATTLE'S BUILDINGS RIVAL MOUNT RAINIER

SIXTH STREET, PORTLAND, OREGON

Courtesy Tacoma Chamber of Commerce

A VIEW OF TACOMA, WITH MOUNT TACOMA (RAINIER) IN THE
BACKGROUND

The wild sea forced the party ashore on some of the rocky islands where an old deserted Indian house afforded shelter from the snow blowing down in a blinding fury from the Olympics.

"The first thing was to search among the rocks along the beach for something to eat, as we were half-starved, and our supper the night before was not sufficient to appease our hunger; and we were quite successful in securing shell-fish along the shore, and our appetites were satisfied for the first time in five days; we also killed a crow, which we found in the village and roasted him before the fire with the understanding that he was to be saved for an emergency. After these culinary arrangements were completed we had time to contemplate the coming night, and it was dreadful to think of; we were fatigued in body and mind and required sleep; we would lie down for awhile, or as long as we could endure the cold and vermin, and then get up and stand around the fire and thus we passed a long miserable night.

"In the morning we found the sea comparatively smooth, but it was rough along the shore rendering it somewhat hazardous to launch our boat, which owing to the awkwardness of some of the company and the extreme roughness of the surf, filled with water but was fortunately not much injured. After repairing the slight damage it had sustained we made a second attempt to launch her, and this time succeeded, not, however, without getting her pretty well filled again and ourselves and our guns completely wet; we bailed the water out of the boat as soon as we got out a sufficient distance to be clear of the breakers, but our arms were in a wretched condition should we have occasion to use them, which might be expected at any time.

"All day we watched for a place to land, but dark found us still in the boat with the wind blowing hard, accompanied with heavy snow squalls during the night which grew so dark we were obliged to keep off from shore for the distance of five or six miles to keep clear of the breakers; but notwithstanding the darkness of the night and the roughness of the sea, our little boat weathered the storm through the long weary night, which was one of great suffering and apprehension.

"At last day dawned, and we could see the snowclad mountains of the coast though the wind continued and the sea was still boisterous; the crow was divided into five equal parts and eaten with great relish; I shall never forget how my portion was enjoyed."

Hancock found as all navigators have learned that the danger here is not from north winds, but from the south where the cold Olympics create fogs dense as wool and the winds whip up the tides to a maelstrom. A few pirate Indians were encountered at various landing places between deep water and high rocks, but as they threatened to strip the whites almost naked in the barter for food, the castaways pushed off through the breakers. It was "snowing and blowing furiously" but they "were kept off the reefs sharp as saws by the roar of the surf," half the crew bailing out water, half pulling on the oar and changing as exhaustion compelled. Ten days were passed tossing in the November storms. Once they were pursued by a pirate Indian crew of fifty swift paddlers; but as the whites had guns and the pirates had none, the dugout went off northward. The explorers of these San Juan waters were now down to no food but the clams ashore and exactly three matches to light a fire.

"We hated to part with them, but it was so bitterly cold we made an effort to light one and failed; a second attempt failed likewise, when the anxiety was intense; some extra shavings were gotten and our last match made us a fire.

"This place was perhaps the roughest we had camped on this expedition; the bank was high and perpendicular so that we could not get up, and were obliged to remain on the beach, which was covered with round rocks about the size of one's head and if we removed them the water would rise in the vacant place, and we preferred having our bed of rocks to lying in the water or sitting up all night.

"At day we launched our boat with the hope of reaching civilization before another night, for we had been so long traveling south and exerting ourselves to the utmost, that we thought we must be somewhere near the entrance of the Straits of Fuca, or perhaps south of it, as at times we were so far out at sea that we could not see everything distinctly.

"We rowed with, if possible, more vigor than any previous day, and about noon met two Indians in a small canoe. I hailed them in the Chinook language or jargon, used by the Hudson's Bay Company and all whites on the Coast in their intercourse with the Indians, and they responded in the same language. I asked how long it would take to reach Victoria, and they said four days."

News carries strangely in Indian lands by what is called "moccasin telegram." Such news had winged its way to the ears of an Englishman—that Captain Grant met on Snake River—residing across the Straits on Vancouver Island. "This kind and considerate person, immediately fitted out a canoe with clothing and provisions and a good crew of Indians, and despatched them in search of us with a letter addressed to the 'Five lost English-men,' in which he said, 'I send you by the bearers of these blankets, clothing and provisions and will soon follow in a canoe myself, hoping to fall in with you.'"

Hancock was a Missouri man. He had come west breathing threatenings and prejudiced deeply against the British on the Pacific Coast. His senti-ment now underwent an amazing change. Captain Grant forwarded the lost adventurers to Victoria, where all were most kindly received.

By 1852, Hancock was back at Neah Bay—Cape Flattery. This time, he erected a block house for protection. Smallpox ran through the Olympic tribes in 1853. It had been contracted by one of the Indian pirates.

"In their distress the Indians concluded I might afford them some relief, and as soon as they would feel the symptoms of the disease, they would come about my house and lie down in the yard to die. They continued this until the dead were so numerous I could scarcely walk about around my house, and was obliged to have holes dug where I deposited fifteen or twenty bodies in each. Still they continued to come about me to die, in such numbers that I finally hauled them down to the beach at a time of low tide, so they would drift away, and even the dogs, during the pestilence, became fat on the bodies of their deceased masters.

"The remaining Indians, after reflecting and mourning over this visitation, concluded that my presence had occasioned all this calamity, as they had never experienced anything like it before; it was with great difficulty I could disabuse their minds of this superstition, but, after a great deal of argument and persuasion on my part, they concluded they might be wrong in this impression, but being determined to have satisfaction from some quarter for the loss of so many of their people, apprehended the Indian who contracted the disease on the schooner, but recovered. As punishment he was taken out in the middle of the Strait of Fuca and placed in a small canoe, barely large enough to hold him, set adrift, without a paddle or anything else. They thought he would drift out to sea and perish, but the night was calm and favorable and paddling with his hands he succeeded in reaching by morning Neah Island, where he was discovered by the natives who went after him and shot him with their muskets."

Great as was the profit from trade, the perils to human life were too risky. Hancock gave up and finally coming down the Coast to Squim Bay near Jamestown, retired to Whidby Island, where he anchored in quiet on the final "sea of matrimony."

And now look back over the Long Overland Trail from the Mississippi to the Pacific two thousand miles—stretching from Lewis and Clark's day roughly to 1857, over half a century! Look back over the longer Racial Trail dim in the historic past covering at least two thousand years, or perhaps before historic annals on stone or parchment, six thousand years, or roughly sixty centuries! We may say it was pagan persecution as to idol worship, or it was lack of pasturage for his flocks sent Abraham trekking up the Euphrates to Palestine about 2000 B.C. Drought sent Jacob and his twelve patriarchal tribal sons trekking to Egypt. Economic persecution sent his descendants under Moses wandering back to their Promised Land for forty years, fighting a way through wilderness raiders sometime about 1400 to 1200 B.C. Dispersion by war scattered the Twelve Tribes up through Russia across Germany and up by sea through the Pillars of Hercules—Gibraltar—to Britain from 800 to 600 B.C. Love of adventure and determination for religious freedom sent the old sea navigators from Columbus to Cartier and Hudson across the billowing Atlantic in ships not so large as many a sailing yacht from 1492 to 1535 and 1610. We may explain that it was purely from trade motives the fur traders pushed up the Great Lakes and down the Ohio from 1660 to 1800. We may add it was the same lure of gain drew Missouri and New York and Baltimore traders to the foot-hills of the Rockies.

It was hard times from 1837 to 1857 forced men in a fever across the Rockies down to the Pacific. The fact remains the Great Racial Movement had gone round the world in a complete circle; and the movement in spite of human motives, low or high, had been a spiral up from lower level of humanity as a hunting and hunted animal to a spiritual rebirth both as to vision and daily living.

We may give the human motive any name. Behind the motive was a Something Greater than the races moved.

Some call that Something Greater X. Some call it Y. Some call it Z. Some call it Destiny. Some call it God. "His Dominion had extended from the rivers to the ends of the earth."

As the culmination of that movement, the Overland Trail stands without a parallel in racial history; and that is why it is held in honor today.

THE END

INDEX